Wanat
Combat Action in Afghanistan, 2008

The Staff of the US Army
Combat Studies Institute

Combat Studies Institute Press
US Army Combined Arms Center
Fort Leavenworth, Kansas

Library of Congress Cataloging-in-Publication Data

Wanat: Combat Action In Afghanistan, 2008

The Staff of the US Army Combat Studies Institute, 2010.

DS371.4123.W36W36 2010

958.104'742--dc22

2010039932

Combat Studies Institute Press publications cover a wide variety of military history topics. The views expressed in this CSI Press publication are those of the author(s) and not necessarily those of the Department of the Army or the Department of Defense. A full list of CSI Press publications, many of them available for downloading, can be found at http://usacac.army.mil/CAC2/CSI/index.asp.

The seal of the Combat Studies Institute authenticates this document as an official publication of the CSI. It is prohibited to use CSI's official seal on any republication without the express written permission of the Director of CSI.

Foreword

On 13 July 2008, nine American Soldiers perished while fighting a pitched battle in the village of Wanat in Afghanistan's Waygal Valley. On that day, the men of Company C, 2d Battalion, 503d Parachute Infantry Regiment, endured four hours of intense close quarters combat and mounting casualties. The contingent of 49 United States and 24 Afghan National Army Soldiers valiantly defended their small outpost against a coordinated attack by a determined insurgent force armed with rocket propelled grenades and automatic weapons. Despite the initial advantage of tactical surprise and numerical superiority, it was the insurgents who ultimately broke contact and withdrew from Combat Outpost Kahler.

Army historians recognized the need to better understand the Battle of Wanat and ensure those who followed learned from the experiences of the courageous Soldiers who defended their outpost with such tenacity. As initial reports from the battle were received, the Combat Studies Institute at Fort Leavenworth, Kansas began to prepare a historical analysis of the circumstances of the Battle of Wanat, launching an exhaustive research effort that produced a comprehensive and compelling example of contemporary history.

This study offers an objective narrative of the events surrounding the Battle of Wanat. It does not seek to draw final conclusions or to second guess decisions made before or during the heat of battle. Rather, it is an implement of learning, allowing the reader to see the events of that day through the eyes of the leaders and Soldiers of Task Force Rock. It is meant to provide context to the chaos and complexity of modern conflict, and to help the reader better understand and appreciate the nature of operations in an era of persistent conflict. Finally, this study serves to honor and preserve the memories of the nine brave men who gave their lives at Combat Outpost Kahler.

Sean B. MacFarland
BG, US Army
Deputy Commandant, CGSC

Acknowledgments

Many people played significant roles in the development of this study from its inception to its completion. Contract historian Matt Matthews proposed the topic, conceptualized the study, initiated the research plan, and executed a number of key oral interviews with participants. When Mr. Matthews transferred to a different project, contract historian Douglas Cubbison took up the Wanat case study. After performing additional research and oral interviews, Cubbison created a working paper upon which later revisions could build. Contract historian Gary Linhart and contract technician Dale Cordes contributed several visual representations of the terrain. Research historian John McGrath of the Combat Studies Institute served as the primary researcher and writer on the final manuscript, revising both text and citations, creating the final graphics, and incorporating new information derived from the documentary record of more recent inquiries. Dr. Donald Wright, CSI's Research and Publications Chief, shared in the writing duties for the final product and provided continuity and direction through various versions of the manuscript. Dr. William G. Robertson, Director of the Combat Studies Institute, provided overall guidance and quality control to the manuscript development process. Editor Carl Fischer worked diligently to see the final manuscript through the editing, layout and publication process.

CSI is indebted to the many officers and Soldiers who sat for interviews and contributed documents in support of this study. These Soldiers include the paratroopers of 2d Battalion, 503d Infantry ("The Rock"), as well as members of the 62d Engineer Battalion, USMC ETT 5-3, and the staffs of the 173d Airborne Brigade Combat Team and 101st Airborne Division (Air Assault), who participated in operations in Afghanistan in 2008.

In preparing this study, the staff at CSI have been constantly reminded of the courage and sacrifice of all those who have served in Afghanistan in difficult circumstances. These thoughts have guided our work in producing what we hope is both a testament to the valor of those who served and a vehicle for learning in the future.

Contents

Page

Foreword iii

Acknowledgements v

List of Figures viii

Symbols Key ix

Chapter 1. Historic and Campaign Background of the Waygal Valley 1

Nuristan Province and the Waygal Valley 1

The Insurgents 8

The Coalition Campaign in Afghanistan, 2001-2008 10

US Operations in Nuristan and Konar, 2001-2007 15

The Deployment of the 173d Airborne Brigade Combat Team (ABCT) to Afghanistan, 2007 23

Chosen Company and the Waygal Valley 39

The 4 July Attack on Bella 50

The Decision to Execute Operation ROCK MOVE 53

Chapter 2. The Establishment of COP Kahler, 8-12 July 2008 69

ROCK MOVE—The Plan 70

Planning and Preparation in Chosen Company 83

The Establishment of COP Kahler, 8-12 July 86

The Terrain at Wanat and the Configuration of the COP 92

The Configuration of OP Topside 100

Operations and Events at COP Kahler, 9-12 July 104

The Enemy, 9-12 July 115

The Eve of the Attack 118

Chapter 3. The Fight at Wanat, 13 July 2008 141

The Attack on COP Kahler 141

The Initial Defense of OP Topside 152

Reinforcing OP Topside 157

Arrival of Attack Helicopter Support 163

Arrival of 1st Platoon Quick Reaction Force 167

The MEDEVACs at Wanat 172

The Consolidation at COP Kahler 176

The Withdrawal from the Waygal Valley 180

Aftermath 182

Chapter 4. Conclusions.. **195**
 Overview 195
 Counterinsurgency in Northeast Afghanistan,
 2007-2008... 200
 Enemy Disposition and Intent: Situational Awareness in
 the Wanat Area 203
 The Delays in Construction of COP Kahler..................... 212
 The Timing of Operation ROCK MOVE: The Relief by
 TF *Duke* 214
 Defensive Positioning 215
 Summary 223
 Closing Thoughts 230

Glossary **239**

Bibliography.. **243**

List of Figures

1. The Waygal Valley xi
2. Theater Organization, Afghanistan 2008 11
3. Array of Forces, Regional Command-East, July 2008 17
4. AO Bayonet, July 2008.. 27
5. AO ROCK, July 2008 29
6. Troops in Contact Incidents by Company, TF Rock, 2007-8............ 31
7. COP Bella 43
8. ROCK MOVE OPLAN 8-9 July 2008 71
9. Wanat, Proposed COP... 81
10. View of Wanat COP looking west from mortar position with 2d
Squad position, the bazaar, and OP Topside's later location in the
background, 9 July 2008 93
11. COP Kahler, 13 July 2008... 99
12. COP Kahler: Looking northwest.. 100
13. OP Topside, 13 July 2008 101
14. The Wanat Garrison, 13 July 2008....................................... 107
15. The Course of the Fight 143
16. OP Topside from the east following the engagement 155

SYMBOLS KEY

UNIT TYPE

unit	□
headquarters	□
infantry	⊠
airborne	⌣
air assault	Y / v
cavalry	⧄
field artillery	●
aviation	◤◥
air cavalry	◤◥
armor	⬭
engineer	ш
brigade support battalion	BSB
special troops battalion	STB

MISC SYMBOLS

camps/FOBs/COPs

closed COPs

HESCO barriers

observation post

Claymore mine

squad position

traffic control point

single concertina wire

double concertina wire

HMMWV-mounted TOW missile

HMMWV-mounted heavy machine gun

HMMWV-mounted automatic grenade launcher

light mortar

heavy mortar

medium machine gun

heavy machine gun

enemy position

landing zone

SYMBOLS KEY (continued)

UNIT SIZE

XXX	**XX**	**X**	**II**
corps	division	brigade	battalion
I	**●●●**	**●●**	**●**
company	platoon	section	squad

⊓

task force (____ size symbol)
Elmts
Elements–part of a unit
(+) reinforced   (-) reduced unit

O

individual paratrooper

BOUNDARIES

regional commands	▬▬▬▬
brigade	▬ X ▬
battalion	▬ ▬ II · ▬
company	········ I ········
provincial	··············

*NOTE: Unless otherwise indicated,
provincial boundaries are
also AO boundaries*

ABBREVIATIONS
(as seen on figures)

ANA	Afghan National Army
BSB	brigade support battalion
CJTF	Combined Joint Task Force
COP	combat outpost
FOB	forward operating base
ISAF	International Security Assistance Force
LRAS3	type of optical surveillance equipment
LZ	landing zone
M240	type of medium machine gun
RC	Regional Command
RC-E	Regional Command–East
STB	special troops battalion
TCP	traffic control point
TOW	type of antiarmor missile

Figure 1. The Waygal Valley.

Chapter 1

Historic and Campaign Background of the Waygal Valley

Afghanistan's history is one of strife and conflict. The people who have lived in what is today Afghanistan have seen a succession of foreign and domestic rulers and conquerors. The first Western invader to enter the region was Alexander the Great who overthrew the previous rulers of the Afghanistan region, the Achaemenid Persian Empire. Alexander continued east from Persia, entering the area from the southeast in 329 BC and operating throughout the region for three years. After passing through the current site of Kandahar (the Pashto equivalent of "Alexandria"), a city he founded, the Macedonian king wintered at "Alexandria in the Caucasus," near the current site of Bagram Air Base. During the next campaigning season, Alexander crossed the Hindu Kush range through the Khawak Pass and conquered the Persian province of Bactria, establishing a Macedonian colony there and marrying Roxana, the daughter of a local noble. The Macedonian then re-crossed the Hindu Kush in 327 BC, and, with part of his army, followed the Kabul River Valley to the Konar River Valley where he came into conflict with local fighters who were probably the ancestors of the modern Nuristanis. Alexander defeated these people but was wounded in the shoulder in the process. He then turned east, crossed through the Nawa Pass into what today is Pakistan and rejoined the rest of his army in the Indus River Valley. There he fought his next series of battles. Although Nuristani folklore often portrays them as being the descendents of Alexander's soldiers, modern scholarship and linguistic evidence indicates a far earlier origin of the Nuristanis. Still, the genes of Alexander's warriors remain alive in Afghanistan.[1]

Nuristan Province and the Waygal Valley[2]

Located in northeastern Afghanistan, Nuristan Province is just south of the highest peaks of the Hindu Kush range, with its modest population of farmers found almost exclusively in steep valleys cut by small river courses between the mountains. This terrain and a lack of all but the most rudimentary infrastructure has historically marked the province as remote and primitive even by Afghanistan's standards. Within Nuristan and Konar provinces, the Waygal River flows south from the Hindu Kush Mountains for 20 miles until it joins the Pech River at Nangalam. The Pech River, in turn, flows into the larger Konar River at Asadabad. The region is spectacularly rugged and divided into numerous small river valleys separated by steep mountain ridges, many in excess of 10,000 feet. The Waygal Valley is located primarily in Nuristan Province but the southernmost five miles are in Konar Province. The provincial boundary which also marks the ethnic boundary between Nuristanis to the north and Safi Pashtuns to the south is located one half mile south of Wanat. All of the valleys of Nuristan and Konar, to include the Waygal Valley, are rocky, deep, narrow, and steep-sided, most of them are classic examples of geological V-shaped valleys. One international observer simply stated, "The terrain is mountainous indeed. This is one of the most topographically forbidding operating environments in the world."[3] Nine Nuristani villages are located in the northern and central Waygal Valley.[4]

While located on the Indian border, during its era of rule in India, the British colonial government rarely became involved with Konar and Nuristan, although the British played a role in the appointment of the Amir of Pashat, the ruler of the eastern Konar region in the 1840s. Individual English explorers sometimes penetrated into the area. One such expedition into eastern Nuristan (then called Kafiristan) became the basis for Rudyard Kipling's 1888 short story *The Man Who Would Be King*. In 1896, after the demarcation of the Durand Line solidified the political borders of his realm, the Afghan Amir Abdur Rahman Khan moved into Kafiristan and subdued the population. As a price for his future protection, he required the Kafiristanis to accept Islam and rechristened them Nuristanis, as they had seen the light of Islam, *nur* being the Arabic word for light. This was part of the process by which Abdur Rahman, a grandson of renowned Afghan leader Dost Muhammad, who ruled in Kabul for 21 years, introduced a stable central government to Afghanistan for the first time in its history.[5]

The next great external intervention in the northeast of Afghanistan occurred in December of 1979 when the Soviet Union sent troops to Afghanistan to rescue and buttress a weak Marxist government that had assumed power the previous year in Kabul. Even before the Soviet intervention, Konar had been the scene of several early rebellions against the Marxist forces. After two successful early offensives along the Pech Valley in the spring of 1980, the Soviets restricted their operations in Konar and eastern Nuristan to the placing of garrisons along the Konar River at major population centers. Soviet successes and brutality in the Pech and Waygal region were such that many mujahedeen families and most of the leadership fled to Pakistan, not to return until the later years of the Soviet war. With that area pacified, most significant heavy fighting was centered along the corridor of the Konar River connecting Jalalabad to Asadabad and Barikowt on the Pakistani border. The Soviets focused on restricting the flow of anti Soviet insurgents and their arms and supplies from Pakistan into Afghanistan through the Konar Valley. The mujahedeen returned to the Pech-Waygal valleys in the mid 1980s. The Soviets and Afghan Marxists executed a brief campaign in the Pech Valley that even penetrated to the Waygal Valley. During this period, Nuristan and Konar saw other fighting between Communist proxies, local landowners and communities, and organized criminal organizations attempting to gain control of the lucrative Kamdesh timber and gemstone interests within the region.[6]

During the civil war in Afghanistan following the Soviet withdrawal and the ensuing Taliban rule from 1996 to 2001, the Taliban maintained only a token presence in the Pech and Waygal Valleys. Nuristan's remote location, its rugged, severely constrained terrain, limited road network, and proximity to the Northern Alliance power center in the Panjshir Valley made a large presence unpalatable to the Taliban. The Nuristanis were also able to play the Taliban off against the Northern Alliance. Neither side attempted to lay a heavy hand on the region out of fear of driving the local population into the arms of its enemies.

Central government influence within the Waygal Valley has historically been limited although this has recently been changing. Similar to other remote areas, there was no permanent governmental administrative presence in the Waygal Valley until the post Soviet era (1993) when a separate Nuristan Province was established and the Waygal Valley became designated as a district within that province. Eventually a district center was established at Wanat which had been a traditional meeting place for the Waygal Valley Nuristanis and the rough road linking the Pech Valley to Wanat was improved sufficiently to allow motor vehicles to reach the administrative center for the first time.[7]

As previously mentioned, two ethnic population groups are predominant in the Waygal Valley: the Nuristanis in the north and Safi Pashtuns in the south. Because of the rugged terrain and steep ridgelines throughout northeastern Afghanistan, the majority of the communities are isolated and relationships between and within the various ethnic groups are extremely complex. The Safi Pashtuns and Nuristanis speak distinctive languages and there are particular dialects within these languages. The Nuristanis especially have a large number of dialects, some of which are so divergent as to constitute separate languages. For centuries, the Nuristanis practiced their own polytheistic religion in a region otherwise dominated by followers of Islam. As previously mentioned, this cultural distinctiveness changed only in the late nineteenth century when Nuristan finally embraced Islam at the forcible demand of the Afghan ruler Abdur Rahman. Nuristan was only established as an independent province in

1993 when it was created from the northern parts of Konar and Laghman provinces.[8]

The Nuristani people in the Waygal Valley differentiate themselves from other Nuristanis by referring to themselves as *Kalasha*. Although the *Kalasha* speak their own distinctive language, the people of the four southernmost villages further identify themselves as *Chimi-nishey,* while the dwellers of the northern villages call themselves *Wai*. The Nuristani population of the Waygal Valley also differentiates itself between *Amursh-kara* and *Kila-kara*. This refers to the type of cheese they make. This is not the minor point that it appears. The type of cheese produced significantly influences how a family organizes its pastoral and dairy activities and this, in turn, reflects the differences between the amount and quality of summer pastures that the people of the northern half of the valley possess compared to the southern half of the valley. Such complicated distinctions validate the convoluted human terrain of the region. It must be noted that even within the same ethnic group, tensions of various types and severity abound between adjacent villages, the majority of whose families are often related. As Sami Nuristani, a resident of the Waygal Valley who is currently a college student in the United States noted, "Be prepared to hear contradicting requests. Also, be open to see some sort of rivalry between the inhabitants of different villages in the valley. You might hear one thing from one village and may hear completely the opposite from another village. It has been there as long as Nuristan existed."[9]

Historically, the small population of Nuristan has depended on the isolation of their compact settlements for military defense. Vast tracts of trackless mountainous terrain surround their villages. These tracts served as effective buffer zones for their communities and could only be exploited by well armed herders who could take their animals there under protection. The Nuristanis controlled the highlands along with the attendant forests, pastures, gem-rich mountains, and water for irrigation that can turn a semi arid land into valuable agricultural fields. After Abdur Rahman imposed peace on the region, the Nuristani population gingerly moved into these buffer areas on the periphery of their settlements. They constructed irrigation systems and agricultural terraces and built rudimentary shelters to use while tending their fields. Given population growth and sustained security, over time these rudimentary shelters were gradually improved and became permanent hamlets. To the south, the Safi Pashtuns had expanded across the lowlands of the Pech and Konar Valleys in the eighteenth and nineteenth centuries at the expense of the previous Dardic speaking inhabitants. The Safis were unable to expand their agriculturally based livelihood into the highland areas adjacent to Nuristani settlements. Accordingly, the lower Waygal Valley became a buffer zone between the Safis and the Nuristanis that saw periods of both cooperation and confrontation. In the early twentieth century when the central Afghan Government unilaterally settled a group of non-Safi Pashtuns from the eastern frontier area of Konar onto traditionally Nuristani land on the west side of the Waygal Valley, the Safi Pashtuns and the *Kalasha* Nuristanis cooperated to eject the newcomers. The area remains Nuristani to the present day. In 1945-1946 when the Pech Safi Pashtuns revolted against the Afghan Government, the central government successfully played the Nuristanis off against the Safis. However, in the *jihad* against the Marxists and Soviets, both groups cooperated successfully. Nevertheless considerable animosity exists within the valley and localized struggles both between the two ethnic groups and among several Nuristani communities are common today.[10]

In Nuristan, the largest unit that has significance is what anthropologists refer to as the corporate community, a process in which a closely interrelated geographic community with common economic interests shares in management and decision-making for the use and disposition of scarce and valuable natural resources. Waygal Village, for example, the northernmost and largest population concentration in the valley, actually is comprised of two different corporate communities, Beremdesh and Waremdesh. Conflicts, usually over resources such as pasture, forests, or water, were frequent between and within the corporate communities of the Waygal Valley and elsewhere in Nuristan. The potential for such conflicts between these distinct corporate communities was one reason why the Nuristanis had an extremely strong exogamy rule. French Anthropologist Claude Lévi-Strauss developed the "Alliance Theory" of exogamy, the practice of marrying outside a local entity such as a family, clan, tribe, or community to build alliances with other groups. According to Lévi-Strauss' theory, such practices result in enhanced opportunities for cultural and economic exchanges and unite diverse organizations that would otherwise engage in conflicts (either military or economic). Nuristani community leaders recognized the need to create at least some bonds between other communities to have social and cultural links to resolve conflicts that might arise, to engage in trade between craftsmen who specialized in products in different communities, and to call on one another for mutual assistance when necessary. Within Nuristan, efforts to act in unity above the level of the corporate community have proven to be difficult and fragile. Some of the current conflict in the region can be traced to the recent dissipation of solidarity within the corporate communities.[11]

In general terms, Nuristani ethnic groups live in homes traditionally constructed into the sides of mountains to conserve limited arable land. The homes are constructed with wooden supports and bracketed in such a manner that they are generally resistant to the frequent earthquakes that plague the region. Families tend to use their first floor for storage and reside on the second floor. Walkways, terraces, and ladders connect families and neighborhoods. Access to the ground or first floor is usually restricted and the ladders that connect residences can be readily removed to enhance security. Structures tend to be clustered or concentrated, literally stacked atop each other, with an extended family living with other such families within a tightly knit community. The Nuristanis' practice what anthropologists refer to as mixed mountain agriculture, where their pastoral activities are a key element that is integrated with their crop cultivation. Essentially, the Nuristanis are subsistence farmers of agricultural land constructed as terraces cut into the hillsides that dominate the region, while livestock is raised on slopes that are too steep to be converted to farmland.[12]

The Safi Pashtuns of the Pech Valley typically reside in compounds. These compounds are enclosed by sturdy walls, sun dried over decades to assume the consistency and strength of concrete and with firing platforms and observation towers incorporated into their design. Each compound houses an extended family. Because the lowland Safi Pashtuns do not have access to the summer pastures of the highlands, they could not maintain economically viable herds of goats or sheep. As a result, the Safi Pashtuns' economy is centered on agricultural cultivation, and the location and maintenance of irrigation canals are extremely important.

Ironically, while Nuristanis generally live in mountainside villages such as Kamdesh and Aranas and Safi Pashtuns live in fortified settlements, in the case of Wanat the opposite is the case. Wanat is located on relatively low land at the junction of two streams and is surrounded by numerous fortified compounds. Meanwhile, the nearest sizeable Safi Pashtun town of Nangalam outside of Camp Blessing, was built on a hillside in a pattern similar to that of Kamdesh and Aranas. This juxtaposition seems to reflect geographical considerations rather than cultural ones in the building styles of settlements.

Nuristan is heavily forested with considerable timber of commercial value. Gem mining is now also a major source of commercial prosperity within both provinces. Criminal cartels control both industries and have frequently exploited these resources to garner individual wealth. The people of Konar and Nuristan have derived little benefit from either product. Within recent years, Konar and Nuristan provinces have seen the introduction of opium poppies as a financially lucrative crop.[13]

Both the Safi Pashtuns and Nuristanis have reputations as warriors. One study noted, "Feuds are an important part of [the] culture and many cultural values are reflected in the feud. For example, masculinity and honor are strong values and provide themes for many stories and songs. Men strive to be fierce warriors who are loyal to their kin, dangerous to their enemies, and ready to fight whenever necessary."[14] However, other anthropologists assert that this reputation is exaggerated and reflects a misinterpretation of the recognition that those who successfully defend their families and communities are afforded. Communities have a tradition of being entirely autonomous and independent, based on the isolation of individual valleys imposed by the rugged terrain. Controversies have traditionally been resolved by the intervention of elders from the corporate community. Individual leaders who can peacefully resolve the inevitable conflicts that arise over access to and the use of constrained resources are considerably respected within their communities. Still, given the poor and unsettled security situation of recent decades, it is uncommon for a household not to have access to weapons for self defense. Although an overly simplistic generalization, it remains valid that Afghan traditional cultures, such as those found in Nuristan, accept the simple physical premise of rule by the strongest, either through rule of force, skill of negotiations, or fulfillment of economic advantages. One anthropological study summarized the Parun Valley as a subsidiary of the Pech River located to the north of the Waygal Valley, "The Parun Valley offers the picture of an encapsulated Kafir culture enclosed by high mountains and an invisible cultural wall, both of which shielded it somewhat against powerful political enemies surrounding the valley."[15] This assessment holds true for Wanat and the Waygal Valley.[16]

Within these remote societies and communities, traditional processes for problem resolution (*shuras*) and respect for individual and family honor are strong, and these two concepts are crucial to comprehending the human terrain in northeastern Afghanistan. A *shura* is an Arabic word for consultation or council. It is a long established process by which households, extended families, and community representatives make corporate decisions. The *shura* system allows Afghan communities and family groups to discuss circumstances and conduct conflict resolution. The system is flexible, and relatively informal. The *shura* is, in essence, a process of negotiation, with the process and its discussions being as significant as the resulting consensus.

In addition to the *shura*, there are a series of informal codes of behavior, referred to as *"kalasha char"* (Kalasha custom) among the Waygali Nuristanis and *"Pashtunwali"* among the Pashtuns, which guides both groups. Although informal, these codes of conduct possess complex expectations of behavior and ethics, which stress honor, self-respect, independence, justice, hospitality, conflict resolution, personal improvement, personal responsibility, charity, forgiveness, worship, and revenge.[17]

The Insurgents

The armed groups that have opposed Coalition operations in Afghanistan are a diverse collection of organizations many of which are tied to specific regions of the country. Konar and Nuristan provinces lie within the sphere of influence of Gulbuddin Hekmatyar's *Hizb-i-Islami*, now known as *Hizb-i-Islami Gulbuddin* (HiG). The HiG was a fundamentalist organization founded by Hekmatyar originally to fight the Soviets and was known to have received considerable support and recognition from the Pakistani military intelligence agency, the Directorate for Inter Services Intelligence (ISI). Although the HiG retained considerable strength and influence in Konar and Nuristan, it was not the only anti Coalition entity influencing events in 2008. There were various Islamic organizations, some of which have their roots in 1980s anti Soviet mujahedeen organizations, others that were closely tied to the Taliban movement and still others that were influenced by the more recent al-Qaeda successes. A number of more radical entities were linked to *Lashkar-e-Tayyiba,* a Pakistan based terrorist organization infamous for its recent attacks in India. In addition to these radical organizations, there were powerful timber, gem mining, and drug (opium) interests that vigorously resisted the establishment of central government control and the trade restrictions, government regulations, and taxation that accompanied it.[18]

Within northeastern Afghanistan, there are three general types of anti Afghanistan forces (AAF): local fighters; dedicated core fighters of the HiG, other fundamentalist groups, and organized criminal factions that are generally Afghan-centric; and the hardcore radical Islamic fundamentalists such as the Taliban and al-Qaeda that can be considered to be transnational. Local fighters are typically recruits from Nuristan and Konar provinces or young men solicited from *madrassa*s and Afghan refugee populations located in Pakistan. They are generally young, unemployed, and poorly educated and are either used as laborers or have received rudimentary training in weapon employment. Economic or material concerns motivate the majority of the local fighters. Their rewards can be a direct cash payment or something as simple as new clothing. Like many young men in Afghanistan, some of these local fighters join strictly for the excitement and to gain a reputation among their peers and within their communities. The local fighters are generally not ideologically motivated and can be recruited away from the AAF simply through regular employment and financial opportunities. More dedicated AAF insurgents will have their operations degraded by the loss of these local fighters, principally because of the absence of transportation and heavy labor and the dilution of their potential recruiting pool.[19]

The core Afghanistan-centric fighters were members of the HiG, other fundamentalist entities, or members of the various drug and lumber cartels. These fighters are generally experienced, highly skilled, well trained, and equipped with state of the art military equipment which is often captured from Coalition forces. These combatants were strongly motivated either by religious ideology or by significant economic or financial interests. Some of them might have been inspired by blood feuds or previous conflicts with American Forces. These fighters tend to be from local districts or provinces or had grown up within regional communities and spoke local dialects. Their predominant sphere of focus and motivation was within northeastern Afghanistan or their immediate home community, district, or province.

The final groups of AAF insurgents in Konar and Nuristan in 2008 were dedicated Islamic fundamentalists or members of the Taliban or al-Qaeda who were often foreign fighters and who frequently operated across international borders and generally espoused a global Islamic caliphate. These foreigners came from a range of Arab nations such as Saudi Arabia or Yemen or from Islamic regions with relatively large, disaffected populations, such as Chechnya or western China. Most of the fundamentalist fighters were based in Pakistan. They were exceptionally dedicated and fanatic and possessed considerable operational experience. They were highly skilled, well trained and armed, and often equipped with state of the art military equipment. Although they possessed fervent and similar religious beliefs to some of the Afghans, they were usually from foreign nations, having come from different cultures and societies and speaking different languages and dialects. They generally had considerable financial and material resources with which to influence both dedicated and local fighters. These fighters were totally dedicated to their cause and unwilling to compromise. Foreign fighters were documented to have been operating in Nuristan as early as 2002 and by 2006 there were an estimated 200 Taliban fighters active there. Small infiltration teams of Taliban, HiG, and al-Qaeda fighters were all in Nuristan in 2007. A recent study of Afghanistan noted that there may have been at any time various AAF or insurgent organizations operating concurrently and entirely autonomously within the same geographic location. This phenomenon of informal competition between different AAF organizations is similar to what occurred within the mujahedeen during the Soviet conflict.[20]

The Coalition Campaign in Afghanistan, 2001–2008

By 2008, the United States and its international partners had been conducting a range of military operations in Afghanistan for seven years. The original mission in October of 2001 was the destruction of al-Qaeda forces responsible for the 9/11 terrorist attacks and the overthrow of the Taliban regime that had given al-Qaeda a safe haven. Those goals had been met rather quickly and by the spring of 2002, Afghanistan had a new government and was seemingly proceeding down the path toward democracy. Coalition forces remained in Afghanistan but in the latter half of 2002 and through 2003, United States units largely resided in a small number of bases from which they mounted periodic security missions.

Opposition to this new political path and the very presence of western military forces in Afghan affairs did not disappear, however. By 2004, there were clear signs that a variety of insurgent and terrorist groups, loosely connected through Taliban leaders and based in Pakistan, were beginning to mount a more focused military effort against the new Afghan Government and the Coalition. The American Government responded by initiating a new counterinsurgency campaign that featured Coalition units taking responsibility for large areas in eastern and southern Afghanistan. In these areas of operations, US commanders, working with the Afghan security forces that the Coalition was training, attempted to win the support of the population by providing security from insurgent groups and using the new Provincial Reconstruction Teams (PRTs) to improve living standards.

Despite the Coalition's introduction of a counterinsurgency approach in 2004, the number of troops and other resources committed to the campaign in Afghanistan remained low when compared to the size of the concurrent effort in Iraq that had begun in March of 2003. Although the territory of Afghanistan was larger than that of Iraq and the Afghan population larger than the Iraqi populace, Coalition troop levels remained below 25,000 through 2004. The majority of these troops belonged to the US Army, which in 2005 had approximately 19,000 Soldiers in Afghanistan. In that

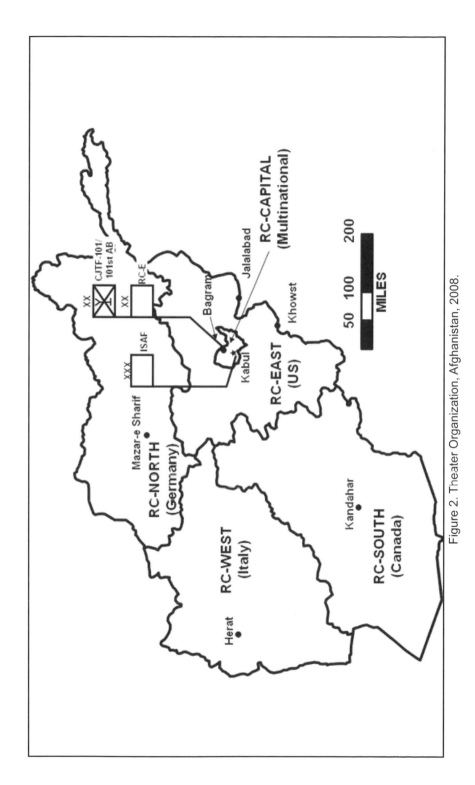

Figure 2. Theater Organization, Afghanistan, 2008.

same year, the US Army deployed more than 140,000 troops to Operation IRAQI FREEDOM (OIF).[21]

This strategic allocation of forces reflected the belief among senior Coalition political and military officials that the situation in Iraq in 2005 was more important and dire than that in Afghanistan. Coalition force levels in Afghanistan did increase over the next three years, almost doubling between 2005 and 2008 with 31,000 of the total number coming from the United States. Still, the resources committed to Operation ENDURING FREEDOM (OEF) in this period remained significantly less than those focused on Iraq, especially after the Bush administration initiated a new campaign approach in January of 2007 that featured a surge in troops in Iraq. The American policy toward Afghanistan between 2002 and 2008 led some US senior military officials to think of OEF as "an economy of force" campaign in the larger Global War on Terrorism (GWOT), suggesting clearly that the main effort of the nation was directed to Iraq. In fact, in December of 2007, Admiral Michael Mullen, Chairman of the Joint Chiefs of Staff, stated publicly that the effort in Afghanistan was "by design and necessity, an economy of force operation. There is no getting around that. Our main focus, militarily, in the region and in the world right now is rightly and firmly in Iraq."[22]

Because Afghanistan was treated as an economy of force campaign, there was only a sparse distribution of Coalition military forces across Afghan territory. Even after the Coalition Command Authority focused American forces solely on the restive areas of the south (Regional Command-South [RC-South]) and the east (Regional Command-East [RC-East]), American units were widely dispersed. After 2004, US battalion sized task forces of approximately 1,000 Soldiers routinely became responsible for areas of operation (AOs) that were the size of small New England States. These units were attempting to create stability and generally win the support of the population in sprawling territories with a very limited amount of troops and other resources.

As the Coalition campaign evolved between 2001 and 2008, the command structure and overall approach of the US effort changed greatly. By 2007, the International Security Assistance Force (ISAF) command, a NATO-led security mission, served as the senior headquarters for military operations in Afghanistan. Combined Joint Task Force-82 (CJTF-82), an organization based on the division headquarters of the 82d Airborne Division and augmented to perform a joint task force role, provided a significant portion of ISAF's forces. Major General David M. Rodriguez, the commander of CJTF-82, had authority for ISAF operations in RC-East.

However, Rodriguez had a second role as commander of forces that were part of CJTF-82 but not formally assigned to the ISAF mission. Many of these forces operated outside RC-East.

In his campaign plan, Major General Rodriguez articulated his mission in the following way:

> In conjunction with the Islamic Republic of Afghanistan, joint, interagency, and multinational partners, CJTF conducts full spectrum operations to disrupt insurgent forces in the combined joint operations area, develops Afghanistan national security capability, and supports the growth of governance and development in order to build a stable Afghanistan.[23]

The "full spectrum operations" noted in this statement was a doctrinal term defined as a combination of offensive, defensive, and stability operations that units executed simultaneously. To do so, CJTF-82 conducted missions along four lines of operation (LOOs): security, governance, development, and strategic communications or information operations. CJTF-82 stated its purpose as building capacity for governance and development, degrading destabilizing forces, and strengthening the Islamic Republic of Afghanistan. The command described its strategic goal as the creation of a "self reliant" Afghanistan that "provides effective governance; is self securing, committed to representative government, economically viable, and rejects narco-production."[24]

To achieve this goal at the tactical level, battalion sized maneuver forces conducted the bulk of the security or combat operations, often termed lethal or kinetic operations. The PRTs, which were ideally manned by both military civil affairs specialists and civilian experts in reconstruction and governmental affairs, owned the lion's share of the development line of operations in a specific province. Concurrently, both the PRTs and the tactical units performed information operations and strived to extend and improve the reach of the democratically elected Government of Afghanistan throughout the region.

In 2007 CJTF-82's forces consisted of only two maneuver brigades located primarily in RC-East, an area roughly the size of Florida. Above the regional command level was the NATO-led International Security Assistance Force (ISAF) which supported the Government of the Islamic Republic of Afghanistan (GIROA) and had authority over both operational units and the civil affairs-oriented PRTs. NATO was the theater strategic headquarters for Afghanistan and directly ran operations in the rest of the country, including RC-South. CJTF-82's major maneuver forces were the

4th Brigade Combat Team (BCT) of the 82d Airborne Division, known as Task Force (TF) *Fury*, which had a large area of operations in the southern portion of RC-East; and the 173d Airborne Brigade Combat Team (ABCT), known as TF *Bayonet,* which operated in the northern portion of RC-East. In addition to these elements, Major General Rodriguez controlled aviation, logistics, and other combat support and service support units as well as various Coalition partner forces. CJTF-82 had its headquarters at Bagram Air Base north of Kabul and its forces were distributed across RC-East on 24 forward operating bases (FOBs) and many additional combat outposts (COPs).[25]

On 10 April 2008, the Headquarters 101st Airborne Division, under the command of Major General Jeffrey Schloesser, replaced the 82d Airborne Division as the senior American operational headquarters in Afghanistan. Schloesser assumed command of CJTF-101 and simultaneously began serving as commander of Regional Command-East for ISAF, like his predecessor Rodriguez. The 101st Airborne Division had recent combat and counterinsurgency experience in both Afghanistan and Iraq and had nearly two full years to train for this deployment. Its senior commanders and staff were well prepared for the mission in Afghanistan.[26]

Like CJTF-82, CJTF-101 operated out of Bagram Air Base and directly controlled operations in the RC-E area. Several of its subordinate commands, including the 101st Sustainment Brigade and the 101st Aviation Brigade, also based at Bagram, supported operations throughout Afghanistan. Within RC-E, in addition to the 173d Airborne BCT, the 4th BCT, 101st Airborne Division (augmented by the 1st Battalion, 503d Infantry, from the 173d) became known as TF *Currahee* and operated in eastern Afghanistan in Khowst, Ghazni, Logar, Wardak, Paktika, and Paktia provinces. CJTF-101 considered TF *Currahee* as its main effort.[27]

CJTF-101's campaign plan built on the basic concepts adopted by CJTF-82 and its subordinate units. Schloesser stated that in 2007 he had visited with US forces in northeastern Afghanistan and sought to "embrace" their approach, an effort he described as a sophisticated campaign to separate the enemy from the people, improve living conditions for the population, and connect Afghans to the institutions of their central government. The commander of CJTF-101 had roughly the same amount of troops and other resources as those available to his predecessor which meant that US forces, especially in the 11 provinces that made up RC-East, continued to be stretched thin across their AOs. To disrupt the insurgents and bring development to local areas, tactical commanders chose to position small units in a large number of FOBs and COPs across sprawling AOs.

Brigadier General Mark Milley, CJTF-101 Deputy Commanding General for Operations, emphasized this salient point, noting, "We had 120 or so combat outposts in Regional Command-East. We had approximately 50 rifle companies or maneuver companies [the equivalent of] about 150 platoons and . . . a lot of these guys were engaging in daily firefights."[28] Thus, by 2007-2008 the standard US practice in RC-East was to man the large number of COPs with platoon sized elements that normally had between 30 and 40 Soldiers. In general, neither Rodriguez nor Schloesser could afford to dedicate more than a single US platoon to any outpost regardless of the local conditions or threat. For this reason, throughout their tenures, the commanders of CJTF-82 and CJTF-101 continuously shifted combat power and the placement of COPs to respond to changing tactical situations and the routine transition of units into and out of the country.[29]

US Operations in Nuristan and Konar, 2001-2007

In a 2007 briefing, the CJTF-82 commander offered an analysis of the security situation in Afghanistan to military and civilian officials. The briefing clearly identified Konar as the only province in RC-East considered a "dangerous environment."[30] Nuristan, the province to the immediate north of Konar, was classified as facing "frequent threats." As noted earlier, these two provinces were home to a fiercely independent population that had historically resisted outsiders encroaching on their authority and customs.

During the first four years of its campaign in Afghanistan, the Coalition chose not to maintain a continuous presence in this isolated and intransigent region. American operations were generally restricted to small commando style raids performed by special operations units attempting to kill or capture high value targets (HVTs) or larger operations by conventional forces that were of limited duration. In 2003 and 2004 some special operations units did establish small bases in the area that were well received by the local communities. However, only in 2005 did the Coalition bring a more permanent presence to the area when a US Marine company began operating in the Pech, Korengal, and Chawkay Valleys in Konar province.

The gradual increase of Coalition military presence in Nuristan and Konar was the result of Coalition realization that the region served as a sanctuary for insurgent and terrorist organizations. A US Special Forces (SF) sergeant major who operated in northeast Afghanistan during this time described Nuristan as "Absolutely an al-Qaeda stronghold because of its remoteness, access to Pakistan, and nearby refugee camps."[31] Further, he stated that the Korengal Valley, a small area south of the Pech River and southeast of the Waygal Valley, specifically had become a terrorist sanctuary that harbored foreign fighters, particularly Arabs. The truth of this comment was reflected in the results of one of the earliest Coalition operations in the area, Operation RED WINGS in June 2005. RED WINGS was a combined conventional and special operations forces (SOF) operation in which US Navy SEALS would support the actions of the Marines recently deployed into Konar by exercising a preliminary reconnaissance mission focused on killing or capturing a powerful local insurgent leader in the Korengal Valley. Accordingly, a four man SEAL Team was inserted onto Sawarto Sar, a high mountain overlooking the Korengal Valley in order to neutralize Ahmad Shah, the local Taliban leader, in advance of operations to be conducted by the Marines. The SEALs were soon compromised by a chance encounter with Afghan goat herders and the team was destroyed in a heavy firefight with a large force of insurgents led by Shah. A rocket propelled grenade (RPG) then shot down a Special Operations helicopter hurrying to the relief of the SEAL Team and 16 SEALs and Army SOF personnel died in the subsequent crash. Of the SEAL Team, only Hospital Corpsman 2d Class (SEAL) Marcus Luttrell survived, being rescued by a local resident who adhered to the Pashtun hospitality code of *Pashtunwali*. The SEAL commander, Navy Lieutenant Michael Murphy, was posthumously awarded the Medal of Honor for his heroism during the firefight, the first such recognition given during Operation ENDURING FREEDOM.[32]

By 2006, the need for more troops in northeastern Afghanistan was apparent. To augment and later replace the small Marine contingent, in April 2006, the 3d BCT, 10th Mountain Division known as TF *Spartan*, mounted Operation MOUNTAIN LION which deployed troops into Konar and Nuristan. The brigade's 1st Battalion, 32d Infantry (1-32d IN) established COPs throughout the Pech River Valley, which runs east-west through the center of Konar Province and was an area of sizeable population. The battalion also set up outposts in two of the capillary valleys off the Pech: the Korengal to the south and the Waygal to the north. Both of these areas were considered potential insurgent sanctuaries and a Coalition presence in these valleys was deemed important in order to prevent them from becoming or continuing to be insurgent sanctuary areas.[33]

The establishment of these outposts (FOBs and COPs) was central to TF *Spartan's* approach to counterinsurgency in eastern Afghanistan. The brigade had adopted an approach that emphasized three critical actions:

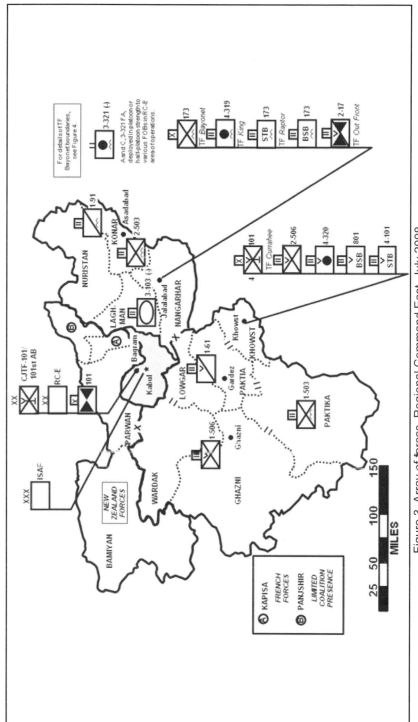

Figure 3. Array of forces, Regional Command East, July 2008.

separating the enemy from the population; securing the population and winning their support by meeting their needs with reconstruction and better governance; and transforming the environment with roads, commerce, and the extension of the Afghan central government so the enemy could no longer survive. Colonel John Nicholson, TF *Spartan* commander, recognized that his AO was so large that he could not ensure that these actions occurred uniformly throughout northeast Afghanistan. Thus, Nicholson focused the Coalition effort on district centers and communities connected by roads to the larger population centers. In these centers and communities, he hoped to create "security bubbles" where his Soldiers could begin their efforts. TF *Spartan* sought to partner closely with the ANA units in the region to magnify its effects and create greater legitimacy for Afghanistan's central government, formally known as the GIROA.[34]

The COPs, usually manned by platoons of 30 to 40 Soldiers and located next to Afghan communities and government entities, played a major role in achieving all three of TF *Spartan's* critical actions. In its 16 months of operations in the region, TF *Spartan* increased the number of FOBs and COPs from seven to 22 in the provinces of Nangarhar, Nuristan, Konar, and Laghman. The new FOBs and COPs enabled the 10th Mountain Division to provide enhanced security to considerable portions of Afghanistan and facilitated GIROA efforts as it attempted to provide services to a larger portion of Afghanistan than it had previously been able to reach. The TF *Spartan* leadership believed that the small bases and outposts were critical for success. Major Paul Garcia, the 1-32d IN operations officer, contended, "The key to our successes in Konar and Nuristan are simple . . . get off the large FOBs and establish outposts located in and among the population. . . . A unit must live with the population day in and day out in order to be effective."[35]

Expansion of these bases enabled TF *Spartan* to employ what has been called the "ink line" counterinsurgency strategy. By constructing new roads and significantly improving existing routes, the counterinsurgents would begin to connect the rural population of eastern Afghanistan to the central government along these "ink lines." However, such a strategy required an extensive logistics support system to supply the significant increase in the number of small positions. Many of the new sites were in extremely rural and isolated locations surrounded by rugged ridgelines and high mountain peaks. The existing road infrastructure was initially either absent or in extremely poor condition and was vulnerable to ambush and improvised explosive device (IED) attack. Thus, in many cases US forces were limited to using helicopters to travel to and supply the bases. Rotary wing assets were scarce and subject to frequent interference by weather conditions, particularly in the winter months.[36]

The 1-32d IN occupied Camp Blessing, an existing installation in the Pech Valley that had been previously used by the Marines, earlier Army units briefly in the area, and SOF elements. Blessing was near the district center for the Pech District of Konar Province and the relatively large town of Nangalam where the Waygal River flowed into the Pech. This post became the major base for operations in the Pech, Waygal, and Korengal valleys. The 1-32d IN's successor unit, the 2d Battalion (Airborne), 503d Infantry (2-503d IN) established its battalion headquarters there. Camp Blessing was named for Sergeant Jay A. Blessing, a US Army Ranger killed in an IED attack in 2003 along the Pech River Road.

With Camp Blessing as a major base camp, the battalion commander, Lieutenant Colonel Christopher Cavoli, constructed two new COPs directly in the Waygal Valley: COP Ranch House near the village of Aranas and COP Bella on the Waygal River next to the tiny hamlet of Bella. These positions, each manned by half of an infantry platoon, were pushed into the remote valley in order to place a Coalition presence there. In addition, Aranas, located roughly 12 miles north of Camp Blessing, had a reputation as an insurgent stronghold. Aranas was one of the largest communities in the Waygal Valley and considerable traffic (north/south and east/west) routinely passed through the town. Captain Douglas E. Sloan, the commander of B Company, 1-32d IN, inadvertently named the Ranch House COP. When initially establishing the outpost, Cavoli remembered that Sloan quipped, "It's pretty big, got a great view. It's clean and well kept. Neighborhood's good. It's one story, a nice ranch house style. I like it."[37] The name stuck.[38]

Cavoli chose the village of Bella as the location of the second COP because the International Medical Corps, a nongovernmental organization (NGO), operated a medical clinic with several doctors and health care professionals there. The clinic was the primary medical facility in the Waygal Valley. Bella was located on the Waygal River, two miles southwest of Aranas and approximately five miles north of Wanat, the district center, and 10 miles north of Camp Blessing. The village of Bella consisted of a few houses, several stores, a restaurant, and a hotel. The COPs at Bella and Ranch House offered reinforced walls for protection, sleeping quarters, and austere living conditions, while Camp Blessing contained more amenities, such as showers, a 24 hour mess hall, a regular weight room, and a dedicated morale, welfare, and recreation (MWR) facility.[39]

Throughout 2006 and 2007, the 1-32d IN performed counterinsurgency operations in the Pech, Waygal, and Korengal Valleys as it attempted to prevent the enemy from using the area as a sanctuary and extend the influence of the GIROA into remote areas. The new Coalition outposts at Bella and Ranch House severely pressured AAF infiltration and exfiltration lines in the valley. This progress was critical because of the considerable AAF presence in the Waygal Valley, including various former mujahedeen entities; al-Qaeda, Lashkar-e-Taiba, HiG, and criminal cartels from the timber trade. During 1-32d IN's tenure in the Waygal Valley, the AAF did not mount direct attacks on US Soldiers, preferring to use mortars, rockets, and occasional distant small arms assaults. The single exception to this occurred on 11 August 2006 when, in an intensive firefight, the AAF killed three Soldiers from B Company, 1-32d IN, while their unit was on patrol between Aranas and Bella.[40]

The 1-32d IN benefited from the 10th Mountain Division's Operation MOUNTAIN LAMB, which specifically focused on the distribution of humanitarian supplies to the population of northeast Afghanistan. Operation MOUNTAIN LAMB was distinctive in that the operation was actually run directly from Fort Drum, NY. This was entirely a non kinetic (non combat) humanitarian operation that entailed the collection and shipment of a large quantity of humanitarian supplies to Afghanistan. Civil affairs operations in northeast Afghanistan had significantly expanded under the 10th Mountain Division's tutelage and the need for humanitarian supplies exceeded the ability of the US Army supply system to provide such specialized nonmilitary items.

In September of 2006, Cavoli decided to replace a decrepit bridge over the Waygal River at Wanat in order to improve ground transportation in the valley. For this mission, the battalion sent a composite force to Wanat that consisted of a platoon of combat engineers from A Company, 27th Engineer Battalion, a theater level engineer unit in direct support of the battalion, a small security contingent from B Company, 1-32d IN, that over time varied in size from a fire team to an entire platoon, and an ANA Company. Once at Wanat, First Lieutenant Andrew Glenn's engineer platoon promptly met with the local elders and hired 50 local laborers to help build the bridge. Glenn provided all of the necessary tools and construction materials. He also purchased bread from the bazaar, and every two or three days, larger purchases of food were made from the local economy. The force informally contracted for laundry services from citizens in Wanat. The ANA Company provided security for the engineers through the establishment of three observation posts (OPs) on the high ground surrounding the bridge site, two to the north and one to the southwest, while US infantrymen supported the OPs. The Afghan and American units in Wanat manned these three OPs with fire teams of about seven ANA or American Soldiers at each location. Another platoon from the same engineer company intermittently performed route clearance missions to locate and eliminate IEDs on the road between Camp Blessing and Wanat and remained overnight at Wanat during these patrols to assist with security.[41]

There were some minor skirmishes as AAF insurgents probed the activities in Wanat but these proved to be ineffective at disrupting the building of the bridge. The engineers established a temporary base in an open field that was essentially inside the environs of the village of Wanat. The field was adjacent to the community bazaar and the mosque and near the Waygal River and Wayskawdi Creek. This comparatively large field provided the engineers with a flat, open staging area necessary to conduct their operations. Glenn's engineers eventually used two segments of World War II surplus Bailey Bridges to construct a major span over the Waygal River and a smaller bridge over the Wayskawdi Creek just to the east. The work took approximately 45 days to complete.[42]

The construction of these two bridges was popular with the community because of the obvious improvements to commerce and transportation that would certainly enhance the town's economic and political status. The project was also popular because it brought jobs directly to the community. Throughout this period, Glenn remembered that relationships with the people of Wanat were positive and beneficial and he felt that the population and community leaders of Wanat were favorably disposed toward the Coalition. When Glenn and his engineers departed Wanat in early November, they left behind an improved infrastructure in the form of two relatively modern bridges. Moreover, in Glenn's mind, he and his engineers had built strong support for and favorable perceptions of the US Army and the Afghan central government.[43]

Despite these newly created ties, 1-32d IN did not establish a permanent presence in Wanat. After the completion of the bridge project in late October of 2006, the battalion's Soldiers pulled out to conduct operations in other parts of the sprawling brigade AO. After October, the GIROA did maintain a small detachment of Afghan National Police (ANP) at the district center in the town. However, Coalition troops appeared in Wanat only intermittently when patrols from the 1-32d IN, and subsequently the 2-503d IN, visited the town.

While the engineer project had brought Coalition goodwill to the Wanat community, the Waygal Valley continued to be a dangerous place for the Americans in 2006. Cavoli's Soldiers found themselves in small skirmishes and suffered indirect fire attacks launched by the AAF in the valley. The 1-32d IN sustained a serious loss in the Waygal Valley on 31 October 2006 when an IED killed three Soldiers, including Sloan, the B Company commander, on the Waygal Valley Road south of Bella. Sloan and the other members of his party, including his replacement as company commander, were driving down the valley after meeting with elders and community leaders to coordinate a range of civil affairs and economic development projects including schools, micro hydroelectric sources, bridges, and roads. His death was greatly mourned by traditional elders and leaders within the valley. Although AAF resistance to the Americans continued into 2007, it decreased in the winter as the heavy snows and cold temperatures reduced combat operations.[44]

As 1-32d IN prepared to redeploy back to Fort Drum in the spring of 2007, its Soldiers believed they had made progress in Konar and Nuristan. Cavoli viewed the success in Wanat as an excellent example of this progress, emphasizing the relationships that his Soldiers fostered in the town:

I like Wanat quite a bit. The people were always good to us. They always gave us tips when trouble was coming. I felt very confident moving about without my armor on, and spent some memorable days drinking *chai* in the little *chaikhana* there. The key thing was the relationship that [First Lieutenant] Andy Glenn and his engineers had established there when they were building the bridge. Glenn was great with the people, and they took him in like a brother. This made the place pretty safe, comparatively speaking.[45]

First Sergeant Jamie Nakano, of the battalion's B Company, asserted that similar ties had been forged between Soldiers and Afghans elsewhere in the Waygal Valley, "The most defining moment for me was making friends with the Afghans that lived in Aranas. They had a distrust of [Americans] because they had not seen Americans for over three years. We were able to build relationships and a remote camp that denied a safe haven for the AAF."[46] Major Scott Himes, the S3 Operations Officer for 2-503d IN, attested to the fact that the Soldiers of 1-32d IN had made inroads in the Waygal Valley, recalling that after his unit deployed to the Waygal Valley in May 2007, Wanat appeared to be amenable to close relations with US Army and Afghan Government troops. Himes viewed

Wanat as "a village that showed the desire to partner with the United States and Coalition forces, including the Afghan National Army."[47] For the Soldiers of Cavoli's battalion, the Waygal Valley had proven to be difficult terrain where the population contained both potential allies and implacable enemies.

The Deployment of the 173d Airborne Brigade Combat Team (ABCT) to Afghanistan, 2007

In May of 2007, TF *Spartan* departed from Afghanistan. Including an unexpected three month extension, the battalion had spent 15 months in Afghanistan. The 173d ABCT replaced the Spartans in northeastern Afghanistan. This unit, the only separate airborne brigade in the Army's force structure, has a relatively short but illustrious history. The unit was established in 1963 on Okinawa as the quick reaction force for the Pacific Command. Under Brigadier General Ellis S. Williamson, the unit specialized in making mass parachute jumps and as a result, its paratroopers earned the nickname "*Tien Bien*" or "Sky Soldiers" from the Nationalist Chinese paratroopers with whom they trained.

The brigade deployed to Vietnam in May of 1965 as the first major US Army ground combat unit to serve there. Theater commander General William Westmoreland initially used the paratroopers as a fire brigade until other major combat units could be deployed. Thereafter, the brigade shifted to several key areas in South Vietnam over the next six years. On 22 February 1967, during Operation JUNCTION CITY, 800 paratroopers from the brigade's 2-503d IN jumped into the rice paddies near Katum in the only combat parachute drop in the Vietnam War. During World War II the 2-503d IN, then part of the 11th Airborne Division, had made a noteworthy parachute drop onto the Island of Corregidor in the Philippines. It was the only large unit combat jump in the Pacific Theater. That operation earned the unit the nickname of "The Rock" in honor of the Rock of Corregidor.

The Sky Soldiers of the 173d fought in the booby trap infested Iron Triangle, blocked North Vietnamese Army (NVA) incursions at Dak To in the Central Highlands, and were the first into the Ho Bo Woods where they discovered the Tunnels of Cu Chi. The brigade engaged in some of the bloodiest fighting of the war in the summer and fall of 1967, culminating in the capture of Hill 875. At its peak in Vietnam, the 173d Airborne Brigade had nearly 3,000 Soldiers assigned. During more than six years of continuous combat, the brigade earned 14 campaign streamers and four unit citations. Sky Soldiers who served in Vietnam received 13 Medals of Honor, 46 Distinguished Service Crosses, 1,736 Silver Stars, and over 6,000 Purple Hearts. There are over 1,790 Sky Soldiers' names on the Vietnam Memorial Wall in Washington, DC. Although relatively new to the US Army, the 173d Airborne Brigade quickly earned an enviable reputation during its extended term of service in the Republic of Vietnam.[48]

The brigade was inactivated on 14 January 1972 at Fort Campbell, Kentucky. In June of 2000, the US Army reactivated the unit as part of an expansion of the paratrooper battalion stationed at Vicenza, Italy, to a full brigade. As such, the 173d served as the US Army Southern European Task Force, the only European based conventional airborne strategic response force. On 26 March 2003 the brigade conducted the largest mass jump since World War II when its paratroopers jumped onto the Bashur Drop Zone in Kurdistan, Iraq, effectively opening a northern front in support of OIF. Nine Sky Soldiers lost their lives during operations in Iraq in 2003 and 2004. Following service in Iraq, the 173d deployed to Afghanistan from March 2005 to February 2006. The brigade headquarters served as the core staff of CJTF-76 in Bagram. Seventeen Sky Soldiers were killed in action during this deployment. After transferring authority to the 10th Mountain Division in February 2006, the 173d returned to Italy. Between February and September 2006, the brigade reorganized into the US Army's new modular brigade combat team configuration and officially became the 173d Airborne Brigade Combat Team (ABCT).

When it completed the transformation process, the Army planned to deploy the 173d ABCT to Iraq in 2007. The brigade began to train for that mission but when the US Department of Defense (DOD) decided in February 2007 to deploy an additional BCT to Afghanistan, the 173d was diverted to that assignment. At the time, the brigade was conducting live fire training at the Grafenwöhr and Hohenfels training centers in Germany. As Specialist Tyler Stafford, a machine gunner with 2d Platoon, C Company, 2-503d IN, later recalled, "We had been working a lot on convoys and urban tactics, and then when we found out we were going to Afghanistan, we had to switch it over to mountainous warfare."[49]

Unfortunately, the comparatively late change of mission did not permit the brigade staff sufficient time to prepare a formal plan for operations in Afghanistan. However, there was time for the unit's leaders to see the terrain on which they would soon be operating. While most of the brigade continued with its mission rehearsal exercise (MRE) at the Joint Multi-National Readiness Center (JMRC) at Hohenfels, the unit's senior leadership performed the pre-deployment site survey (PDSS) in Afghanistan. While the 173d ABCT leadership was not present for the majority of the MRE and could not benefit from the exercise, their absence provided an enhanced training opportunity for subordinates and junior officers. Because of the late notice of the 173d's deployment to Afghanistan, the JMRC staff made efforts to adjust the MRE from Iraq focused to Afghanistan focused training but the result was a hybrid that contained elements of both.

The 173d ABCT then redeployed from the training sites in Germany to unit garrison sites in Germany and Italy, a time consuming process. As Colonel Charles Preysler, the 173d ABCT commander, remembered, "Immediately upon completion of the MRE, we rolled home as fast as we could because it was Easter weekend and we went on block leave. We came back from leave and eight days later we deployed."[50] The shortened timeline meant that the 173d ABCT did not have opportunities to perform a command post exercise or conduct detailed intelligence analysis of the region of Afghanistan in which they would soon be operating.

Despite the change in deployment, the brigade was able to make some adjustments to individual and small unit level training as noted by Specialist Stafford above. However, because many senior leaders in the brigade prioritized combat and medical skills, there was far less time for any comprehensive cultural familiarization with Nuristan or Konar or for any dedicated language instruction and no time for detailed technical or physical preparation for mountain warfare. In Preysler's view, the switch in deployment destinations had made the 173d ABCT's arrival in Afghanistan a "pretty tough way to come into combat."[51]

During the PDSS in early 2007, the 173d ABCT leadership worked closely with that of TF *Spartan* and came away impressed with the counterinsurgency approach of Colonel John Nicholson and his subordinates. Preysler essentially adopted the objectives and methodology used by CJTF-82 at the operational level and TF *Spartan* at the tactical level. Lieutenant Colonel William Ostlund, who deployed with the 173d ABCT in 2007 as commander of 2-503d IN, stressed the continuity between TF *Spartan* and the Sky Soldiers. With the Soldiers of 2-503d IN taking over the parts of the provinces of Nuristan and Konar in which the 1-32d IN had operated, Ostlund noted that he heavily relied on the approach devised by Cavoli and his staff.[52]

This continuity of approach also applied at the theater level when in April of 2008, 11 months after the deployment of the 173d, CJTF-101 took command from CJTF-82 and adopted its predecessor's campaign framework. According to CJTF-101 deputy Milley, "We took the 82d campaign plan, modified it slightly and then executed [it]."[53] In this way, the Coalition approach in Afghanistan maintained stability throughout 2007 and into 2008. For units like the 173d ABCT therefore, the arrival of the new higher headquarters did not signal a major shift in operational practices in northeast Afghanistan.

However, while the leaders of the 173d ABCT had confidence in the general framework of the TF *Spartan* approach, they held some reservations about some of its details, particularly the extreme dispersal of troops on small and distant COPs. For example, Lieutenant Colonel Jimmy Hinton, the 173d's intelligence officer, felt that their predecessors had "gone too far, too fast" and established bases in the steep isolated valleys of northeast Afghanistan that were too difficult to supply and secure. Accordingly, as early as the summer of 2007, leaders in the 2-503d IN and 173d ABCT contemplated the closing of some of these bases, including the two in the Waygal Valley that could only be supported by helicopters.[54]

When the 173d ABCT arrived in northeast Afghanistan in the spring of 2007, CJTF-82 augmented it with additional forces and the organization became known as TF *Bayonet*. During its tour of duty, TF *Bayonet* maintained its headquarters at FOB Fenty at the Jalalabad Airfield. One of its two organic infantry battalions, the 1st Battalion, 503d Airborne Infantry, was detached to TF *Fury* (the 4th BCT, 82d Airborne Division) and later to its follow on unit, TF *Currahee* (the 4th BCT, 101st Airborne Division) for the duration of the deployment. This detachment left TF *Bayonet* with five battalions of all types. Three of these formations were configured as combat elements: 2-503d IN; the 1st Squadron, 91st Cavalry, organized as a reconnaissance, surveillance, and target acquisition (RSTA) squadron; and the 4th Battalion, 319th Field Artillery (FA), partially reorganized as an infantry unit. The two other battalion sized elements in the task force were support units that were based at FOB Fenty: the 173d Special Troops Battalion and the 173d Support Battalion. These two battalions supported operations throughout TF *Bayonet's* AO. During 2008, the 173d ABCT received aviation support from TF *Out Front* based on the 2d Squadron, 17th Cavalry (Air Cavalry) from the 101st Airborne Division that deployed to FOB Fenty in January of 2008. Additionally the PRTs, which operated in each of the four provinces in the AO, provided the bulk of the funds and management for the construction of roads, schools, and other projects as well as expertise in governance, medical operations, and other noncombat affairs. The PRTs became key assets in TF *Bayonet's* campaign and worked closely with Colonel Preysler as well as with the individual battalion commanders who had responsibility for the smaller

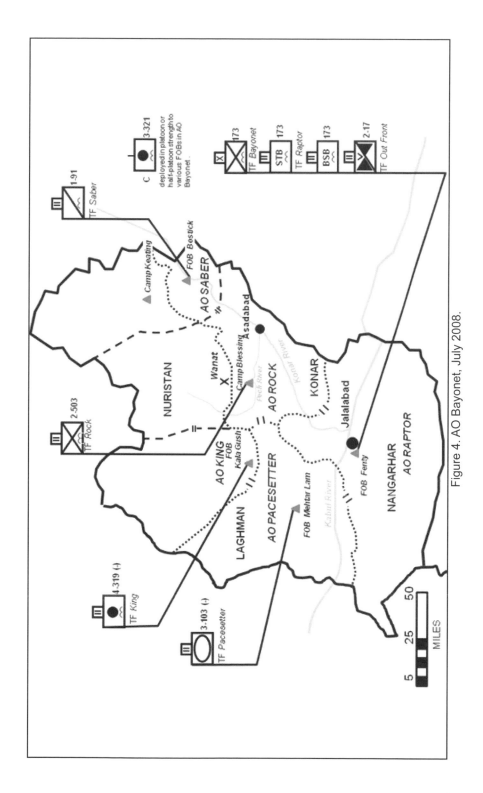

Figure 4. AO Bayonet, July 2008.

27

AOs in the provinces. Finally, in March of 2008, the 3d Battalion, 103d Armor (Pennsylvania Army National Guard) arrived in Afghanistan and was attached to TF *Bayonet* to conduct operations in Laghman Province.[55]

This relatively small set of units was responsible for a large AO consisting of Nuristan, Nangarhar, Konar, and Laghman provinces, an area of 15,058 square miles and with an Afghan population of two million. The latter were divided into 20 ethno linguistic groups, most of which extended across provincial boundaries. The TF *Bayonet* AO was about half the geographic size of the State of Maine and included the important cities of Jalalabad and Asadabad, 125 miles of border with Pakistan, the infamous Tora Bora Mountains where Coalition forces almost caught Osama bin Laden in December of 2001, the Afghan side of the renowned Khyber Pass, and numerous other passes from Pakistan into Nuristan and Konar provinces. Running through this AO on a north-south axis was the Konar River, which was one of the major insurgent infiltration routes from Pakistan into Afghanistan. To provide security and stability, TF *Bayonet* had approximately 3,000 US Soldiers spread across its five battalions excluding TF *Out Front*.[56]

Colonel Charles Preysler, the commander of TF *Bayonet*, was a 1982 Reserve Officers' Training Corps (ROTC) graduate of Michigan State University and a career infantryman with extensive service in the 75th Ranger Regiment. Preysler had previously commanded the 2d Battalion, 187th Infantry, of the 101st Airborne Division, in Operation ANACONDA in Afghanistan in March, 2002, and in the invasion of Iraq in March, 2003. He later returned to Afghanistan with the US Southern European Task Force (Airborne) in 2005, serving as the J3 Operations Officer for CJTF-76 in 2005-2006. Accordingly, Preysler had considerable experience in Afghanistan, although his prior service had not been in the northeastern part of the country.

Preysler, like his predecessors, faced multiple challenges with limited resources. His plan can be seen as a careful balance between the need to secure the major population centers where economic growth and Afghan Government legitimacy could be cultivated and the expansion of the Coalition presence into less populated areas. For Preysler, the two major populated areas that held the most promise were Nangarhar Province and the Pech River Valley in Konar Province. As noted earlier, the Pech Valley runs east-west and thus serves as a major line of communication in the region. In Nangarhar, the most heavily populated of the four provinces in his AO, Preysler initiated a major economic program called "Nangarhar Inc.," which sought to develop local businesses and attract investments

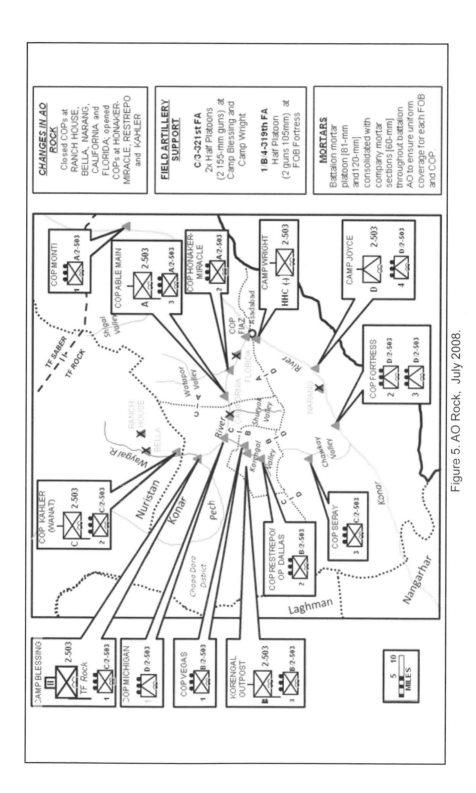

Figure 5. AO Rock, July 2008.

from both inside and outside the country as a way of providing stability and security to northeast Afghanistan.[57]

To augment the developmental projects in these two regions, TF *Bayonet* sought to expand security and economic development into less populated areas and thus continued to man the small bases and outposts where development was more challenging. In 2007 and 2008, the Soldiers of the task force often found themselves in small COPs in the Konar, Pech, and Korengal Valleys, all of which were somewhat isolated and located near insurgent forces keen on driving them away.

TF *Bayonet* depended heavily on its maneuver elements, and particularly on its sole remaining infantry battalion, 2-503d IN. Preysler tasked that unit with responsibility for most of Konar Province and the central portion of Nuristan Province. In general, the battalion's mission was to secure the Pech Valley while fostering security and development in the adjacent Watapor, Korengal, Waygal, and subsidiary valleys that ran like smaller capillary veins from the main artery of the Pech Valley. This was a daunting mission for the battalion sized force that became known as TF *Rock*.

The TF *Rock* AO was mountainous and large, consisting of 2,300 square miles, roughly half the size of the State of Connecticut. The AO had a population of approximately 525,000 Afghans divided into 10 ethno linguistic groups that were in competition with each other, and had been for thousands of years, although the Pashtuns were the dominant and largest of these groups. While it was obviously impossible for a single battalion to have a significant presence everywhere in such an extensive territory, the battalion commander, Lieutenant Colonel William Ostlund, divided his AO into four individual company AOs focused on the Pech Valley and the most important of the capillary valleys. In each company AO, the paratroopers manned small bases from which they conducted security, reconstruction, and other counterinsurgency related missions. By 13 July 2008, there were 14 of these broadly dispersed bases, including one site, COP Fiaz, which was manned principally by an Afghan police unit. (See figure 5.)[58]

Command and control in areas of operation like AO Rock was difficult. Because of the rugged terrain, distances between bases, and the constant threat of IEDs and ambushes, commanders at the company and battalion levels had to take a decentralized approach. This meant making daily choices about which units to visit, which Afghan leader to meet, and which school or community center opening to attend. The practice

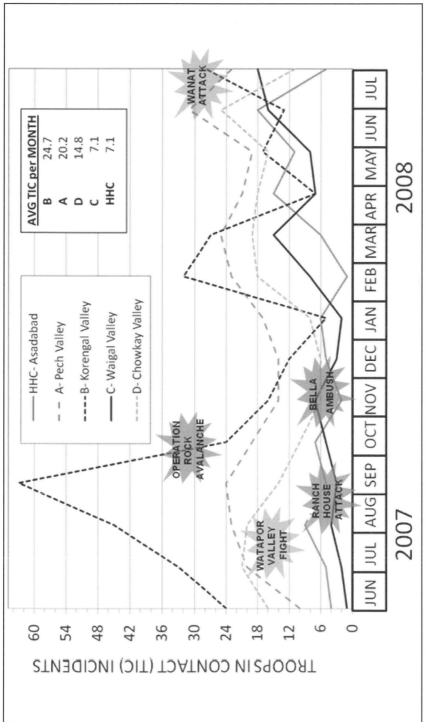

Figure 6. Troops in Contact Incidents by Company, TF *Rock*, 2007-8.

of battlefield circulation in northeast Afghanistan in 2008 meant that a battalion commander could not expect to meet with each of his company commanders on a daily basis. Moreover, when crises erupted, transportation shortages and security concerns almost always prevented battalion and company commanders from traveling expeditiously to personally supervise the actions of subordinate units. In many cases, commanders led by communicating through radio and digital systems. This type of decentralized command and control was not optimal but it was integral to a counterinsurgency campaign in which the relatively limited troops were spread broadly across large areas of operations.

Given the need to spread its forces, TF *Rock* focused on two areas during its deployment. The first of these was the Pech River Valley. Able Company, with three platoons, had primary responsibility for the valley, inheriting from the 10th Mountain Division a series of outposts connecting Camp Blessing at Nangalam with the provincial capital at Asadabad where the Pech and Konar Rivers met. During TF *Rock's* tour, A Company consolidated several of its smaller bases into a single new base called Honaker-Miracle located next to the Watapor District Center in the Pech Valley. The Watapor Valley, a capillary valley that ran north from its junction with the Pech Valley, proved to be a chronic problem for the company. The battalion's first major combat action took place there in July of 2007 and resulted in the deaths of the two paratroopers for whom the later COP Honaker-Miracle was named. Apart from securing the Watapor, the construction and security of the Pech Valley road was the main mission of Able Company. The road, located on the north bank of the Pech River, was the lifeline for both Coalition forces and commerce and reconstruction in the valley. Coalition authorities had long tried to widen and pave the road through the valley from Asadabad to Camp Blessing. After many delays and abortive starts, engineers began a final effort to complete the road's construction in April of 2007 during the 1-32d IN's tenure. Construction continued under the 2-503d IN and was completed in early 2008. Able Company provided security for the road both during and after its construction. Although enemy activity in the nearby Watapor Valley remained relatively high throughout the TF *Rock* period, the Able Company paratroopers focused on countering the enemy's campaign to disrupt the construction and traffic on the Pech River road.[59]

If developing the Pech Valley was TF *Rock's* primary mission, the security of the six mile long Korengal Valley was very close in importance. The Korengal was a capillary valley running south from its junction with the Pech Valley several miles east of Nangalam. The area was relatively small but its population, as previously discussed, was restive. The high rate of enemy activity forced TF *Rock*, as it had its predecessor, to place an entire infantry company in the valley. That unit, Battle Company, took over several combat outposts from the 1-32d IN and built another one (Restrepo) with each occupied by a platoon sometimes reinforced with additional elements. This allocation of forces was understandable. As has already been discussed, despite its compact nature, the Korengal had been an enemy stronghold since local insurgents wiped out a SEAL team and shot down a Chinook helicopter killing 16 special operations troops in June of 2005 on the slopes of Sawtalo Sar Mountain just to the east of the Korengal. In 2007 and 2008, the Korengal was by far the most active area in AO Rock. The TF staff tracked and compared combat activities in its company sectors throughout its tour and found that almost 40 percent of all enemy contacts (troops in contact or TICs) took place in the Korengal (see figure 6). Enemy action in the Korengal was highest for TF *Rock* during the 2007 summer campaigning season but insurgent activity remained elevated throughout the battalion's tour of duty there. By comparison, the Pech Valley had the next highest rate of enemy contact with slightly less than 30 percent of all TICs.[60]

The remaining third of TF *Rock's* incidents was divided between the Waygal Valley, where Chosen Company operated and other areas in Konar province. The TF *Rock* staff and tactical operations center were located at Camp Blessing. Other elements of the Headquarters and Headquarters Company (HHC) secured the military facility at the provincial capital of Asadabad and conducted various other functions along the provincial roads. Destined Company, the weapons company with its three remaining platoons, and a rifle platoon attached from Chosen Company, operated in a sector along the Konar River, which included the volatile Chawkay Valley extending northwest from the Konar River toward the Korengal Valley.

By July of 2008, Chosen Company had responsibility for a sector that included the Waygal Valley, an area extending 30 miles north from Nangalam into central Nuristan; the Chapa Dara District which formed the extreme western portion of both the Pech Valley and Konar Province; the central Pech Valley area around Camp Blessing; and the Shuryak Valley extending south from the Pech east of the Korengal Valley. To cover this area the company had three platoons; a small antitank platoon from Company D, which manned a small base called Michigan on the Pech River at the northern end of the Korengal Valley and its remaining two rifle platoons. Operationally one of Chosen Company's rifle platoons normally served as the TF *Rock* quick reaction force (QRF) at Camp Blessing while the other platoon garrisoned the posts in the Waygal Valley. The two rifle platoons rotated between these missions. The unit did not permanently station troops in Chapa Dara and the Shuryak Valley. In the Waygal Valley, the Chosen Company commander had to disperse his one available platoon between two combat outposts during much of TF *Rock's* deployment. The paratroopers in the Waygal Valley did indeed come into contact with the enemy and some of the actions were intense. The combat incidents in the valley, however, paled in comparison to those in the Korengal or Pech, representing only about a tenth of TF *Rock's* total combat activities during its tour in northeast Afghanistan.[61]

Augmenting the approximately 1,000 members of TF *Rock* were an additional 400 Americans that included US Marine embedded training teams (ETTs) who advised the Afghan forces as well as other US Soldiers who provided combat support functions. A further 2,500 Afghan security personnel from the ANA, the ANP, the Afghan Security Guards (ASG), and the Afghanistan Border Police operated in the area and conducted a variety of missions with TF *Rock*. Yet this total force was still quite small given both the size of the AO and the size of the population in the area. The 1,400 US troops in the AO represented the entire Coalition force available to conduct counterinsurgency operations in an area populated by 525,000 Afghans. This fact meant that there were two US Soldiers per 1,000 Afghan citizens. When the Afghan security forces are added to this total, the ratio of all security forces—both Afghan and US—increases to approximately six security personnel per 1,000 Afghans.[62]

A ratio of six security personnel per 1,000 residents is far below the normal threshold for effective troop density as suggested by various studies of successful and unsuccessful counterinsurgency and other contingency operations. One study proposed a force structure of one brigade (approximately 5,000 Soldiers) per 483,141 inhabitants. This figure was derived from the comparison of troop density ratios in successful historic stability and contingency operations. The study suggested that a minimum force density for police operations of 4.1 security personnel per 1,000 inhabitants is necessary in these operations and an overall troop density of 13.26 Soldiers per 1,000 inhabitants is the minimum necessary for success. TF *Rock's* strength was far below this threshold, not even amounting to the necessary force structure to perform routine police protection in a stable secure environment which Nuristan and Konar were certainly not.[63]

Faced with this imposing challenge, Ostlund and his paratroopers arrived and began operating in northeast Afghanistan in May of 2007. Ostlund was a former enlisted Ranger who received an infantry commission through the University of Nebraska Army ROTC program in 1989. Like Preysler, Ostlund had extensive infantry and Ranger experience. He had also earned an advanced degree in international relations from Tufts University.

Ostlund would later state that his unit benefited from the lessons of his predecessors in TF *Spartan*. He recalled the role that the commander of 1-32d IN played during TF *Rock's* deployment:

> Colonel Chris[topher] Cavoli, the battalion commander, subsequently went to [George C. Marshall European Center for Security Studies] Garmisch-Partenkirchen, Germany and taught COIN. He and I stayed in continuous contact and sought continuity of thought and action. He remained as a friend and mentor who understood the fight, had a strong mind, and time to think and offer advice as he reflected on his actions in Konar.[64]

In developing TF *Rock's* campaign plan, Ostlund took guidance from TF *Bayonet* while adopting much from the approach taken by Cavoli and 1-32d IN. Like Cavoli, Ostlund contended that "gaining and maintaining the support of the Afghan population" was the decisive effort in his campaign.[65] Still, he concluded that in view of the terrain in his AO and his limited number of troops, TF *Rock* would never be able to clear enemy forces from the AO; hold or secure those areas that were cleared; and build infrastructure, governance, and gradually improve the capacity of the ASF. The TF *Rock* commander contended that he "didn't have enough forces to 'clear, hold, and build' in one of my valleys, much less the 10 or 15 that we were responsible for."[66]

Instead of "clear, hold, and build", Ostlund believed he had the right resources to "separate, stabilize, and engage." "Separate" entailed clearly identifying the AAF as detriments to local security and progress by using information operations, negotiations, and relationship building with local Afghan leaders known as "key leader engagements." "Stabilize" involved United States and Afghan units pushing the enemy away from population centers using lethal (i.e. combat) and nonlethal (i.e. noncombat) operations. In this stage of the campaign, Coalition forces would become close allies with local leaders. Once these alliances fostered stability, the unit would inject money in the form of reconstruction projects to create the prosperity that would assist in the retention of popular support. The final part of this approach, "engage", included increasing stability and the fostering of healthy connections between local populations and national institutions such as the representatives of the GIROA and the ANP.[67]

Like most American tactical level leaders in Iraq and Afghanistan, the TF *Rock* commander and his company commanders sought the right balance of combat and noncombat operations to create stability and progress in their areas of responsibility. If their campaigns began to lean too heavily on lethal operations, they might cause casualties among noncombatants or damage civilian property, both outcomes that would alienate the population from the Coalition cause. However, reluctance to use lethal operations especially in response to direct attacks on Coalition forces, Afghan security elements, or the population, would likely cause local populations to doubt the ability or will of the Coalition to engage the AAF and create a secure environment. Likewise, if combat operations were not accompanied by the right type of reconstruction and governance efforts, Afghan communities might not see the tangible benefits offered by the GIROA and remain essentially neutral in the larger conflict as they waited to see whether the AAF or the Coalition and its Afghan allies won decisively.

In its efforts to diminish the significant influence of the AAF in Konar and Nuristan, TF *Rock* certainly conducted combat operations. In an article for the US Army's *Military Review* in the summer of 2009, Ostlund stated that his TF had become involved in 1,100 engagements with the AAF in its 14 month deployment. In support of these firefights, his unit had called in 5,400 fire missions (36,500 howitzer/mortar rounds) and 3,800 bomb or gun runs from fixed or rotary wing aircraft. Additionally, his troops fired 131 Javelin and tube-launched, optically-tracked, wire-guided (TOW) antitank missiles. As a result of these combat actions, 26 Soldiers in the TF lost their lives and another 143 were wounded.[68]

As a result of collateral noncombatant casualties, or the enemy fueled perception of such, the Coalition use of indirect fire and close air support (CAS) became controversial. As early as July of 2002 for example, US Army Special Forces in Oruzgan Province in southern Afghanistan directed the bombing of what they believed was a concentration of Taliban. The attack allegedly caused dozens of casualties, including women and children. The Afghan Government believed the Americans had mistakenly targeted a wedding party, formally protested to the Coalition, and forced the US military headquarters to begin an investigation.[69]

The Coalition continued its airstrikes against enemy targets in Afghanistan between 2003 and 2005 but in 2006, according to a Human Rights Watch study, the number of civilian deaths attributed to Coalition bombs made a sudden leap to 116. In 2007, the study claimed that the deaths more than tripled to 321. In one of the 2007 incidents, US forces in

Kapisa Province in central Afghanistan used indirect mortar fire and CAS against a house at which they had observed two armed insurgents enter after having fired a rocket at an American base. According to a US military spokesperson, the bombs destroyed the house. Afghan sources asserted that the attack killed five women, three children, and an elderly man. The attention generated by this incident and others like it that led to a growing number of civilian casualties induced US Army General Dan K. McNeill, the NATO military commander in Afghanistan, to institute stricter revised rules of engagement (ROE) in May of 2007 for the use of CAS in cases where civilians might be endangered. The revised ROE emphasized the use of proportional attacks only when an imminent threat to Coalition forces was clearly identified and only after positive identification of enemy combatants at the targeted location. TF *Bayonet* units disseminated and enforced the new ROE.[70]

The new rules of engagement were based on Coalition forces having a complete understanding of a situation that was often hard to come by in the chaotic violent engagements in which they became involved. Making the task far more difficult was the enemy's blending with the population and their documented practice of using civilians as shields. Despite the most careful adherence to the 2007 rules of engagement and the strong commitment to win the support of the population, troops in the heat of battle could direct attacks against positively identified enemy that inadvertently led to civilian casualties.[71]

In Konar province in October of 2007, for example, TF *Rock's* Battle Company, operating in the Korengal Valley, called in fire from an AC-130 gunship on a residential compound in the village of Yaka China into which they had seen armed insurgents run. The company commander on the scene felt that his Soldiers were in imminent danger from the insurgents and coordinated for CAS. Ostlund, watching video feed of the situation from an unmanned aerial vehicle (UAV), concurred with the decision and authorized the attack. While the CAS killed insurgents, Battle Company Soldiers quickly discovered that the attack had also killed five and wounded 11 others, all of whom were women or children. US Army helicopters immediately evacuated the wounded to the medical aid station. However, despite immediate mediation with the village elders by the Battle Company's commander and a promise to bring an $11 million road project to the area, the elders ultimately chose to continue to support the insurgents against the Coalition.[72]

As noted earlier, the insurgent enemy in the Korengal Valley generated the most attacks or troops in contact (TIC) incidents for the Soldiers of TF

Rock. The Pech Valley saw a significant number of TICs. Leaders in these regions of TF *Rock's* AO used indirect fire as well as direct engagements in response to enemy actions. In the Waygal Valley the insurgents mounted lesser resistance to TF *Rock* than did the enemy elements in the Korengal or the Pech. There the battalion's Chosen Company had responsibility for stabilizing the security situation and extending the influence of the GIROA. However, as will be shown below, the local population in this valley proved to be particularly resistant to Coalition efforts, and the Soldiers of Chosen Company found themselves in a number of minor firefights some of which required the use of CAS and artillery strikes. Captain Matthew Myer, the Chosen Company commander, recalled that his subordinate leaders did request and receive indirect fire support and directed those missions against a variety of targets including civilian buildings but Myer contended that his paratroopers, like those of Battle Company in the Korengal, followed the 2007 rules of engagement. This meant that they requested indirect fire against structures from which enemy fire was coming or against buildings that they confirmed had been abandoned by the local population and used by insurgent groups. Myer also noted that whenever possible, his men attempted to work with local leaders and use other intelligence means before targeting any structure in the valley.[73]

Throughout the campaign in the TF *Rock* AO, Ostlund, Myer, and other leaders in the battalion made a concerted effort to win over local populations with the reconstruction and governance projects that offered both employment and a better quality of life. These nonlethal operations had the potential to undermine the power of the insurgents in the AO, thus making actions such as the attack at Yaka China far less likely. The TF *Rock* commander viewed nonlethal actions, such as reconstruction projects, as the most effective "weapons" in his unit's campaign but acknowledged that they were often far more difficult to use because of the involvement of various organizations including higher headquarters that closely monitored how money was spent and how projects progressed. Ostlund expressed his frustrations with the slowness of the reconstruction effort by comparing it with the relatively free hand he and his leaders had in using indirect fire and CAS against enemy targets. In a briefing completed in 2008 after they returned from Afghanistan, the leaders of TF *Rock* wrote, "Millions [of dollars] in ordnance = no questions asked – thousands in non lethal effects = many questions over many days/weeks."[74]

To help with the complex reconstruction effort, Ostlund relied heavily on the Konar PRT which was based in the provincial capital of Asadabad. The PRT's focus in 2007 and 2008 was on the construction of roads and bridges, especially in the Konar and Pech River Valleys, as well as clinics and other government buildings throughout the valleys of the AO.[75] US Navy Commander Larry LeGree, who led the Konar PRT in 2007, contended:

> We've seen it everywhere else, where once we've built roads through some of these valleys and we built bridges that connect population areas, the economics just go through the roof and now you get people above bare subsistence living where they're susceptible to enemy influences, get them to where they care about starting a small business, selling excess commodities, and getting to secondary and tertiary markets.[76]

A study completed by the US Army Strategic Studies Institute reinforced LeGree's assertion arguing that the road building campaign launched by the Konar PRT in 2007 had done a great deal to win popular support and create greater stability. The study noted that IED attacks along the main valley road dropped precipitously between 2006 and early 2008. Further, a survey conducted by the US Agency for International Development (USAID) documented the link between the Pech road construction and the growing stability and new economic opportunities.[77]

By the end of 2008, the PRT reported spending $43 million on infrastructure projects that affected all 14 districts of Konar province and several adjoining districts in Nuristan. TF *Rock* contributed to the reconstruction effort by sponsoring $2.2 million of additional projects funded by the Commander's Emergency Response Program (CERP). One of the key targets for the infrastructure building effort was the Waygal Valley. The local communities of that valley were only tenuously connected to the rest of Konar and Nuristan provinces and were heavily influenced by the AAF. The TF *Rock* and the Konar PRT commanders sponsored the construction of a new district center in Wanat, which was completed in June of 2008. Further, they hoped to build a modern road through the valley so that the Waygal population might benefit from the greater stability and economic progress seen in the Pech Valley and other regions of the province.[78]

Chosen Company and the Waygal Valley

Chosen Company had held responsibility for the Waygal Valley since TF *Rock's* arrival in northeast Afghanistan in mid 2007. The company had established a strong reputation during earlier combat deployments and the Soldiers had adopted as their informal mascot, the popular Marvel Comics hero "The Punisher," a "lone soldier standing between evil and the community, willing to do the job that nobody else will, taking out the bad guys." The Chosen paratroopers privately purchased and universally wore "punisher skull" patches embroidered with the proud words "Chosen Few."

Captain Matthew Myer, whose father had served 27 years in the Infantry, commanded the company. Myer was a 2001 graduate of the US Military Academy and had previously deployed to Iraq with the 4th Infantry Division in 2003. Within the battalion, Myer was a well regarded company commander, known for possessing a calm contemplative leadership style which was balanced by the aggressive, dynamic approach of the company's first sergeant, First Sergeant Scott Beeson. As already briefly mentioned, although Chosen Company organizationally contained three platoons, throughout the Afghanistan deployment one platoon (3d Platoon) was detached to Destined Company. Thus, Myer only had two platoons (his 1st and 2d Platoons) to operate within the Waygal Valley. Although Myer gained a third platoon from D Company early in 2008, this platoon spent its period under Myer's control as the garrison for COP Michigan in the Pech Valley and was not available for operations in the Waygal area.

Typically, one rifle platoon provided the garrison for the two isolated COPs in the valley. Thus, half the platoon or approximately 20 Soldiers manned COP Ranch House near the town of Aranas and the other half served at COP Bella in the village of Bella. Augmenting the US Soldiers at these COPs were Afghans assigned to local ASG units and those ANA elements that operated in the valley. Usually an ANA infantry platoon was stationed wherever a US infantry platoon was. After the closure of Ranch House in October of 2007, the garrison at COP Bella was expanded to a full US platoon and an ANA platoon. The platoon not serving at the COPs remained at Camp Blessing as the TF *Rock* quick reaction force (QRF), frequently performing operations throughout TF *Rock's* AO. Periodically, the two platoons rotated between these two duties.

Chosen Company was the economy of force effort within TF *Rock* and a lack of combat power constrained Myer throughout the entire deployment. In essence, Chosen Company's main mission was to secure COP Ranch House and COP Bella, using them to separate the AAF from local communities while beginning to stabilize the security situation in the Waygal Valley to the extent possible.[79]

In July of 2008, the leader of Chosen Company's 2d Platoon was First Lieutenant Jonathan P. Brostrom, 24. Brostrom was a 2006 Army

ROTC graduate of the University of Hawaii. While a cadet, he had earned the Air Assault, Airborne, and US Navy Scuba Diver badges. Following graduation from Ranger School, Brostrom was assigned to Italy and then deployed to Afghanistan in June of 2007. Brostrom planned to make the Army a career and hoped to eventually become a Special Forces officer. He had initially served as TF *Rock's* Assistant Operations Officer and by July of 2008 he had been the 2d Platoon leader for eight months with considerable combat experience, mostly at COP Bella.[80]

The first several months of Chosen Company's tour of duty in the Waygal Valley had been relatively peaceful with little enemy contact. That changed however, in August of 2007 after Myer publicly fired the incompetent and corrupt local ASG chief at COP Ranch House. Shortly thereafter, at dawn on 22 August 2007, 60 or more insurgents attacked the Ranch House in an attempt to overrun the outpost. At the time, the garrison consisted of approximately 25 paratroopers, half of the company's 1st Platoon, augmented with small detachments of ASG and ANA.

The ASG proved to be the outpost's Achilles heel. Unlike the regular ANA combat formations, the ASG were locally recruited, low quality security personnel responsible for serving as gate guards and providing static defense from guard towers. They had minimal training, limited responsibilities, and were only equipped with small arms for individual defense. The ASG were not organized or expected to participate in sustained combat. ASG weakness gave the insurgents a chance for success. When the early morning attack began with a heavy barrage of RPGs, the ASGs promptly withdrew, creating a gap in the perimeter that allowed a number of insurgents to penetrate the defenses of the outpost. Hand to hand combat followed. Ultimately, CAS strikes directly on the Ranch House assisted the paratroopers in repulsing the AAF. In the action eleven paratroopers were wounded, some with life threatening injuries. The ASG and ANA each sustained one member killed in action.[81]

Throughout the fall of 2007, the paratroopers at COP Ranch House continued to receive indirect and small arms fire. Because of the outpost's vulnerability, its relative isolation from the Aranas community and its dependency on helicopters for resupply, TF *Rock* decided to abandon the Ranch House position on 2 October 2007. While this certainly reduced the Coalition presence in the valley, the decision made sense to those who feared another large attack especially in the coming winter months when the weather would be far worse and support would be more difficult to provide. Equally important was the fact that the decision was not a sudden one. As early as the PDSS, TF *Bayonet* and TF *Rock* leaders had been concerned about the isolation of the Waygal COPs and had discussed the possibilities of closing some of the outposts.

Predictably, the Taliban and HiG presented the decision to abandon COP Ranch House as a victory, claiming that they had driven the Americans out. They made a lengthy propaganda video that depicted insurgents seizing and occupying Ranch House in a deliberate attack. Notwithstanding the fact that Coalition forces had clearly abandoned Ranch House before the video was made, this tape demonstrated a formidable psychological operations and information operations (IO) effort on the part of the insurgents and, according to one Afghan source, constituted an AAF propaganda success.[82]

Following the closure of the Ranch House, TF *Rock* leaders obtained agreements from elders in the Waygal Valley to provide security, both in the northern portion of the valley near Aranas and in the south closer to Nangalam. However, on 9 November 2007, violence again erupted when the AAF ambushed a Chosen Company 1st Platoon patrol moving to COP Bella following a s*hura* in Aranas. The casualties were heavy. First Lieutenant Matthew C. Ferrara, the platoon leader who had won the Silver Star in the Ranch House battle, was killed along with four of his paratroopers, one Marine NCO serving as an ANA advisor and two Afghan soldiers. An additional eight American and three ANA Soldiers were wounded in the ambush.[83]

From the fall of 2007 through the spring of 2008, implacable enemy forces and an ambivalent population in the Waygal Valley continued to hinder TF *Rock's* efforts there. Direct engagements with the enemy that required artillery or CAS were relatively rare, numbering from three to 10 per month between September 2007 and February 2008. However, as the weather improved in March 2008, the number of attacks of this sort increased.[84] Still, as Captain Benjamin Pry, the TF *Rock* Intelligence officer, stated; the enemy "wasn't always effective but the threat was always there."[85] Further, Pry asserted that intercepts of insurgent communications confirmed that COP Bella was almost always under surveillance. The Soldiers manning COP Bella focused on securing their site and consequently only made contact with the local population when they were on patrol. One machine gunner from Chosen Company recalled, "We also didn't go off the FOB unless there was a patrol."[86] Most of the meetings with local authorities were conducted by the senior NCOs and officers who attended *shuras* periodically. However, those meetings produced limited results.

Figure 7. COP Bella looking westerly.

Pry and other senior officers in TF *Rock* understood the vulnerability of COP Bella. However, as Pry explained, the lack of troops meant there were few options as long as the command needed to maintain a presence in the valley. He contended:

> [Bella] was definitely a high threat area but there was little the Coalition forces were able to do about it because of limited mobility and lack of assets. . . . We didn't have the right amount of intelligence collection assets, rotary wing assets, or close air support. We just had a limited number of assets to put against that problem but that was happening everywhere in theater. Everyone was starving for assets and to do stuff up in that area, you need more than most.[87]

Battalion Commander Ostlund later contended that during TF *Rock's* deployment, the Waygal Valley presented the single greatest challenge. He called it the one area "that no matter what we did we were just not effective."[88] TF *Rock* had attempted to develop relations with the population in the valley and had supported the Konar PRT's construction of the new district center in Wanat as one way of showing the Coalition's good will. The overall situation in the valley, however, did not significantly improve. Ostlund explained that in his estimation, the lack of a road connecting Camp Blessing to Bella, Aranas, Wanat, and many other valley communities was the critical factor in the failure to foster support from the population in the Waygal. The battalion commander argued that roads connecting his bases to outposts were critical to the success enjoyed by TF *Rock* elsewhere in the AO, contending, "I attribute that to having a trafficable road everywhere else all the way to our forces so that we could have persistent presence, connect with the population, and wear down their resistance. We could wear down the enemy's desire to hang out with the population and be at risk of being killed or captured."[89] Utmost in Ostlund's mind was the vulnerability of COPs Ranch House and Bella which could only be supported by dangerous helicopter resupply missions. That weakness, Ostlund believed, forced the Soldiers to focus heavily on securing their bases. As early as the fall of 2007, the TF *Rock* commander considered these two outposts to be symbolic of the Coalition presence but incapable of serving as platforms for the "separate, stabilize, and engage" approach.[90]

The lack of progress and the ability of the AAF to retain influence in the Waygal Valley frustrated the Soldiers of TF *Rock* and Chosen Company. After the attack on COP Ranch House, one member of Chosen Company told an Army historian that he was offended by the lack of gratitude from some of the residents in the Waygal Valley, "We built them a school and gave them money for roads. A lot of times, I gave the workers clothes for their kids and shoes for their kids. I gave them blankets. We'd give them food and they complained that we didn't do enough for them."[91]

Ostlund too felt this frustration. After the 9 November 2007 ambush, he attempted to influence the population of Aranas and nearby villages by freezing all reconstruction projects planned for the Aranas area until the local leaders could assist the Coalition in fostering security in the Waygal. Ostlund announced this policy at *shuras* with Aranas officials on 21 and 24 November 2007. At the latter meeting, which took place in Nangalam, he was joined by Captain Myer, the Pech River district police chief, and the local ANA battalion commander. The TF *Rock* commander made it clear that unless the leaders of Aranas assisted the Coalition in driving out the AAF, they would not get support in the form of reconstruction projects. A summary of the meeting stated that both Ostlund and Myer told the Aranas elders that "if they want money, projects, and support, then they need to be part of the process instead of being part of the problem."[92] Both US officers hoped that as the officials from Aranas saw Bella, Wanat, and other valley communities receive the benefits of the Coalition reconstruction efforts, they would swing their support away from the AAF and to the side of the GIROA and TF *Rock*.[93]

It is important to note that TF *Rock* Soldiers continued to engage the Aranas officials in the winter of 2007. On 15 December, Lieutenant Brostrom, whose platoon was at the time manning COP Bella, met in Bella with the men of the Aranas *shura*. Brostrom emphasized the TF *Rock* position about the need for security in the Aranas area before US Soldiers could return to implement projects. Unfortunately, despite assurances to TF *Rock* leaders, the Aranas officials did not have the inclination or the ability to assist the Coalition in identifying and eliminating the AAF influence in their area.[94]

In January 2008, Chosen Company lost another key leader. At COP Bella, in the early morning of 26 January 2008, the platoon sergeant for 2d Platoon, Sergeant First Class Matthew Ryan Kahler, led a predawn patrol to visit guard stations manned by the ASG to monitor alertness. There had been previous problems with the ASG falling asleep or leaving their sentry stations to warm themselves at stoves inside the buildings. As Kahler and his patrol reached one guard post, which had not responded to their radio calls, he stepped to the front, warning one of the paratroopers, "This could be dangerous."[95] As he moved forward, calling out to the silent bunker, an ASG member suddenly leaned out, shot, and killed Kahler. Although a subsequent Army Regulation (AR) 15-6 investigation ruled that it had been an accidental discharge, the paratroopers in Kahler's platoon believed the guard had deliberately shot their platoon sergeant. From that moment, relationships between the ASG, ANA, and Chosen Company became increasingly tense. Sergeant Erik Aass, company radio-telephone operator (RTO), recalled that after the incident, many of the Soldiers became "very suspicious of the ASG."[96] In contradiction of Islamic and regional traditions, the Chosen Company leadership received no regrets or condolences from local families, communities, or government officials, further affecting the already weak relationships between Americans and Afghans. After the November ambush and this shooting, there were indications that many Soldiers in 2d Platoon no longer fully trusted the people of the Waygal Valley or the ASG. To replace Kahler, Staff Sergeant (later Sergeant First Class) David Dzwik transferred from a squad leader position in the 1st Platoon to become the 2d Platoon's platoon sergeant.[97]

In its recalcitrance, the population of the valley was not merely expressing traditional xenophobia and a desire for isolation. Facing legitimate threats and dangers from the insurgents active in Nuristan, the residents of Bella, Wanat, and other communities could not be seen as supporting the Coalition unless they were being adequately protected by the American paratroopers and ASF, including the ANA and ANP. Without adequate security, or improvements to their quality of life that were worth risking their lives for, the residents of the Waygal Valley remained at best uncommitted. Dr. David Katz, an anthropologist and expert on Nuristani culture, has argued that the population's reluctance to work more closely with central authorities was simply a self defense measure taken to protect itself against local fighters who were opposed to any outside influences. Counterinsurgency expert David Kilcullen has argued that this attitude affects the larger Afghan population as well, suggesting, "The majority of Afghans simply want security, peace, and prosperity and will swing to support the side that appears most likely to prevail and to meet these needs."[98] In 2007, Chosen Company was attempting to show the population of the valley that the Coalition did intend to prevail.

Throughout the late fall and winter, the slow campaigning season in Afghanistan, the paratroopers at COP Bella received harassing fire, and efforts to resupply the position remained difficult. TF *Rock* had considered transferring operations of the COP from Bella to Wanat as early as their PDSS to Afghanistan in February 2007. However, in late 2007, neither CJTF-82 nor TF *Bayonet* made that decision despite the concerns of Major General Rodriguez, the commander of CJTF-82, that Bella would face an overwhelming attack or that a cargo helicopter would be shot down while resupplying the COP. Rodriguez's successor, CJTF-101 commander Schloesser visited COP Bella and along with his deputy, Brigadier General Mark Milley, shared this apprehension. Schloesser commented later, "I was concerned, to be quite frank, first and foremost about Bella. It's where we had the indicators that there was some massing of insurgents."[99]

In the early spring of 2008, TF *Bayonet* moved closer to the final decision to evacuate Bella and to construct a new COP at Wanat. The TF *Bayonet* Executive Officer, Lieutenant Colonel Peter Benchoff, recalled that on 7 March 2008, Colonel Preysler directed his staff to begin work on this operation. Hines recollection is that Major Jack Rich, the TF *Bayonet* operations officer, told Ostlund and the TF *Rock* operations officer, "'We really want you to look at moving to Wanat. Come up with a course of action. I'm going to send our brigade engineer to go recon and we'll get this thing moving.'"[100] At the same time, Milley recalled ongoing discussions between Preysler, the TF *Bayonet* commander, and the CJTF-101 staff about the closure of COP Bella and its replacement with a new outpost at Wanat.[101]

Planning for the actual construction of the combat outpost began in the TF *Bayonet* staff. The engineer site reconnaissance conducted in March allowed the TF *Bayonet* logistics section to develop a list of requirements for the new COP at Wanat. By May, Colonel Preysler then sent an Operational Needs Statement (ONS) to the CJTF engineer section, a document that requested "design support and construction" of the new COP. The construction of that outpost was set to begin in early June. That statement became part of the Joint Facilities Utilization Board (JFUB) process that determined priorities, funding, and other requirements for construction in Afghanistan. When it became clear in May that all critical assets for the operation would not be available until after June, the start date for construction of the new base at Wanat was shifted to 1 July 2008. Finally, in early June, the JFUB approved the design and build plan for the COP at Wanat.[102]

The design for the COP was very detailed. In early May, the 420th Engineer Brigade had finalized plans for an outpost that had an inner perimeter surrounded by seven foot high walls and triple strand concertina wire. The facility would also have guard towers, hardened barracks, showers, and a latrine. Construction would involve both US military engineers and local Afghan construction contractors. The original design package included a detailed construction schedule that included key milestones and required 17 weeks for the completion of the COP. In June, a modified schedule was issued that reduced the schedule to eight weeks. While the TF *Rock* executive officer, engineer officer, contracting officer, logistics officer, and other staff members would become involved in coordinating construction contractors and gathering materials, the battalion relied on the engineer design and timeline as the overall plan for the construction of the new COP at Wanat.[103]

For leaders in TF *Rock*, the move to Wanat promised not only to solve the problems related to COP Bella but also to breathe new life into their effort in the Waygal Valley. The town was the Nuristani community located farthest south in the valley and thus was the closest to the American military and Afghan government facilities in the Pech Valley. The Waygal District Center and the ANP District Headquarters were located at Wanat, and a relatively modern road extended the five miles from Camp Blessing near Nangalam in the Pech River Valley to within one mile of Wanat. The final mile was unimproved but with a minimal construction effort, this road could be completed to provide excellent ground trafficability to Wanat. Ostlund later contended that he had hoped to move to the town since TF *Rock's* arrival in 2007:

> We targeted Wanat for over a year as a place where we could
> effectively progress along the lines of operation (LOOs)
> of security, governance, economic development, and IO.

Wanat would position a base that was in close proximity to a new district center, a new police station, a market, and a population center and was accessible by air and ground [lines of communication].[104]

By the spring of 2008, Ostlund considered Wanat to be the right site to begin a series of reconstruction projects worth $1.4 million. The funding came from previously allocated resources which were to be used at Aranas. TF *Rock* had frozen all projects there after the Ranch House attack. Captain Devin George, the Chosen Company executive officer (XO), emphasized another benefit of an American move to Wanat which was the potential the town presented for the development of the ASF in the valley. George noted, "We would be co-located with the district government so we could mentor them so they could police themselves up. We wanted to help them develop their government so they could do something other than just guard the district center and not really affect anything outside of their one kilometer [security] bubble."[105]

In conjunction with the TF *Bayonet* decision to begin planning the move, TF *Rock* initiated negotiations with Afghan leaders in Wanat beginning in April to obtain permission to use land within or adjacent to the village for a COP. The discussions between TF *Rock* and Wanat community leaders regarding where and when such an outpost would be established made the planning of the operation a protracted affair. Previously, the Coalition had carried out land use negotiations through the Afghan Ministry of Defense, which typically resulted in no payment to the actual landowner for the Coalition's use of his property. This created considerable ill will.

In an attempt to prevent such heavy handedness, the Army established Contingency Real Estate Support Teams (CREST), small groups of real estate specialists operating at the division/CJTF level under the staff engineer. These teams researched land ownership and negotiated directly with the landowners to ensure they received equitable and direct payments for use of their property. Standard procedures required that these land arrangements be formalized with the community and landowner prior to Coalition occupation.[106]

Appropriate for locations where security was well established, the use of the CREST process at Wanat was problematic. Discussions between TF *Rock* and the Wanat district leaders were formally held on 20 April, out of which came a document signed by the Afghans, authorizing use of land in the town for a new combat outpost. By this time, however, the AAF were actively operating in close proximity to the community and the Afghan elders and community leaders had made it clear to TF *Rock* leaders that formal arrangements would leave them exposed to the insurgent repercussions. The AAF would perceive the elders as having actively cooperated with the Coalition forces and central government of Afghanistan. At a *shura* on 26 May, these local leaders expressed a desire that the Coalition forces simply occupy the land and then pay for its use after the fact in order to provide them with political cover and deniability against insurgent threats. Such an approach would have provided the Wanat elders with a lever that they could use against the insurgents as they could then complain that the insurgents had not "protected" them against the American occupiers.[107]

The s*hura* on 26 May did not go well. Both Ostlund and Myer felt they were being "put off" by the elders and that the meeting was being deliberately drawn out. The *shura* was not, in any measure, positive. In fact, in a gross violation of well established cultural traditions, the elders did not eat lunch with the TF *Rock* officers. During the return from Wanat to Camp Blessing, the convoy was involved in a large ambush that seriously wounded two paratroopers. The American officers felt that the elders had specifically delayed the *shura* so that the ambush could be established. A follow up *shura* on 8 June went no better and the American officers believed that only their pointed declaration of "spy planes and bombers" over the valley deterred another ambush. Clearly, there were elements within the population of Wanat and the valley that did not want Coalition forces to establish a base in their town. Yet the difficulties of maintaining COP Bella persisted and TF *Rock* continued to plan for the move to Wanat. Myer recalled that he had designated his 2d Platoon as the unit to establish the COP and that he and Brostrom discussed the operation frequently in late spring and early summer. Myer noted that on visits to Wanat for the *shuras* during this period, he and Brostrom carefully considered where to construct the COP and how Brostrom would position his vehicles. Their planning included discussions about which town officials needed to be engaged in the early days of the construction of the COP and how the ANP stationed in Wanat could be integrated into COP operations.[108]

Pressure to execute the move to Wanat grew in early July as the paratroopers of TF *Bayonet* approached the end of their deployment and began meeting the advance teams of the brigade that would replace them. That unit, 3d BCT, 1st Infantry Division (ID), known as TF *Duke*, was preparing to take full responsibility for the AO by the end of July 2008. However, TF *Duke* had fewer Soldiers and resources than TF *Bayonet*.

The connection between TF *Duke's* deployment and the Bella/Wanat operation had been on the minds of the CJTF senior staff since April 2008. Original concerns at the CJTF level focused on the need for Colonel Preysler to remove the COP at Bella and establish the COP at Wanat before TF *Bayonet* departed Afghanistan. Simply put, senior Coalition leaders concurred with the need for the mission but did not want to give TF *Duke*, which was smaller and essentially unfamiliar with the terrain and population, the mission of conducting that complex operation in the hostile environment of the Waygal Valley. Instead, they chose to have the experienced units of TF *Bayonet* and TF *Rock* execute the operation in Bella and Wanat even if it meant that the paratroopers involved were in the final weeks of their extended deployment and would quickly relinquish the COP to their replacements. General Schloesser asserted that he chose TF *Bayonet* for the mission because the command was "the best prepared unit at that point, my most experienced unit in Afghanistan, and there was no one who knows Konar and Nuristan like them."[109] Colonel Preysler, the TF *Bayonet* commander, contended that the need to position TF *Duke* for success was the overwhelming reason for his decision to launch the operation in Wanat in the final weeks of TF *Bayonet's* tour in northeast Afghanistan. Agreeing with Preysler were Battalion Commander Ostlund and Company Commander Myer.[110]

The 4 July Attack on Bella

While TF *Rock* prepared to evacuate COP Bella, the battalion's intelligence officers expected an insurgent attack on the outpost. This belief seemed to be realized on 3 July when an insurgent mortar round severely wounded Specialist Gabriel Green at Bella. When the AAF launched yet another mortar attack the next day, Myer directed a team of two AH-64 Apache gunships to fire on a pair of pickup trucks believed to be fleeing from the AAF mortar firing position. The Apaches destroyed the trucks and the mortar fires on Bella, which had been increasing for several weeks, ceased. In the remaining four days of Bella's occupation, the AAF initiated no further attacks on the closing outpost. Seemingly, the air strikes had broken the back of the pending enemy attack and, in fact, signals intelligence which was later confirmed by Schloesser, indicated that the insurgent leader in the Waygal District, Mullah Osman, had in fact, been wounded in the counterstrikes and several insurgents were killed. Thus the Apache attack disrupted the insurgent command and control at a critical time.[111]

Despite this, and predictably, AAF propaganda portrayed the Apache attack as yet another instance of a callous and indiscriminate American attack on innocent civilians, since the attack had apparently killed and injured several civilians who were also in the targeted trucks. The insurgents claimed that the Apaches arbitrarily attacked the members of the staff of the Bella Medical Clinic, who were simply fleeing the area in response to a Coalition warning to evacuate in advance of the closure of the Bella COP. The insurgents were supported in their claims by both the Nuristani provincial governor, Tamin Nuristani, and the Waygal District Chief, Ziaul Rahman. When Nuristani appeared on the *Al-Jazeera* Arabic television network with his claims three days before the attack on Wanat, Afghan President Hamid Karzai summarily removed him as provincial governor.[112]

TF *Rock* and TF *Bayonet* officers unhesitatingly contend that UAV coverage clearly revealed that the engaged vehicles were fleeing from confirmed indirect fire attack sites that were actively harassing COP Bella. To support the assertion that enemy mortar crews had been inside the trucks, TF *Rock* noted a cessation of insurgent indirect fire attacks following the 4 July helicopter strike. Ostlund stated that forensic examinations conducted on some of those killed disclosed the presence of gunpowder, that weapons were found within the vehicles, and that TF *Rock* believed some of the dead to be known insurgents. However, because the vehicles allegedly contained at least one identified guard from the Bella Medical Clinic, the presence of gunpowder and weapons could be explained otherwise. Pry, the TF *Rock* Intelligence Officer, asserted that the pickup trucks initially contained civilians departing from Bella but that insurgents forced their way on board to provide them with "human shields" to facilitate their escape from the attack site and in effect launched their attack to lure the Americans into causing civilian casualties. The CJTF-101 commander recognized, however, that in striking at the insurgents in the pickup trucks, the helicopter gunships had killed civilians.[113]

The relationship of the 4 July incident to the later action at Wanat is a matter of some dispute. The AR 15-6 investigation conducted by TF *Bayonet* ultimately concluded that there was "insufficient evidence" to prove that there were non combatant civilians among the casualties in the pickup trucks but the investigation did keep Myer away from Wanat for several days.[114]

Despite the controversy and TF *Bayonet*'s attempt to address the issues raised by some local Afghan leaders, Pry thought the incident had minimal impact:

> The amazing thing was the lack of outcry. Yes, some people were mad because some civilians were hurt. No one disputes

the fact that there were some civilians there. What was amazing is that almost everyone that was hurt was brought back to Blessing. They conducted first aid on most of them and I think one or two of them were MEDEVAC'd [medically evacuated] through US means. They found vehicles for the rest through the Afghan National Security Forces (ANSF) and drove them out to Asadabad. We tried to question everyone who was there and one of the common themes was that they were made to do it. They said, "They hopped in our vehicles. They shot at you guys and then they ran back in the vehicles." As the helicopters flew by, I think someone even shot at one of them. It became clear pretty quick that civilians were involved but they were unwilling participants with the AAF that were conducting an attack. They were put in harm's way and almost used as shields.... When we were talking to everybody, they told us how many people were in the vehicles and there were four males aged 20 to 30 who we couldn't account for. No one would say who they were because they were all scared to talk about it. It wasn't like the valley turned against us after that.[115]

Despite Pry's view, one Afghan media source claimed that the incident enraged other provincial officials who threatened to shut down the local government in protest. A former Wanat resident told an American journalist, "The [US] air attack on 4 July opened a way among the people for the militants to preach against US forces."[116]

From afar, former Waygal Valley resident Sami Nuristani contended that there was a direct correlation between the event at COP Bella and the subsequent attack on Wanat:

I think July 4 was a disaster both for the people of Waygal Valley and the Coalition forces. The aftermath of the Bella incident led to the [Wanat] attack, the link is very obvious[ly] mostly caused by the anger over the death of innocent civilians in Bella. I have known two of the deceased in that incident. Most people believe that the locals were so angered by the Bella incident that they even cooperated (or simply did not report to the Americans) with those who attacked the [Wanat] outpost. The attack certainly changed people's support for the US Army given the fact that they killed the very people who had helped them or were very cooperative to them.[117]

There is some circumstantial evidence supporting this assertion. When Brostrom arrived at Wanat on 8 July 2008, one of the first acts by the local Afghan elders was to hand him a list of the casualties from the helicopter attack. The platoon leader forwarded the names to Myer. Clearly, the attack was very much on the minds of Wanat leaders.[118]

TF *Rock* did try to mitigate any tensions caused by the attack by arranging for a meeting between unit leaders and the local ANP chief, the district governor, and the local ANA battalion commander. The Afghan officials reviewed the forensic evidence confirming the gunpowder residue on some of the victims and then went on local radio to offer the Coalition version of the events surrounding the attack. Neither TF *Rock* nor TF *Bayonet* leaders, however, offered formal apologies. To complicate matters for TF *Bayonet*, another Coalition air attack on what was later determined to be a wedding party in adjacent Nangarhar Province on 6 July resulted in numerous civilian casualties.[119]

The 4 July attack took place in the midst of the final preparations for ROCK MOVE, the operation to close Bella and occupy a position at Wanat. Originally projected for execution on 1 July, the operation was delayed because of illumination conditions. This meant that the paratroopers of 2-503d IN would have to execute the operation even closer to the end of their tour of duty in Afghanistan.[120]

The Decision to Execute Operation ROCK MOVE

In early July 2008, the first Soldiers of TF *Duke* began arriving in Konar Province and started the formal transition process with TF *Rock*. Against this background, the TF *Rock* leaders and staff officers put the finishing touches on the plan to disestablish the COP at Bella and establish a new COP at Wanat. TF *Rock* assigned this operation—ROCK MOVE— to Chosen Company. ROCK MOVE was classified as a Level One Contingency Operation, one which required resources from outside TF *Bayonet* such as UAV and other intelligence collection support, as well as higher level coordination to integrate those assets. Such operations required approval from the CJTF-101 commander, Schloesser. On 3 July 2008, Schloesser approved the general concept of the operation.[121]

However, the details of the operation required the approval of Schloesser's Deputy, Milley. Ostlund briefed the ROCK MOVE plan first to his brigade commander, Preysler, on 6 July 2008 and then to Milley the next day. Myer attended the latter briefing remotely as he was still acting as the on site commander at Bella. Ostlund recalled questions about the weather and the support that would be available to Brostrom and his men if they were attacked while establishing the new COP at Wanat. In the briefing, Ostlund explained that he and his staff had mitigated those concerns by reinforcing the US platoon with a platoon of 24 Afghan soldiers. For local fire support, the TF *Rock* commander planned to attach a mortar section equipped with a 120-mm mortar and a 60-mm mortar, and a vehicle-mounted TOW missile launcher to Brostrom's command. Additionally, Ostlund intended that Myer's company headquarters would co-locate with the platoon at Wanat, which would also have the priority of fires during the operation from the two 155-mm howitzers located at Camp Blessing and two at Asadabad. A Predator UAV and other intelligence platforms would provide the platoon information about the Wanat area and offer early warning of any impending attack. Convinced that the plan was complete and comprehensive, Milley approved it and ordered TF *Rock* to execute ROCK MOVE beginning the next day, 8 July 2008.[122]

In terms of the enemy threat, the ROCK MOVE planners considered the greatest threat to the operation to be an attack on Bella while it was being evacuated that either disrupted the operation or shot down one of the transport helicopters moving supplies and troops. Considered equally dangerous was an ambush of the 2d Platoon while it moved by road to Wanat or immediately after it arrived there. On the other hand, the intelligence specialists and combat commanders felt that the most likely enemy activity during the course of the operation would be possible mortar and small arms sniping at ground personnel and aircraft at both Bella and Wanat and possible ambushes and IED attacks on the road between Camp Blessing and Wanat. TF *Rock* expected to have sufficient available manpower and firepower to repulse or neutralize these likely insurgent efforts at disrupting the execution of ROCK MOVE.[123]

By this time, Chosen Company's tour of duty in the Waygal Valley was down to about two weeks. All of the paratroopers' personal gear with the exception of their weapons, rucksacks, and combat equipment, had been shipped home. Chosen Company and TF *Rock* had spent over 14 months conducting complex and intensive counterinsurgency operations in the Waygal Valley. By the summer of 2008, the Soldiers of Chosen Company and TF *Rock* were more than familiar with the AAF that they fought against. Indeed, TF *Rock* reported that the company had fought 48 engagements with the enemy in the Waygal Valley during those 14 months. Only eight of those actions had been initiated by the Coalition. The Soldiers of TF *Rock* knew how the insurgents fought, they understood their tactics and how they preferred to employ their weapons, and they respected the AAF as tough, determined, committed, and skilled fighters.

However, as noted earlier, actual interaction between the population and the paratroopers had been limited. Generally, Chosen Company's time in the Waygal Valley had proven to be frustrating, and after 14 months of operations, progress was difficult to measure.[124]

Viewed from beyond the confines of the Waygal Valley, TF *Rock* had experienced considerable success with a counterinsurgency approach in its AO, much of that based on road construction and expansion in the Pech and Konar Valleys. The paratroopers of TF *Rock* had achieved some progress in the considerably more volatile Korengal Valley, one of the task force's main efforts. However, concomitant success was not achieved within the Waygal Valley, where the Soldiers of Chosen Company found themselves devoting a great amount of effort to their own security. The actions of the enemy and the reactions of the US Soldiers in the valley led to more than a modicum of mutual distrust between the Soldiers and the Waygal Valley population. Against this background, the withdrawal from COP Bella and the occupation of COP Kahler in Wanat moved forward.

Notes

1. Frank L. Holt, *Into the Land of Bones, Alexander the Great in Afghanistan* (Los Angeles: University of California Press, 2005); John Prevas, *Envy of the Gods, Alexander the Great's Ill-Fated Journey Across Asia* (Cambridge, MA: Da Capo Press, 2004); Shaista Wahab and Barry Youngerman, *A Brief History of Afghanistan* (New York, NY: Facts on File, 2007), 43.

2. Information on Nuristan predominantly comes from three sources: Max Klimburg, "The Situation in Nuristan," *Central Asian Survey* 20, no. 3 (2001): 383–390; Richard V. Weekes, ed., "Nuristani," in *Muslim Peoples, A World Ethnographic Survey* (Westport, CT: Greenwood Press, 1978), 292–297; and Richard F. Strand, "The Current Political Situation in Nuristan," http://users.sedona.net/~strand/Current.html (accessed 12 February 2009).

3. David Kilcullen, *The Accidental Guerrilla: Fighting Small Wars in the Midst of a Big One* (New York: Oxford University Press, 2009), 107.

4. Dr. David Katz of the Naval War College, an expert on Nuristan, reviewed this chapter. Also see David J. Katz, *Kafir to Afghan: Religious Conversion, Political Incorporation and Ethnicity in the Väygal Valley, Nuristan* (Ph.D. Thesis, University of California, Los Angeles, 1982); Schuyler Jones, *Men of Influence in Nuristan: A Study of Social Control and Dispute Settlement in Waygal Valley, Afghanistan* (New York: Seminar Press, 1974), 25. The village of Wanat itself is located at a height of 3773 feet. See Katz, 74. The boundary between Nuristan and Konar in the Waygal Valley has been controversial. On some maps the boundary appears north of Wanat, making the village a part of the Pech district of Konar Province. The Nuristanis consider the ethnic boundary to be the provincial boundary. The central government tacitly agreed to this interpretation as the district capital for the Waygal District of Nuristan is now considered to be Wanat and a new district center was built there in 2007. The Nuristanis claim any place where Nuristanis live to be de facto parts of Nuristan including large areas of northeastern Kunar Province. Ironically, large parts of western Nuristan contain Pashai-speaking inhabitants.

5. Christine Noelle, *State and Tribe in Nineteenth-Century Afghanistan: The Reign of Amir Dost Muhammad Khan (1826-1863)* (London: RoutledgeCurzon, 2004), 37. The British and Russians drew up the Durand Line in 1894 to mark the western border of British India with Afghanistan and effectively make an indsependent Afghanistan into a buffer state between the two great powers.

6. Combat actions in the Konar Valley region are documented in Colonel Lester W. Grau, ed., *The Bear Went Over the Mountain: Soviet Combat Tactics in Afghanistan* (Washington, DC: National Defense University Press, 1996); Colonel Ali Ahmad Jalali and Lester W. Grau, *The Other Side of the Mountain: Mujahideen Tactics in the Soviet-Afghan War* (Quantico, VA: US Marine Corps, 1995); Stephen Tanner, *Afghanistan: A Military History from Alexander the Great to the Fall of the Taliban* (Cambridge, MA: Da Capo Press, 2002), 245–246.

For more on the timber criminal interests in Nuristan, see Antonio Giustozzi, *Koran, Kalashnikov, and Laptop, The Neo-Taliban Insurgency in Afghanistan* (New York: Columbia University Press, 2008), 64–65. The destruction of the Nuristan forests and looting of the timber to finance the mujahedeen during the Soviet-Afghanistan War is briefly discussed in Rob Chultheis, *Night Letters, Inside Wartime Afghanistan* (New York: Orion Books, 1992), 124–126. The current use by the Taliban of gemstones and timber to finance their operations has been recently discussed in Animesh Roul, "Gems, Timber, and Jiziya: Pakistan's Taliban Harness Resources to Fund Jihad," *Terrorism Monitor* 7, no. 11 (30 April 2009), http://www.jamestown.org/programs/gta/single/?tx_ ttnews%5Btt_news%5D=34928&tx_ttnews%5BbackPid%5D=26&cHash=4d18 a44d9a (accessed 13 October 2009). For a good first person account of the Pech uprising against the Marxists and Soviets, see David B. Edwards, *Before Taliban: Geneologies of the Afghan Jihad* (Berkeley: University of California Press, 2002), 132-166.

7. Katz, 77.

8. Wahab and Youngerman, *A Brief History of Afghanistan*, 16–17.

9. Sami Nuristani, e-mail to Douglas R. Cubbison, Combat Studies Institute, Fort Leavenworth, KS, 2 March 2009. Dr. David Katz has carefully reviewed the discussion of these ethnic groups. The Pashai, who live in the Korengal Valley, in parts of the Pech Valley west of Nangalam and in western Nuristan, speak a separate Indic (Dardic) language (Pashai). For the purposes of this study, the Pashai and Safi Pashtun are discussed together. For a detailed discussion of the Nuristani people of the Waygal Valley, see Katz, *Kafir to Afghan*.

10. Katz, 133, 155-6, 176-7.

11. This anthropological discussion is provided for background information, but has no direct bearing on the Battle of Wanat.

12. Lennart Edelberg, "The Nuristani House," in *Cultures of the Hindu-Kush, Selected Papers from the Hindu-Kush Cultural Conference Held at Moesgard 1970,* edited by Karl Jettmar (Wiesbaden, Germany: Franz Steiner Verlag, 1974), 120.

13. First Lieutenant Erik Jorgensen, interview by Douglas R. Cubbison, 2007.

14. "Pashai," *World Culture Encyclopedia*, http://www.everyculture.com/ Africa-Middle-East/Pashai.html (accessed 12 February 2009).

15. Max Klimburg, "The Enclaved Culture of Parun in Former Kafiristan," *Asien* 104 (July 2007): 70.

16. George H. Wittman, "Afghan Proving Ground," *The American Spectator*, 6 March 2009, http://spectator.org/archives/2009/03/06/afghan-proving-ground/ print (accessed 6 March 2009).

17. Katz, 135, 174, 213, 246-250, 256; Marcus Luttrell, *Lone Survivor: The Eyewitness Account of Operation Redwing and the Lost Heroes of SEAL Team 10* (New York: Little, Brown and Company, 2007), 285-6.

18. Mohammad Yousaf, *Afghanistan, The Bear Trap* (Havertown, PA: Casemate, 2001), 40–41, 105, 119, 208; Seth G. Jones, *In The Graveyard of Empires, America's War in Afghanistan* (New York: W.W. Norton and Company, 2009), 30–34; Kilcullen, *The Accidental Guerrilla*, xviii–xix. The same term is used by Jones, 77–79.

19. Captain Benjamin Pry, interview by Douglas R. Cubbison, Combat Studies Institute, Fort Leavenworth, KS, 6 May 2009, 6; For discussions of local fighters, see Giustozzi, *Koran, Kalashnikov, and Laptop*, 41.

20. Note that this assessment is an expansion of that promulgated by Giustozzi, *Koran, Kalashnikov, and Laptop*, 33–43, and supported by the insightful analysis provided by Kilcullen, *The Accidental Guerrilla*, 83–87; Giustozzi, *Koran, Kalashnikov, and Laptop*, 35, 68, 101; Jones, *In The Graveyard of Empires*, 228.

21. Senate Committee, *Statement of Secretary of Defense Robert M. Gates, Senate Armed Services Committee, Tuesday, September 23, 2008*, 6; Department of the Army G3, *US Army Troop Levels in OEF Spreadsheet*, 2008.

22. Robert Burns, "Mullen: Afghanistan Isn't Top Priority," *USA Today*, 11 December 2007, http://www.usatoday.com/news/washington/2007-12-11-3963072919_x.htm (accessed 6 November 2009).

23. CJTF-82, "CJTF-82 Command Brief," 14 February 2008, slide 7.

24. CJTF-82, "CJTF-82 Command Brief," 14 February 2008, slides 9, 23; Brigadier General Mark Milley, interview by Douglas R. Cubbison and Dr. William G. Robertson, Combat Studies Institute, Fort Leavenworth, KS, 18 and 20 August 2009, 33.

25. CJTF 82, "Tier I OPD AAR" Briefing, undated, RC-East Geometry slide.

26. Major General Jeffrey Schloesser, interview by Douglas R. Cubbison and Robert Ramsey, Combat Studies Institute, Fort Leavenworth, KS, 5 August 2009, 1–3; Milley, interview, 18 and 20 August 2009, 4–5.

27. The 1-503d Infantry had previously served under TF *Fury* (4th BCT, 82d Airborne Division). When TF *Currahee* (4th BCT, 101st Airborne Division) replaced TF *Fury* in April 2008, the paratrooper battalion continued to serve under the new brigade until it redeployed in July 2008.

28. Milley, interview, 18 and 20 August 2009, 33.

29. Schloesser, interview, 5 August 2009, 3.

30. CJTF-82, "CJTF-82 Command Brief," 14 February 2008, slide 16.

31. Sergeant Major D. Utley, "Konar Valley," *Long Hard Road, NCO Experiences in Afghanistan and Iraq* (Fort Bliss, TX: US Army Sergeants Major Academy, October 2007), 53–56.

32. For Luttrell's experience see Marcus Luttrell, *Lone Survivor: The Eyewitness Account of Operation Redwing and the Lost Heroes of SEAL Team 10* (New York: Little, Brown and Company, 2007).

33. Colonel Michael A. Coss, "Operation Mountain Lion: CJTF-76 in Afghanistan, Spring 2006," *Military Review* (January–February 2008): 26.

34. 3d Brigade Combat Team, 10th Mountain Division, *Spartan Review, After Action Report, Afghanistan 06–07*, Fort Drum, NY, May 2007, 5-4, 6-24.

35. 3d BCT, 10th Mountain Division, *Spartan Review*, page 5-16. A FOB is formally defined by the US Army as any secured forward position that is used to support tactical operations. The term "combat outpost" is not formally defined by the US Army, but is generally used to describe any post that is smaller or less permanent than a FOB. In practice, Soldiers of all ranks tend to use the two terms interchangeably.

36. The "ink line" strategy is fully articulated in Kilcullen, *Accidental Guerrilla*, 87–95; and in Douglas R. Cubbison, "The Crossed Swords Tribe of Afghanistan: The 10th Mountain Division and Counterinsurgency Excellent in Afghanistan, 2006," 57–62 (unpublished manuscript).

37. Colonel Christopher Cavoli, e-mail to Douglas R. Cubbison, Combat Studies Institute, Fort Leavenworth, KS, 15 March 2009.

38. Captain Matthew Myer and and First Lieutenant Matthew Ferrera, interview by Major David Hanson, 305th Military History Detachment, Camp Blessing, Afghanistan, c. August-Septembetr 2007, 5. As early as November 2003 US Army Rangers and troops from the 1st Brigade, 10th Mountain Division, had first visited Aranas at the same time that Camp Blessing (originally called Camp Catamount) was first established.

39. The area of Bella was also familiar to US forces prior to the establishment of a COP there. In October 2003, the US Air Force bombed a house in the village of Tazagul Kala, just south of Bella. The house was presumed to be occupied by HiG leader Gulbuddin Hekmatyar. In November 2003, US Army troops from the 1st Brigade, 10th Mountain Division, surveyed the site of the bombing. While close associates of Hekmatyar had been killed in the airstrike, the HiG leader himself had not been present. See "Uphill Pursuit for Afghan Warlord,' *Christian Science Monitor*, 22 December 2003, http://www.csmonitor.com/2003/1222/p06s01-wosc.html/(page)/CSM-Photo-Galleries/In-Pictures/Space-Photos-of-the-Day/Space-photos-of-the-day-06-22 (accessed 17 July 2010); Kevin Dougherty, "10th Mountain Division Improves Base for Incoming Unit," S*tars and Stripes,* May 15, 2007, http://www.stripes.com/news/10th-mountain-division-improves-base-for-incoming-unit-1.64019 (accessed 17 August 2010)

40. The three soldiers were Specialist Rogelio R. Garza, Jr., Private First Class Andrew R. Small, and Private First Class. James P. White, Jr. See "Three Soldiers Killed in Enemy Attack," *DiversityinBusiness.com,*

http://www.diversityinbusiness.com/Military/Casualties/2006/Mil_Cas_20608.
htm (accessed on 16 August 2010).

41. Captain Andrew Glenn, e-mail to Douglas R. Cubbison, Combat Studies
Institute, Fort Leavenworth, KS, 20 August 2009; Cavoli, e-mail, 15 March 2009.

42. Glenn email, 20 August 2009.

43. Captain Andrew Glenn, interview by Douglas R. Cubbison, Combat
Studies Institute, Fort Leavenworth, KS, 2 April 2009, 1–4. When Wanat was
searched following the 13 July 2008 engagement, they discovered memorabilia
from this project including a 27th Engineer Battalion commemorative coin. See
Major Scott Himes, interview by Douglas R. Cubbison, Combat Studies Institute,
Fort Leavenworth, KS, 25 April 2009, 4.

44. Cavoli, e-mail, 15 March 2009. Typically insurgent activity in Afghanistan
was greatly reduced in the winter.

45. Cavoli, e-mail.

46. First Sergeant Jamie Nakano, "1SG Jamie Nakano, Infantry," in *Afghan
Company Commander After Action Review Book, Operation Enduring Freedom
VII*, ed. Lieutenant Colonel Tony Burgess, 64 (West Point, NY: US Army Center
for Company Level Leaders, US Military Academy, 2007).

47. Himes, interview, 25 April 2009, 2.

48. Edward F. Murphy, *Dak To, The 173d Airborne Brigade in South
Vietnam's Central Highlands, June–November 1967* (Novata, CA: Presidio Press,
1993); Bob Breen, *First To Fight, Australian Diggers, New Zealand Kiwis and
US Paratroopers in Vietnam, 1965–1966* (Nashville: The Battery Press, 1988).

49. Corporal Tyler M. Stafford, interview by Douglas R. Cubbison, Combat
Studies Institute, Fort Leavenworth, KS, 10 February 2009.

50. Colonel Charles Preysler, interview by Major Kevin Ellson, Center for
Army Lessons Learned (CALL) Theater Observation Detachment Liaison Officer
to Combined Joint Task Force (CJTF) 101, 3 September 2008, https://call2.army.
mil/toc.asp?document=4655 (accessed 18 February 2009).

51. Preysler, interview, 3 September 2008.

52. Colonel William Ostlund, interview by Contemporary Operations Study
Team, Combat Studies Institute, Fort Leavenworth, KS, 19–20 March 2009, 4.

53. Milley, interview, 18 and 20 August 2009, 13.

54. Lieutenant Colonel Jimmy Hinton, interview by Douglas R. Cubbison,
Combat Studies Institute, Fort Leavenworth, KS, 18 March 2009, 10; Schloesser,
interview, 5 August 2009, 5; Milley, interview, 18 and 20 August 2009, 15–16;
Himes, interview, 25 April 2009, 2; Major Brian T. Beckno, interview by Douglas
R. Cubbison, Combat Studies Institute, Fort Leavenworth, KS, 2 July 2009, 4–5;
Exhibit 6a (Operations Officer, 2-503d IN, interview) to US Central Command
(CENTCOM), "Re-investigation into the Combat Action at Wanat Village, Wygal
District, Nuristan Province, Afghanistan, on 13 July 2008 (Redacted), 9.

55. The 3-103 AR replaced a previous ARNG organization with the same mission, 1-158th IN, from Arizona, which had deployed in March 2007 and also been attached to TF *Bayonet*. The 1-158th IN had, in turn, replaced a Connecticut ARNG unit, 1-102d IN, which had originated the Laghman mission in December 2006.

56. The population figures are from Afghanistan Research and Evaluation Unit, "Updated Population Estimates for Afghanistan," *Afghanistan Research Newsletter*, http://www.areu.org.af/index.php?option=com_frontpage& Itemid=25 (accessed 13 August 2009). There is no census for Afghanistan so these numbers are approximate.

57. Colonel Charles Preysler, interview by Major Kevin Ellson, 3 September 2008, US Army Center for Army Lessons Learned, Fort Leavenworth, KS, 8 September 2008.

58. 2-503d IN, "Thoughts on COIN/OEF VIII" Briefing, slide 16; "Updated Population Estimates for Afghanistan;" TF *Rock*, "NTC Observer Controller" Briefing, 12 December 2007, slide 17; TF *Rock*, TF *Rock* RIP/TOA Back Brief," 16 June 2008, slide entitled "TF *Rock* Pre-RIP."

59. Ostlund, interview, 19–20 March 2009, 8, 15; Michael Moore and James Fussell, *Afghanistan Report 1: Kunar and Nuristan: Rethinking US Counterinsurgency Operations* (Washington, DC: Institute for the Study of War, 2009), 21, 31, http://www.understandingwar.org/files/Afghanistan_Report_1.pdf (accessed 5 April 2010).

60. TF *Rock*, "TIC Asset Tracker" Spreadsheet, 22 July 2008.

61. TF *Rock*, "TIC Asset Tracker" Spreadsheet, 22 July 2008; Exhibit 16a (Captain, Company Commander, 2d Platoon, C Company, 2-503d IN, interview) to US Central Command (CENTCOM), "Re-investigation into the Combat Action at Wanat Village, Wygal District, Nuristan Province, Afghanistan, on 13 July 2008 (Redacted), 36-7; TF *Rock*, "CONOP ROCK MOVE," PowerPoint Presentation, 7 July 2008, slide 9; Chosen Company's sector was expanded to include COP Michigan about halfway through its tour when TF *Saber*, the unit to the right (northeast) of TF *Rock* transferred one of its troops to TF *Raptor* (the Brigade Special Troops Battalion) in Nangarhar Province and TF *Rock* then assumed responsibility for two districts in Kunar Province formerly in AO Saber. Able Company's boundaries were adjusted to include these new districts and Chosen company assumed responsibility for COP Michigan and received the 1st Platoon, Destined Company, formerly attached to Able Company, to garrison the COP. See Exhibit 30b (COL, Deputy Brigade Commander, 173d ABCT, interview) to US Central Command (CENTCOM), "Re-investigation into the Combat Action at Wanat Village, Wygal District, Nuristan Province, Afghanistan, on 13 July 2008 (Redacted), 65.

62. Major Brian Beckno, e-mail to Douglas R. Cubbison, Combat Studies Institute, Fort Leavenworth, KS, 29 July 2009.

63. John J. McGrath, *Boots on the Ground: Troop Density in Contingency Operations* (Fort Leavenworth, KS: Combat Studies Institute Press, 2006), 148.

64. Colonel William Ostlund, e-mail to Douglas R. Cubbison, Combat Studies Institute, Fort Leavenworth, KS, 23 February 2009.

65. 2-503d IN, "Thoughts on COIN" Briefing, slide 15.

66. Ostlund, interview, 19–20 March 2009, 4, 5.

67. Ostlund, 5.

68. Colonel William B. Ostlund, "Tactical Leader Lessons Learned in Afghanistan: Operation Enduring Freedom VIII," *Military Review* (July–August 2009): 9.

69. Linda D. Kozaryn, "New Weapons Cache Found: Oruzgan Deaths Investigated," *Defend America*, 8 July 2002, http://www.defendamerica.mil/archive/2002-07/20020708.html (accessed 19 November 2009). Every US action in Nuristan resulted in an enemy claim of massive civilian casualties. A prime example is the 6 April 2008 raid against an insurgent stronghold in the town of Shok in Doab District in western Nuristan by US SF and Afghan Commandos. The six hour firefight was so intense that ten SF soldiers were later awarded the Silver Star Medal for the action. Yet articles appearing in Islamic and European news sources soon claimed the US forces had "massacred" civilians indiscriminately. In reality, the insurgents had no reservations about using civilians as human shields. This situation reoccurred during the 4 July 2008 Bella action, which is discussed later in this work. See "Narrative from Shok Valley Battle in Afghanistan," *Army Times*, 15 December 2008, http://www.armytimes.com/news/2008/12/army_battlenarrative_121508w/ (accessed on 19 July 2010); and "The Massacre in the Do'ab District, Nuristan," *RAWA News*, 29 April 2008, http://www.rawa.org/temp/runews/2008/04/29/the-massacre-in-the-do-8217-ab-district-nuristan.html (accessed on 19 July 2010).

70. Human Rights Watch, *"Troops In Contact": Airstrikes and Civilian Deaths in Afghanistan* (New York, NY: Human Rights Watch, 2008), 13; Carlotta Gall and Abdul Waheed Wafa, "9 From One Family Die in U.S. Strike Near Kabul," *New York Times*, 6 March 2007, http://www.nytimes.com/2007/03/06/world/asia/06afghan.html?_r=1&scp=2&sq=march%206%202007%20gall&st=cse (accessed 20 November 2009); Gall and Wafa, "9 From One Family Die in U.S. Strike Near Kabul;" The briefing used by TF *Bayonet* to explain the 2007 Rules of Engagement was titled "TF *Bayonet* CDRs ROE Refresher" and was dated 15 May 2007.

71. The Taliban practice of shielding has been documented in Human Rights Watch, *"Troops In Contact": Airstrikes and Civilian Deaths in Afghanistan,* 25–28.

72. Elizabeth Rubin, "Battle Company is Out There," *New York Times,* 24 February 2008, http://www.nytimes.com/2008/02/24/magazine/24afghanistan-t.html?pagewanted=1&_r=1 (accessed 20 November 2009); Rubin, "Battle

Company is Out There." In a recent work, Sebastian Junger, a reporter then embedded with Battle Company, presents this incident more sharply. Yaka China was an insurgent stronghold and US airstrikes were ordered only after surveillance sources directly saw enemy groups moving in and around specific locations in the village. See Sebastian Junger, *War* (New York: Hachette Book Group, 2010), 94-100.

73. Captain Matthew Myer, e-mail to Donald P. Wright, Combat Studies Institute, Fort Leavenworth, KS, 7 December 2009.

74. 2-503d IN, "Thoughts on COIN" Briefing, slide 25.

75. 2-503d IN, "2d Battalion (ABN), 503d IN, 173d ABCT, AO Rock Overview, 26 July 2008" Briefing, slide 93.

76. Soraya Sarhaddi Nelson, "Westerners Play Pivotal Role in Afghan Rebuilding," *National Public Radio Morning Edition* transcript, 20 May 2008, http://www.npr.org/templates/transcript/transcript.php?storyId=90599416 (accessed 20 November 2009).

77. Carter Malkasian and Gerald Meyerle, *Provincial Reconstruction Teams: How Do We Know They Work?* (Carlisle Barracks, PA: Strategic Studies Institute, 2009), 19.

78. 2-503d IN, "2d Battalion (ABN), 503d IN, 173d ABCT, AO Rock Overview, 26 July 2008" Briefing, slide 92; "TF *Rock*/ PRT Nuristan," June 2008, PowerPoint briefing, slides 4, 7. Although Wanat is in Nuristan Province, the Konar PRT supervised this project based on geographical expediency.

79. Captain Matthew Myer, interview by Matt Matthews, Combat Studies Institute, Fort Leavenworth, KS, 1 December 2008, 1; Sergeant First Class David Dzwik, interview by Douglas R. Cubbison, Combat Studies Institute, Fort Leavenworth, KS, 2 April 2009, 11; 2-503d IN, "Thoughts on COIN" Briefing, slide 9; Exhibit 33b (Platoon Sergeant, 2d Platoon, C Company, 2-503d IN, interview) to US Central Command (CENTCOM), "Re-investigation into the Combat Action at Wanat Village, Wygal District, Nuristan Province, Afghanistan, on 13 July 2008 (Redacted), 21-2.

80. 1LT Jonathan Brostrom and SSG David Dzwik, interview with Major David Hanson and Sergeant Wickham, 305th Military History Detachment, Camp Blessing, Afghanistan, 2 May 2008.

81. Sergeant Brandon Aird, "Medic Recognized for Actions During Insurgent Assault," *Outlook* 41, no. 15 (15 April 2008): 1; Sergeant Brandon Aird, "Sky Soldier Awarded Distinguished Service Cross," *Army.mil/news,* http://www.army.mil/-news/2008/09/17/12493-sky-soldier-awarded-distinguished-service-cross/ (accessed 19 February 2009).

82. Video of the Taliban "attacking" the vacant Ranch House position is available at http://theunjustmedia.com/clips/afgha/July08/noor/noor.htm (accessed January 2010).

Conversations between Douglas R. Cubbison and Sami Nuristani in summer 2009 noted that the video remains widely popular and frequently viewed in Afghanistan.

83. Major David S. Hanselman. "The Bella Ambush 9-10 November 2007: Bravery Under Fire," unpublished paper presented at the Conference of Army Historians, Arlington, VA, 30 July 2009.

84. TF *Rock*, "TIC Asset Tracker" Spreadsheet, 22 July 2008.

85. Pry, interview, 6 May 2009, 4.

86. Stafford, interview, 10 February 2009, 3.

87. Pry, interview, 6 May 2009, 4.

88. Ostlund, interview, 19–20 March 2009, 10.

89. Ostlund, interview.

90. 2-503d IN, "2d Battalion (ABN), 503d IN, 173d ABCT, AO Rock Overview, 26 July 2008" Briefing; "1st Battalion, 32d Infantry Regiment" Web site, http://www.drum.army.mil/sites/tenants/division/3BCT/1-32INF/afghan.asp (accessed 22 September 2009).

91. Staff Sergeant Erich Phillips and Specialist Jason Baldwin, interview by Master Sergeant Richard Gribenas, 305th Military History Detachment, 7 October 2007, 13.

92. TF *Rock*, *07 11 24 Aranus Shura, Posted*, 2 December 2007, 1.

93. TF *Rock*, *07 11 24 Aranus Shura*.

94. TF *Rock*, *07 12 15 Aranus Shura 15DEC07*, 16 December 2007.

95. Army Regulation (AR) 15-6 Investigation on SFC Kahler KIA, contained within CJTF-101, "Army Regulation 15-6 Investigation into Battle of Wanat (Redacted, Unclassified Version)" (Bagram Air Base, Afghanistan, 21 October 2008).

96. Sergeant Erik Aass, interview by Matt Matthews, Combat Studies Institute, Fort Leavenworth, KS, 13 January 2009, 4.

97. AR 15-6 Investigation on SFC Kahler KIA, 21 October 2008; Aass, interview, 13 January 2009, 4; Dzwik, interview, 2 April 2009. 3.

98. Kilcullen, *The Accidental Guerrilla*, 66. Kilcullen's entire second chapter on Afghanistan, 2006–2008, comprehensively addresses this topic, so crucial to comprehending events in the Waygal Valley in June and July 2008; Katz, *Kafir to Afghan*, passim.

99. Schloesser, interview, 5 August 2009, 5, 6.

100. Himes, interview, 25 April 2009, 3.

101. Milley, interview, 18 and 20 August 2009, 17; Exhibit 21b, (LTC, Brigade XO, 173d ABCT, interview) to US Central Command (CENTCOM), "Re-investigation into the Combat Action at Wanat Village, Wygal District, Nuristan Province, Afghanistan, on 13 July 2008 (Redacted), 5.

102. Exhibit 18 (Operational Needs Statement) to US Central Command (CENTCOM), "Re-investigation into the Combat Action at Wanat Village, Wygal District, Nuristan Province, Afghanistan, on 13 July 2008 (Redacted); Exhibit 22a (Major, Brigade Engineer, 173d ABCT, interview) to US Central Command (CENTCOM), "Re-investigation into the Combat Action at Wanat Village, Wygal District, Nuristan Province, Afghanistan, on 13 July 2008 (Redacted), 10-12; Exhibit 26 (Summary of the Construction of the US Portion of COP Wanat) to US Central Command (CENTCOM), "Re-investigation into the Combat Action at Wanat Village, Wygal District, Nuristan Province, Afghanistan, on 13 July 2008 (Redacted). 9-11; Colonel William Ostlund, email to Donald P. Wright, Combat Studies Institute, Fort Leavenworth, KS, 10 September 2010.

103. Exhibit 6a (Major, Operations Officer, 2-503d IN, interview) to US Central Command (CENTCOM), "Re-investigation into the Combat Action at Wanat Village, Wygal District, Nuristan Province, Afghanistan, on 13 July 2008 (Redacted), 15; Exhibit 14b (Major, Battalion XO, 2-503d IN) to US Central Command (CENTCOM), "Re-investigation into the Combat Action at Wanat Village, Wygal District, Nuristan Province, Afghanistan, on 13 July 2008 (Redacted), 10-11, 23-25; Exhibit 27a (CPT, Battalion S4, 2-503d IN, interview) to US Central Command (CENTCOM), "Re-investigation into the Combat Action at Wanat Village, Wygal District, Nuristan Province, Afghanistan, on 13 July 2008 (Redacted), 7-9; Exhibit 26 (Summary of the Construction of the US Portion of COP Wanat) to US Central Command (CENTCOM), "Re-investigation into the Combat Action at Wanat Village, Wygal District, Nuristan Province, Afghanistan, on 13 July 2008 (Redacted). 19; Exhibit 51b (CPT, Contracting Coordinator, HHC/ 2-503d IN, interview) to US Central Command (CENTCOM), "Re-investigation into the Combat Action at Wanat Village, Wygal District, Nuristan Province, Afghanistan, on 13 July 2008 (Redacted). Passim;

104. Lieutenant Colonel William Ostlund and Captain Matthew Myer, joint e-mail to Douglas R. Cubbison, Combat Studies Institute, Fort Leavenworth, KS, 23 March 2009.

105. Captain Devin George, interview by Matt Matthews, Combat Studies Institute, Fort Leavenworth, KS, 15 October 2008, 5; Lieutenant Colonel William Ostlund and Captain Matthew Myer, joint e-mail to Douglas R. Cubbison, Combat Studies Institute, Fort Leavenworth, KS, 23 March 2009.

106. Lieutenant Colonel Julian Smith, interview by Douglas R. Cubbison, Combat Studies Institute, Fort Leavenworth, KS, 10 June 2009, 5–6.

107. Lieutenant Colonel William Ostlund, "Battle of Wanat Storyboard and Brief" Briefing, 16 July 2008, slide 3; Exhibit 61 (LTC, 2-503d IN, statement), CJTF-101, "Army Regulation 15-6 Investigation into Battle of Wanat (Redacted, Unclassified Version)" (Camp Blessing Afghanistan, 17 July 2008), 1; Exhibit 23 (Authorization from Wanat District Leadership to Build a Coalition Combat Outpost, 20 April 2008) to US Central Command (CENTCOM), "Re-investigation into the Combat Action at Wanat Village, Wygal District, Nuristan Province, Afghanistan, on 13 July 2008 (Redacted).

108. Ostlund, "Battle of Wanat Storyboard and Brief" Briefing, 16 July 2008, slide 3; 108.   Myer, e-mail, 18 November 2009.

109. Schloesser, interview, 5 August 2009, 7.

110. Schloesser; Milley, interview, 18 and 20 August 2009, 17; Colonel Charles Preysler, e-mail to Douglas R. Cubbison, Combat Studies Institute, Fort Leavenworth, KS, 5 May 2009, 5.

111. Ostlund, "Battle of Wanat Storyboard and Brief" Briefing, 16 July 2008, slide 4; Schloesser, interview, 5 August 2009, 6; Ostlund, e-mails, 24 February 2009 and 8 May 2009; Exhibit 106 ("AR 15-6 Investigation (Findings and Recommendations)—COP Bella Allegation of Non-Combatant Casualties, 4 July 2008"), CJTF-101, "Army Regulation 15-6 Investigation into Battle of Wanat (Redacted, Unclassified Version)" (FOB Fenty, Afghanistan, 26 July 2008).

112. "Karzai Axes Leader for US Rebuke," *Al Jezeera. net*, 10 July 2008, http://www.thefreelibrary.com/ Karzai+'axes+leader+for+US+rebuke'.-a0181341406 (accessed on 19 July 2010); for the anti-American view of the incident, see "The Massacre at Aranas on the Waygal River, Nuristan Province," *RAWA News*, 16 July 2008, http:// www.rawa.org/temp/runews/2008/07/16/the-massacre-at-aranas-on-the-waygal-river-nuristan-province.html?e=http:/amyru.h18.ru/images/cs.txt? (accessed 19 February 2009). The International Medical Corps, which operated the Bella Medical Clinic, stated in a news release dated 8 July 2008 that "three of its staff members were killed, and another severely injured" and that "the International Medical Corps personnel were killed while leaving their village following warnings of an imminent attack." This press release claimed that the dead were Dr. Nemetalluh, Nurse Naeem, and Dr. Najeebullah and that one of the seriously wounded was a Dr. Zainab.See International Medical Corps Press Release, "International Medical Corps Mourns the Loss of Three Humanitarian Workers in Afghanistan; Another Injured," http://www.imcworldwide.org.uk/news.asp? pageid=5&nid=2 (accessed 14 August 2009).

113. Exhibit 106, CJTF-101, "Army Regulation 15-6 Investigation into Battle of Wanat (Redacted, Unclassified Version)" (FOB Fenty, Afghanistan, 26 July 2008). Ostlund, e-mails, 24 February 2009 and 8 May 2009; Pry, interview, 6 May 2009, 4-5.

114. Myer, interview, 1 December 2008, 6; Exhibit 106, CJTF-101, "Army Regulation 15-6 Investigation into Battle of Wanat (Redacted, Unclassified Version)" (FOB Fenty, Afghanistan, 26 July 2008), 7.

115. Pry Interview, 6 May 2009, 5.

116. David Tate, "US Had Warning of Attack in Nuristan," *A Battlefield Tourist,* 28 July 2008, http://www.battlefieldtourist.com/content/2008/07/ (accessed 2 April 2009); Omer Sami, Moeed Hashimi, and Wali Salarzai, "NATO Airstrike Kills 22 Civilians in Nuristan,*" Pajhwok Afghan News*, 5 July

2008, http://www.pajhwok.com/viewstory.asp?lng=eng&id=57969 (accessed 16 November 2009).

117. Nuristani, e-mail, 2 March 2009.

118. Aass, interview, 13 January 2009, 4.

119. Ostlund and Myer, e-mail, 23 March 2009; "US Planes Hit Afghan Wedding Party, Killing 27," *The Sydney Morning Herald,* 7 July 2008, http://www.smh.com.au/news/world/us-planes-hit-afghan-wedding-party-ki lling-27/2008/07/07/1215282687896.html (accessed 8 September 2009); "Afghanistan Says U.S. Airstrike Hit Wedding Party," *New York Times,* 6 July 2008, http://www.nytimes.com/2008/07/06/world/asia/06iht-afghan.4.14278415. html (accessed 8 September 2009).

120. Exhibit 6a (Operations Officer, 2-503d IN, interview) to US Central Command (CENTCOM), "Re-investigation into the Combat Action at Wanat Village, Wygal District, Nuristan Province, Afghanistan, on 13 July 2008 (Redacted), 19-20.

121. Milley, interview, 18 and 20 August 2009, 18.

122. Milley, interview, 18 and 20 August 2009, 22; Myer, e-mail, 15 October 2009; Ostlund, e-mails, 24 February 2009 and 8 May 2009.

123. TF *Rock*, "CONOP ROCK MOVE," PowerPoint Presentation, 7 July 2008, slides 5, 7.

124. Ostlund, "Battle of Wanat Storyboard and Brief" Briefing, 16 July 2008, slide 2.

Chapter 2

The Establishment of COP Kahler, 8-12 July 2008

Operation ROCK MOVE called for the establishment of a new tactical base in an area that was known to be dangerous. The American experience in Afghanistan and Iraq had demonstrated that a new base, such as a forward operating base (FOB) or a combat outpost (COP), was most vulnerable to attack in the first few days of its inception. At this time, Soldiers as well as civilian contractors, if they were present, were busy constructing protective barriers, guard towers, and stone walls. Often, units emplaced defensive obstacles, such as concertina wire and antivehicle ditches while clearing fields of fire, establishing the best possible positions for heavy weapons systems, and setting up permanent and redundant communications. A certain amount of disruption was attendant as heavy construction was underway and different contractors and workers circulated through the new post.

From an insurgent's perspective, outposts like the Wanat COP represented a number of threats. First, the Coalition used them to launch regular patrols and interact with the local population, degrading the ability of the insurgents to operate freely. Secondly, once the base was established, any insurgent attack might engender hostility from the adjacent community, risking its alienation from the insurgent's cause. Further, the base represented more than just the threat of a larger Coalition force providing greater security in the immediate area. The US troops and local security forces introduced jobs to a community, often hiring local workers to help operate dining facilities and perform other menial tasks. Local National (LN) trucks rolled in and out and required fuel and servicing. Construction workers and local materials of various types, such as concrete and wood, were needed. Once in place, the outpost extended the Coalition's presence and authority and held the potential to convert the adjacent community from neutrality or hostility to benevolence toward the central government.

The new COP at Wanat, which 2d Platoon of Chosen Company named unofficially after its slain platoon sergeant, Sergeant First Class Matthew Ryan Kahler, represented all of these threats to the insurgent groups in the Waygal Valley. While COP Kahler was at its most vulnerable in its initial occupation, the outpost remained at risk until the exterior stone wall planned to encircle the base was completed. Against all previous experience and expectations, the insurgent force actively operating in the Waygal Valley chose to exploit this window of opportunity and attack the position in this period after initial occupation but before all the fortifications had been completed. This chapter describes Task Force (TF) *Rock's* plan to emplace the COP and the actions taken to establish the outpost in the first five days before the enemy attack.

ROCK MOVE – The Plan

Between March and June 2008, as recounted in the previous chapter, TF *Rock* made plans for ROCK MOVE, the operation that would disestablish the COP at Bella and establish COP Kahler in Wanat. One of the most critical components of the planning process was the finalization of the physical layout of the new COP. The theater level 420th Engineer Brigade, supported by elements of the brigade's Company C, 62d Engineer Battalion, TF *Bayonet's* main construction engineer asset, prepared a surveyed engineering design for a complex and formidable base. That design included an exterior stone wall; an interior barrier wall; a formal entrance control point; guard towers; permanent barracks; a potable water system with pump house, shower, and laundry facilities; and a waste water system complete with a leach field. The interior wall and guard towers would be fashioned from products manufactured by the HESCO Barrier Company and in wide use in both Iraq and Afghanistan. The barriers were woven metal baskets made of steel mesh lined with heavy fabric; were easily erected and filled with sand, dirt, or other materials by Soldiers on the construction site; were installed rapidly; and provided excellent protection against direct and indirect fire attacks.

While the engineers developed the construction plan, the TF *Rock* staff prepared the plan for the operation. At the same time, Chosen Company Commander Myer and 2d Platoon Leader Brostrom did their own planning. They reconnoitered the proposed COP location during the *shura*s in Wanat in the spring of 2008. The end result was the detailed battalion level plan for ROCK MOVE that was, as previously discussed, briefed to and approved by General Milley on 7 July 2008.[1]

Under ROCK MOVE, Chosen Company's mission was to use both ground and air movement to "realign US and ANA [Afghan National Army] forces in Nuristan province [in order to] deny freedom of movement [to the enemy] and consolidate US forces for upcoming [relief in place] with 1-26 IN."[2] The realignment was the evacuation of COP Bella and the establishment of a new COP at Wanat. The creation of an outpost at Wanat was the initial step in setting conditions that would allow for "improved security, governance, and economic development" in the valley. ROCK MOVE defined ultimate operational success as the safe removal of the paratroopers and equipment from COP Bella, the establishment of COP Kahler, the disruption of AAF in the valley, and the local acceptance of a Coalition base in Wanat.[3]

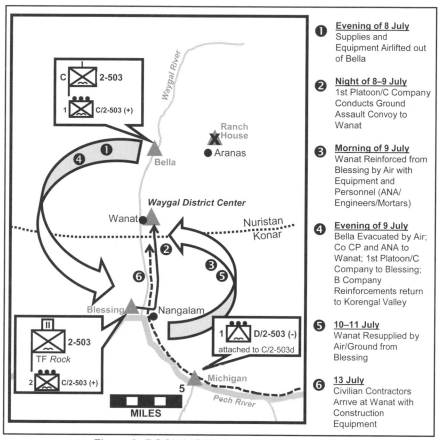

Figure 8. ROCK MOVE OPLAN, 8-9 July 2008.

The operation itself consisted of a series of concurrent and consecutive maneuvers. First, there was the withdrawal from COP Bella, currently manned by C Company's 1st Platoon, augmented with two squads from B Company. This realignment was a two day long operation to be conducted on 8 and 9 July. On the first day, two Chinook helicopters from TF *Out Front* would move equipment from Bella to Camp Blessing after dusk. On the second day, again after dusk, the Chinooks would withdraw the personnel at Bella, moving the 1st Platoon to Camp Blessing and the two B Company squads, which had augmented the Bella garrison in its last days, directly to their home base in the Korengal Valley. Since Wanat would have been occupied during the previous night, some of the equipment and personnel, notably part of a platoon of ANA soldiers and Chosen Company Commander Myer, would move directly from Bella to Wanat.[4]

The second maneuver was the establishment of the position at Wanat. During the night of 8/9 July, C Company's 2d Platoon, augmented with attached elements, would move by ground convoy in high-mobility multipurpose wheeled vehicles (HMMWVs) from Camp Blessing to Wanat and establish a hasty position there on the site of the proposed COP. Ostlund and Myer felt that it was important that the initial occupation of the COP site occur in darkness to retain tactical surprise. By dawn on 9 July, the residents would find 2d Platoon already in place securing the site at which the new COP would be constructed.[5]

Accordingly, for a brief period on 9 July, both Bella and Wanat would coexist. On the morning of the 9th, TF *Rock* would use the Bagram based helicopters of the two-Chinook Pech Resupply run to bring additional personnel and supplies from Camp Blessing to the new Wanat position. These additions included the bulk of the mortar section and its equipment, part of the ANA platoon, the supporting engineers and their equipment, and additional ammunition and barrier materials. As stated above, after dark, as the final act in the withdrawal from Bella, the Chinooks would transfer the ANA platoon and Captain Myer from Bella to Wanat.[6]

Ostlund assumed some risk when he decided, upon a recommendation from Myer, to execute ROCK MOVE on 8 July. Prior to the initiation of the operation, the officers discovered that although the construction materials were already staged at Camp Blessing, the Afghan company contracted to bring heavy construction equipment to the Wanat COP and then assist in constructing its defenses would not arrive until 13 July, later than anticipated. Ostlund, Myer, and the battalion operations officer, Major Scott Himes, agreed that soldier labor and the augmentation of the platoon with an engineer squad and a Bobcat front end loader (then at Bella) could adequately prepare the COP defense in the six days until the civilian equipment operators arrived with their machinery.[7]

One of the reasons that Ostlund chose to continue with ROCK MOVE on 8 July was the lunar illumination cycle. The AN/AVS-6 night vision goggles (NOG) used by the pilots of the CH-47D Chinook cargo helicopters that would be used in ROCK MOVE had certain safety limitations. The NOGs required at least 25 percent lunar illumination and a 30 percent or better lunar elevation angle above the horizon. Because the moon rises and falls during the course of the night, TF *Bayonet* codified 30 minute blocks of darkness based on the amount of risk involved inherent in the lunar illumination cycle. If both conditions were met, an hour was considered green, or optimum for the use of Chinooks. If only the illumination percentage condition was met, the period of time was classified yellow, or cautious. With an illumination angle of less than 30 percent, the pilots could still see but less clearly, requiring them to proceed more slowly than under the green conditions. A 30 minute block was considered red or high risk, when both conditions were not met.[8]

Given the estimate of the enemy situation, TF *Bayonet* Commander Preysler and TF *Rock* Commander Ostlund considered a night evacuation to be essential to ROCK MOVE's success, with Chinook vulnerability reduced in the darkness. The initial projected date for the operation was 1 July but the first seven nights of the month were completely in the red cycle. Accordingly, Ostlund delayed the execution of ROCK MOVE until the evening of 8 July, the earliest green and yellow time blocks available. On 8 July, conditions were green from 1930 to 2000 hours, yellow from 2000 to 2330 hours, and red thereafter. On 9 July the green period increased to an hour, from 1930 to 2030, with the yellow condition lasting from 2030 to 2230, with red conditions the rest of the night. Green conditions lasted only in the early evening hours from 8 to 12 July. Yellow and red periods dominated for most of the rest of the month. While the delay of civilian construction contractors was inconvenient, to wait for their arrival to start the operation would put the helicopters at greater risk in night operations. The commanders chose to proceed with ROCK MOVE while the moon provided the optimum illumination for Chinook operations.[9]

To provide a measure of operational security, the Americans did not tell the residents of either Bella or Wanat that the realignment would begin on 8 July. Key leaders from CJTF-101 down to the TF *Rock* level were concerned about the vulnerability of TF *Out Front's* helicopters as they flew through the deep valley and approached Bella for the evacuation of the men and material at that COP. In the days following the arrival of 2d Platoon, TF *Out Front* would deliver heavy equipment and supplies to the paratroopers at Wanat. After six days, members of the Afghan construction company would arrive and provide the heavy construction support that would build the walls and other facilities of the base. At this point, Ostlund commented that the infantrymen of the 2d Platoon would be there to provide security for the contractors as they built the COP.[10]

The increasingly dangerous enemy situation around Bella played a key role in Ostlund's decision to execute ROCK MOVE in the battalion's waning days in Afghanistan. The TF *Rock* intelligence section assessed the insurgent forces in the Bella and Wanat areas to number between 130 and 150 experienced fighters under the leadership of Mullah Osman, a Nuristani from the northern Waygal Valley village of Waygal. Osman was not a formal member of the *Hizb-i-Islami Gulbuddin* (HiG) or any specific insurgent group. He worked, however, with a wide range of AAF elements in Nuristan and Konar provinces, using intimidation and, if necessary, overt force to retain influence over the local leaders in the Waygal Valley. Since Osman was reportedly wounded at Bella on 4 July, the leadership in any possible insurgent operations against Wanat shifted to a younger local AAF leader, Mawlawi Sadiq Manibullah. Manibullah was the son of an Aranas elder who had had previous connections to HiG elements in northeast Afghanistan and was influential in Wanat. In an insurgent video released some months after the attack, Manibullah identified himself as the leader of the assault on Coalition forces at Wanat.[11]

Because of the shortage of Coalition troops, Osman's forces enjoyed freedom of maneuver in much of the valley, particularly in the villages east of Bella and Wanat. These AAF elements had been responsible for the attacks on COP Bella in June and July 2008. When necessary, Osman had shown that he could bring in insurgent groups from the Korengal and Watapor valleys to launch larger attacks on Coalition forces. Coalition intelligence also believed that fighters from other Islamic countries, including terrorists associated with al-Qaeda, had been active in northeast Afghanistan and at times had traveled through the Waygal Valley and worked with the local insurgents.[12]

Pry, Task Force *Rock*'s intelligence officer, believed that Osman had become "absolutely furious" when he discovered that the Coalition planned to establish a base in Wanat. Pry's assessment in the ROCK MOVE plan was that Osman had focused his anger and his forces primarily on the US Soldiers stationed at COP Bella. In Pry's opinion, the insurgent leader would most likely place mortars and other heavy weapons in positions to overlook COP Bella to attack any Coalition force – especially aircraft – that might come to support or evacuate the outpost. The intelligence officer thought that the insurgents might also launch direct attacks on the observation posts (OPs) located on the high ground above Bella and perhaps on the COP itself.[13]

For Osman, however, any Coalition attempt to establish a base at Wanat was totally unacceptable. Pry had indications that in early July, the insurgents who lived near Wanat had moved north to participate in operations against COP Bella. However, Pry also believed that these elements had established weapons caches in the high ground surrounding

Wanat. According to the assessment in the ROCK MOVE plan, the insurgents planned to move from Bella back to the Wanat area within 24 to 48 hours of the Coalition's move into Wanat. Osman's local forces, with the support of any neighboring insurgent groups and foreign fighters he might recruit, would launch any attack that would follow. Pry did have reports that contingents of foreign fighters had entered the Watapor Valley, one ridgeline to the east of the Waygal Valley, in May or June 2008.[14]

One of the main reasons Ostlund and Myer were willing to set up the Wanat COP immediately and then risk waiting for the arrival of the civilian construction crew was the TF *Rock* officers' appreciation of the enemy's probable actions. While the Americans thought it was possible for the enemy to attack the new COP at Wanat during its construction, Pry believed that this was not the most *likely* insurgent course of action. Instead, in the ROCK MOVE plan, the intelligence officer thought that the most likely enemy move would be a gradual escalation of activity in the Wanat area, occupying OPs around Wanat, and emplacing improvised explosive devices (IEDs) on the road leading from Camp Blessing north to Wanat.[15]

Myer, the Chosen Company commander, shared the view of a gradual enemy response. Based on patterns established in attacks on COP Ranch House and other actions, Myer believed that the insurgents would gradually move major weapons into positions around Wanat and then fire both rockets and mortar rounds into the COP to "dial in" the proper range. According to Myer, "We thought if they were going to do a large scale attack, they're going to first refine all the assets they wanted to utilize to do that and then after something like 90 days, then they're going to try to do a large scale attack like they did at the Ranch House."[16] Platoon Sergeant Dzwik concurred with this assessment, "I was expecting an attack. I thought the enemy would make their presence known. I was expecting harassing fire from any one of the high ground in every direction. I did not think the village itself would let the AAF [Anti-Afghan Force] turn their village into a battle zone."[17]

US commanders and staffs at higher levels, including Ostlund and the CJTF-101 intelligence officer, had seen this pattern across northeast Afghanistan and assumed that the AAF would follow suit at Wanat. CJTF-101's commander, Schloesser, certainly shared this belief. He described the enemy's general pattern of scattered indirect and small arms fire against small Coalition bases as "almost a routine way for the enemy to measure what we were doing in any new established outpost or vehicle patrol base . . . to try to understand what our tactics, techniques, and procedures were going to be and assess us for about a week or two before actually trying to pressure that respective outpost…That's exactly what I believed we were going to see there at Wanat."[18]

As noted in the previous chapter, Ostlund had reinforced the platoon with a number of assets. Organizationally, out of a table of organization and equipment (TOE) strength of 39, Brostrom had 29 paratroopers available in his platoon at Wanat, divided into three rifle squads, a weapons squad, and a headquarters element. The weapons squad, which by TOE consisted of nine members divided into two three-man machine gun crews and two two-man close combat antiarmor teams equipped with the Javelin antiarmor missile system, manned only the two three-man M240 machine gun teams at Wanat. Although the platoon did not man its Javelin teams, it did bring the weapons system to Wanat. The platoon headquarters consisted of the platoon leader, the platoon sergeant, the medic, the radio-telephone operator (RTO), and the forward observer.[19]

On paper, the three rifle squads each contained nine paratroopers including a staff sergeant squad leader, two sergeant team leaders, and six junior enlisted men. The squad was divided into two four-man fireteams, each armed with two M4 assault rifles, an M203 40-mm grenade launcher and an M249 squad automatic weapon (SAW). The three squads of the 2d Platoon at Wanat maintained strengths of between five and seven squad members. The platoon contained a designated marksman, a soldier specially trained and equipped with an M21 sniper rifle. This individual was not a sniper but was trained to "improve a squad's precision engagement capabilities at short and medium ranges."[20]

Although organizationally a paratrooper rifle platoon normally has no vehicles, for service in Afghanistan, Brostrom's platoon received an M114 armored HMMWV for each rifle squad and one for the platoon headquarters. Because these HMMWVs mounted heavy weapons in their cupolas, their presence greatly enhanced not only the platoon's mobility, but also its firepower. Two of the HMMWVs mounted M2 .50-caliber heavy machine guns. The other two vehicles carried Mk-19 40-mm automatic grenade launchers. The initial occupation and defense of COP Kahler would be based on these vehicular weapons. As the COP matured, the defense would be built around the heavy weapons.

For ROCK MOVE, Ostlund reinforced the 2d Platoon with a platoon of 24 soldiers from the ANA's 2d Company, 3d *Kandak* (Battalion), 2d Brigade, 201st Corps. This force included three US Marines of an embedded training team (ETT) which advised the ANA platoon. The

Afghans were armed with AK-47s and RPGs. The Marines brought with them an M240 machine gun. Half the ANAs would arrive at Wanat via Chinook from Camp Blessing on the morning of 9 July. This group would set up a traffic control point on the Waygal Valley road just south of the COP site. The other half would arrive that night by Chinook directly from Bella.[21]

To provide immediate fire support, the 2d Platoon would bring two mortars and a tube-launched, optically tracked, wire guided (TOW) missile launcher system mounted on an M114 HMMWV to Wanat. The TOW launcher and its squad of three paratroopers would provide responsive and highly accurate direct fire against distant targets. The TOW had proven extremely valuable in the mountainous terrain of Konar and Nuristan provinces. As the TF *Rock*'s executive officer (XO), Major Brian Beckno recalled, "We fired that TOW in direct fire mode on any Taliban we saw in our sights that we considered a threat. The locals called that one weapon system the 'Finger of God.' We had confirmed kills with that weapon system."[22] The six-man mortar section would provide indirect fire support using a 120-mm mortar and a 60-mm mortar. Both the mortars and the TOW launcher would be placed within the new COP. Myer considered the TOW and mortar systems to be essential. He would have recommended canceling ROCK MOVE if he had not received these assets.[23]

Once COP Bella was evacuated, the 2d Platoon would have the priority of fires from both a section of 155-mm howitzers based at Camp Blessing and a similar section based at Asadabad. The platoon would also be able to call for fire support from the AH-64 Apache attack helicopters of TF *Out Front*. However, because helicopters were a limited asset in Afghanistan, the Apaches would not be permanently placed on station above the Waygal Valley. If the 2d Platoon needed attack helicopter support, TF *Out Front* would divert Apaches flying other missions to Wanat or dispatch aircraft being held on standby as a quick reaction force (QRF) at the Jalalabad Airfield. Reaction time differed depending on the situation but according to Lieutenant Colonel John Lynch, the TF *Out Front* commander, once his Apache pilots received the alert, it would take approximately 30 minutes to fly from Jalalabad to Wanat by the most direct route.[24]

TF *Rock* had arranged for the attachment of an engineer squad from C Company, 62d Engineer Battalion (Heavy), to support ROCK MOVE. The squad, consisting of six Army engineers, would arrive in Wanat with a small Bobcat front loader to help the infantry by filling HESCO containers but also by helping the platoon improve its position in Wanat. Brostrom and Dzwik would make broad use of HESCOs within the COP.[25]

In total, including all of these assets at Wanat, the strength of the force at the outpost would be 44 US Soldiers, three US Marines, and 24 Afghan soldiers. TF *Rock* had thus made 71 personnel available for the initial establishment of the base. Myer himself and two members of his headquarters staff were to join the 2d Platoon on the evening of the 9th, flying in directly from Bella. Ultimately, TF *Rock* planned for a garrison of 74 American and Afghan military personnel at the new COP.

For Milley, the CJTF-101 deputy commander, the size of the force at the new COP was significant. He had approved the operation because of the relatively large force assigned to the Wanat portion of the operation. Milley recalled that he viewed ROCK MOVE as a "company-minus" operation because of the two infantry platoons and the planned presence of the company headquarters. In his opinion, given the enemy situation briefed to him by TF *Rock*, Ostlund had allocated the right amount of troops to the mission. Reacting to the relative dearth of manpower for operations in Regional Command–East (RC-East) in 2007 and 2008, Milley had commented:

> In terms of combat power, that's a significant amount of combat power for what I had previously seen, what I had studied, and what I had observed and over the course of the 15 months, 75 is still a significant amount of combat power anywhere in Afghanistan . . . 75 guys is a lot of guys and if properly used and employed, then that's a significant amount of combat power.[26]

As previously mentioned, the long range plan for the construction of COP Kahler relied on the use of civilian contractors. TF *Rock* had issued several contracts to Afghan construction companies to build the camp. The major contract went to a construction firm based in Jalalabad which would provide heavy equipment and operators. The period of the contract was from 1 July to 25 December 2008, with the actual start date being contingent on the date of occupation of the site by Chosen Company. In contracts approved before ROCK MOVE but not finalized until 11 July, a construction company from Asadabad was slated to provide an earth fill service for fighting positions and the HESCO barriers, and the laying of gravel. The contracts were awarded to the nearest local businesses with the capability to perform the job. This project was scheduled for completion by 28 July. A contract bid to build a stone wall around the COP, which was posted in late June, was still pending. There was also a contract for laborers at Wanat with a labor management company based in Kabul that was carried over from Bella. Accordingly, TF *Rock* intended that civilians would do the bulk of the construction work at Wanat. This was the procedure that the unit followed when it constructed several other COPs in the Korengal and Pech valleys. However, as mentioned above, the company from Jalalabad was unable to assemble and move its equipment to Wanat before 13 July. According to Myer, this delay happened because the construction company initially anticipated a start date of 3 July but when ROCK MOVE's start date was moved back, the company returned its equipment to Jalalabad. When the Afghans were told of the new required date, 9 July, the construction company was unable to reassemble its equipment and move it to Wanat before 13 July. Therefore, by necessity, the 2d Platoon's paratroopers and their attached engineers would do the early work on the COP's defenses.[27]

In addition to providing the Wanat garrison with fire support and engineers, Ostlund also ensured that the 2d Platoon was equipped with or supported by various intelligence assets. In its inventory, TF *Rock* had two Long Range Advanced Scout Surveillance Systems (LRAS3). The LRAS3 is a ground-mounted thermal system allowing around the clock surveillance. Ostlund gave one of the devices to Brostrom. The battalion commander believed this piece of equipment was critical to the 2d Platoon's successful accomplishment of its mission. Moreover, the TOW missile launcher attached to the platoon was not only an excellent direct fire weapon but it came equipped with an Improved Target Acquisition System (ITAS). The ITAS also provided 24 hour long range surveillance capability. Detailed technical specifications of these two systems are classified but the two systems, although limited to line of sight views, provided Brostrom's troops with formidable night vision and long range surveillance capabilities. Myer regarded these two systems highly.[28]

CJTF-101 had also agreed to support ROCK MOVE with other powerful intelligence, surveillance, and reconnaissance (ISR) assets. These resources, which included aerial signals intelligence (SIGINT) platforms that monitored radio and telephone communications and unmanned aerial vehicles (UAVs) that provided real time and full motion video (FMV) observation of terrain and events, were highly valuable and scarce. In RC-East, CJTF-101's primary FMV assets were a single Predator UAV and one MQ-12 Warrior-Alpha UAV. The other Predator UAV under CJTF-101's control was permanently committed to Regional Command-South (RC-South) and thus unavailable to TF *Rock*. The primary theater level SIGINT asset was "Red Ridge," a fixed wing, medium altitude SIGINT platform. Because of a dedicated translator, the Red Ridge intercepts were almost immediately available to the supported units.[29]

The UAVs with their full motion capabilities were powerful systems but could not be counted on to detect enemy fighters on all occasions. In fact, in the mountainous and forested terrain of northeastern Afghanistan, using UAVs to find small groups of insurgents was exceptionally difficult. Lieutenant Colonel Pierre Gervais, the CJTF-101 Intelligence Officer, described using the optics on a UAV to search for insurgents as "looking through a soda straw...it's hit or miss."[30] However, when SIGINT or HUMINT reports suggested the location of suspected insurgent groups; UAVs could be directed to precise spots to make positive identification and to gather greater information. Coalition forces used this method of coordinating or "cross cueing"; imagery, human, and signals intelligence across Afghanistan in 2008.

Predator and Warrior-Alpha were not the only UAV assets operating in RC-East. In fact, TF *Bayonet* deployed to Afghanistan with two types of organic UAV systems: the RQ-7 Shadow and RQ-11 Raven. TF *Out Front* also deployed to Afghanistan with the MQ-5B Hunter UAV, a system similar to the Shadow. TF *Bayonet* had four Shadow platforms comprising one complete system. A system includes a launcher, recovery equipment, maintenance equipment, and two radio control vans. The Shadow had to be operated out of Jalalabad Airfield because it required a regular landing strip, a rare commodity in northeastern Afghanistan, in order to be recovered. During its 14 month deployment, TF *Bayonet* considered constructing an alternate location at Camp Blessing to extend the reach of the Shadow but there were terrain and space limitations at the camp and Jalalabad was more central to the brigade's overall area of operation (AO). In any event, the Shadow could not be operated within the Waygal Valley because of the rugged terrain in the valley that blocked the radio signals needed to guide the UAV. For all of these reasons, TF *Bayonet's* Shadow and Hunter systems could not reach Wanat and support TF *Rock* during ROCK MOVE.[31]

TF *Bayonet* had also deployed with a number of Raven UAV systems. The Raven was a smaller, highly portable system that required only a single operator, could be carried in a rucksack, and recharged from a HMMWV. The drone had a six nautical mile radius of operation and a 90 minute single flight endurance. The Raven mounted an infrared (IR) camera system that provided an "over the hill" capability, was fully night capable, and was "launched" by literally being thrown into the air by hand. In Afghanistan in 2007 and 2008, TF *Bayonet* distributed the Raven systems to its subordinate battalions.

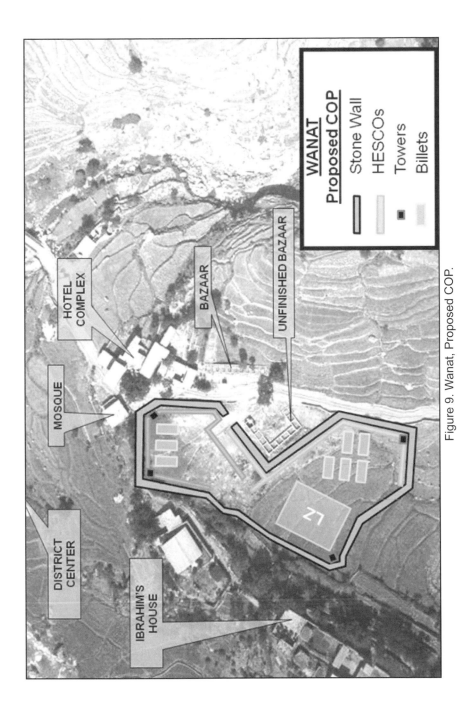

Figure 9. Wanat, Proposed COP.

Unfortunately, the Raven also possessed reduced capabilities and numerous vulnerabilities which restricted and degraded its optimal employment throughout this period. Within the difficult terrain dominated by the precipitous ridges and valleys, the Raven had to be carefully employed due to cross winds and variable drafts that severely constrained its utility. The mountains also had an adverse effect on the radio signals that operators used to control the UAV. TF *Rock* had not enjoyed much success with the Raven system during its year in Afghanistan and the Raven clearly had limited applications. TF *Rock* could easily have deployed a single Raven to COP Kahler and perhaps used it as a deterrent at night over Wanat when the winds in the Waygal Valley decreased. However, the possibility of losing a Raven and the subsequent requirement to mount a patrol to find the aircraft meant that TF *Rock* did not consider its use to be a worthwhile risk in ROCK MOVE or in many of the operations that preceded it.[32]

Given the limitations of the Shadow and Raven systems, TF *Rock* relied heavily on the FMV and SIGINT assets controlled at the CJTF level. To manage these systems, CJTF-101 held a daily intelligence synchronization meeting which was attended by Deputy Commander Milley; the CJTF intelligence officer, Lieutenant Colonel Gervais; and the CJTF operations officer, Colonel Christopher Pease. Through this meeting, CJTF-101 managed ISR assets 96 hours forward. Assets were initially apportioned to a particular brigade sized command for planning purposes and then 72 hours out, they were formally committed. The brigade would then be responsible for planning the use of these assets in accordance with its priorities and operations. The theater command subsequently adjusted the actual allocations that a brigade received based on a variety of factors. During daily operations, the true hours flown varied based on weather, maintenance issues, or higher priority events intervening such as a report of Coalition troops in contact (TIC) with the enemy.[33]

Working with the TF *Bayonet* staff, Captain Pry requested FMV and SIGINT coverage for ROCK MOVE from 8 through 17 July. Pry hoped for ten days of ISR coverage because in his estimation, the paratroopers would need that amount of time before they emplaced and filled all the HESCO barrier walls at the COP. He sought 12 hours of SIGINT and 24 hours of FMV per day but realized that TF *Rock* was unlikely to receive this amount of coverage given the demands on the ISR systems. Indeed, there were a number of operations and events in Afghanistan in the second week of July 2008 that demanded attention from the CJTF headquarters and its ISR resources. In mid June, a number of insurgents had escaped from the ANA-run Sarposa Prison in Kandahar and the investigation into that event was still ongoing. On 26 June, insurgents ambushed a Coalition convoy in the Tangi Valley of Wardak province and tortured, killed, and mutilated three American National Guardsmen. The Coalition responded with an offensive operation to find the insurgent group that committed the brutal attack. During ROCK MOVE, the operations in the Tangi valley were still ongoing and would require ISR support. In the two weeks before the Wanat attack and the two weeks following that assault, there were over 60 insurgent attacks in southern Paktika and Khowst provinces and an additional 20 attacks along the Konar and Nangarhar provincial border areas.[34]

Despite these concurrent operations and crises, when ROCK MOVE began on 8 July, Pry had received confirmation from the CJTF that adequate ISR would be available for the first 72 hours of the operation. Thus, while TF *Rock* had requested ISR coverage for a full ten days, Pry was unsure how much coverage would actually be apportioned after 10 July. Changing priorities, weather, and other factors would likely affect ISR coverage over Wanat. So, in addition to the LRAS3 and ITAS systems noted above, TF *Rock* planned to supplement this higher level ISR support with its own internal SIGINT assets.

The battalion had available a number of commercially produced integrated communications (ICOM) radio scanners which were able to intercept insurgent radio communications. Chosen Company had an interpreter who typically listened into insurgent broadcasts on these scanners. More importantly, TF *Rock* enjoyed direct support from two low level voice intercept (LLVI) teams equipped with the state of the art AN/MLQ-40(V)3 Prophet system from TF *Bayonet*'s military intelligence company.[35]

Planning and Preparation in Chosen Company

As noted earlier, the planning for ROCK MOVE at the company and platoon levels began long before July 2008. Myer and Brostrom knew that the move to Wanat was likely before their departure from Afghanistan and had been thinking about the operation throughout the spring and early summer. Myer and Brostrom had visited Wanat several times for *shuras* and had discussed the operation generally and the layout of the COP specifically. Brostrom's platoon sergeant, Sergeant First Class David Dzwik, recalled being with Myer at Wanat in the spring when the company commander was designating key positions, including OPs. Dzwik stated that in the months leading up to ROCK MOVE, the platoon leadership had a good understanding of where they would go and what they had to do in Wanat. He stated, "The [company] commander had set up where he was envisioning the positions which was pretty much where we set up. We knew the area so we knew from pictures we took and from visiting the positions, where we were going to go."[36]

In the first week of July, Myer and Brostrom attended TF *Rock* briefings of the ROCK MOVE plan to higher headquarters. Dzwik recalled that he was also present at one of these briefings. Thus, the company and platoon leadership were very familiar with the plan for the operation, including the attachments and support that the 2d Platoon would receive. By 6 July, Brostrom and Dzwik understood that ROCK MOVE was likely to be approved and they began making final preparations for the operation.[37]

The TF *Rock* staff did not issue a formal operations order to Myer or Brostrom before ROCK MOVE. According to Myer, this was not an oversight but standard TF practice after 14 months in Afghanistan. Instead of issuing traditional written operation orders, the experienced TF *Rock* staff and its company level leaders often used fragmentary orders (FRAGOs) and officers like Myer and Brostrom used troop leading procedures to ensure that platoons and squads had a clear understanding of missions and tasks. In the case of ROCK MOVE, Chosen Company and the 2d Platoon had been arguably preparing, albeit sporadically, for months. The details of the operation were contained in the briefing slides for the 7 July 2008 briefing to Milley, although most of these details had been worked out before that date. In addition to this briefing, on 7 July, Lieutenant Colonel Ostlund met privately with Brostrom to review the mission and the assets that had been attached to 2d Platoon for ROCK MOVE.[38]

The 2d Platoon paratroopers took a number of steps to plan and prepare for the mission in Wanat. While the platoon did not mount a formal rehearsal of concept, Dzwik later remembered that his troops conducted precombat checks on 7 and 8 July. At the same time Myer and Brostrom received briefings from the squad leaders about the mission and their specific tasks. Dzwik considered these backbriefs as tantamount to an informal rehearsal.[39]

One of Brostrom's squad leaders remembered these pre-operation preparations. Staff Sergeant Jonathan Benton, the platoon's 2d Squad leader, recalled that Brostrom did not conduct a formal rehearsal or create a sand table model of the COP to use in briefing his subordinates. The process was a bit less formal:

What we were briefed and what we were told was that we were going to go there and establish a forward operating base and we would be there until 1st Infantry Division came out to [relieve] us. Our impression was that we were going out there to establish a stationary position, to build up walls and defensive positions, and establish relations with the local populace in order to stay there in a permanent situation.[40]

Benton asserted, "We knew what was out there and what we had to work with. . . . Lieutenant Brostrom did the best he could. He did an awesome job with what time he had and was able to put us in positions to try to support one another."[41]

Understandably with the end of their deployment within sight, some members of the 2d Platoon felt some anxiety about the move to Wanat. With only 13 days of duty in Afghanistan remaining after over 14 months of continuous operations, many of the men were looking forward to returning home. All of them had already shipped their personal items back to Italy and only retained a single rucksack with immediate living gear, their combat equipment, and weapons. Stafford remembered, "None of us wanted to go [to Wanat]. We had about 13 days left before we were scheduled to get out of there on the choppers and we were all really pissed off that we had to go. We knew the intel[ligence] reports of massing enemy attacks and very high risk missions, so not a lot of us wanted to go."[42]

Some of the paratroopers expected the worst to happen as they began establishing the new COP. Sergeant Jesse Queck, one of the mortarmen, recalled, "*No one* [his emphasis] in the company wanted to do this Wanat thing. We all knew something bad was going to happen. I mean, guys were writing on their facebook pages to pray for them, they felt like this mission was the one they weren't coming back from."[43] Dzwik stated that he also expressed concerns about ROCK MOVE to the Chosen Company first sergeant. The platoon sergeant feared that there would be a lack of assets to reinforce the COP and foresaw potential problems with logistical support while the incoming forces from the 1st Infantry Division (ID) relieved the paratroopers. He thought those issues would become especially problematic if the plan's assumptions about the enemy and local population proved incorrect. However, Dzwik also noted that he believed the plan for ROCK MOVE was essentially sound and acknowledged that some amount of risk is inherent in all combat operations.[44]

Brostrom shared some of these uncertainties about the mission to establish COP Kahler. Before ROCK MOVE was approved, Brostrom spoke privately with his peers about his concerns. He talked at Camp Blessing with First Lieutenant Brandon Kennedy, an officer in Able Company and Brostrom's best friend, who remembered that Brostrom's doubts centered on the pro insurgent stance of the population in the Wanat area, "The topic came up about the Wanat mission. He told me he did not like it. He said he thought it was a bad idea and he knew he was going to get [messed] up because the last four times he had gone up there, he had been ambushed or IED'ed every time, often with very good effects."[45] Brostrom told another officer in Afghanistan, that based on the intelligence he had seen, any Coalition base established in Wanat was almost certainly going to be attacked by significant enemy forces.[46]

Kennedy recalled that Brostrom was also worried about the assets he would have for the mission. According to Kennedy, the 2d Platoon leader "expressed concerns to me about the number of men he was taking with him for the mission (I think he told me it would be around 23–24 plus some ANA, who he felt didn't really count toward combat power anyway) and that he was also concerned about the terrain surrounding the area."[47] Around 1 July, a week before ROCK MOVE would begin, Brostrom discussed these issues with his boss, Captain Myer. Myer recalled that his 2d Platoon leader did not request specific resources but was seeking ways to mitigate the risks associated with the operation. As the company commander remembered, "That is when we decided to make sure he had a 120-mm mortar tube and attach a weapons truck (up-armored HMMWV with TOW missile and ITAS) as well as additional ISR (LRAS3)."[48] Brostrom mentioned to Kennedy that Captain Myer had addressed his concerns by arranging for the direct and indirect fire support. Despite this fire support, Kennedy felt that Brostrom retained some anxiety about his platoon's role in ROCK MOVE.[49]

Regardless of these personal doubts and concerns, the burden of keeping the platoon focused on the mission and motivated to accomplish it fell primarily on Brostrom and Dzwik. The platoon sergeant stated that he did not change the routine of combat checks and drills in preparation for the operation, and he simply told the Soldiers that they had come here to do 15 months of a job, not 14 months. In his opinion, by July 2008, the platoon was a tightly knit highly efficient organization and that its focus on mission accomplishment never slipped.[50]

The Establishment of COP Kahler, 8-12 July

ROCK MOVE began on schedule and was executed with few glitches. Suprisingly, the enemy did not interfere with any of the air movements.

Bella was evacuated after dusk on the second day (9 July) with Myer on the last helicopter out of the site. At Myer's request, the garrison there had been reinforced four days earlier with two squads from B Company in the Korengal Valley. Myer feared an attack from the relatively large AAF force known to be in the vicinity. He also wanted to use the extra manpower to help expeditiously load supplies because of his concern that the insurgents intended to shoot down a helicopter during the evacuation. The faster the uploading, the less the time the Chinooks would be in the enemy's crosshairs. Myer recalled, "I had a feeling that the enemy was trying to do a large scale attack on Bella because they knew we were going to vacate it. They could do a large attack and then say they forced us out of Bella."[51] The TF *Rock* officers were also concerned because in early June, the insurgents fired upon and disabled a civilian contracted Mi-8 "Hip" helicopter on a routine run delivering food to Bella. The landing zone at Bella was closed for three days until the helicopter could be recovered, leaving the garrison stranded without a means of resupply or medical evacuation. This incident clearly showed Ostlund the vulnerability of the Bella position. In any event, after the 4 July Apache attack, the AAF near Bella remained dormant. Aircraft had been routinely fired upon for some weeks before the Apache attack. After that event, the Chinooks were unmolested as they came and went at Bella.[52]

Sergeant Erik Aass, Myer's RTO, recalled that the company commander:

> decided that we should leave it standing and just make an announcement that we were donating the buildings to the villagers. Either way, the Taliban were going to claim that they drove us off. This way, we could twist the argument and say we were giving something to the villagers. If the Taliban then chose to take it over, then we could say they stole it from the villagers.[53]

With all the controversy concerning the 4 July Apache strike, he decided, on his own initiative, to go first to Blessing in order to facilitate the completion of the pending AR 15-6 investigation of the attack. Because of the Coalition's sensitivity concerning possible civilian casualties, this investigation had become a priority for TF *Bayonet*. Since Myer was the officer who directed the air strike, he was obviously a key witness in any investigation. His participation in that process meant that Myer remained at Camp Blessing on 10 July to be interviewed and to coordinate the interviews of other members of Chosen Company who had been involved in the 4 July action at Bella. Myer participated in the investigation on 10

July. On 11 July, RCP and aircraft availability issues prevented him from moving to Wanat. However, on the 12th, he was able to catch a CH-47 flight to the new COP.[54]

With COP Bella safely closed, many senior officers such as Colonel Preysler, and even Myer, felt that the most dangerous portion of ROCK MOVE was over. TF *Rock* transferred all materials and all American personnel to Camp Blessing and some of the Class IV (construction materials) and Class V (ammunition) were subsequently moved to COP Kahler on 9 July. Myer had chosen to personally oversee the actions at Bella in early July, an effort that contributed to the COP's successful evacuation without any casualties. While Myer did not personally supervise the planning and preparation of the establishment of the COP at Wanat, he was aware of the details and had a team of experienced officers and NCOs in the company doing the preparations.[55]

On the evening of 8 July, 2d Platoon, Chosen Company, departed from Camp Blessing after sunset in a ground assault convoy for the 90 minute long drive to Wanat. The convoy contained five HMMWVs; one for each of the three rifle squads, each reinforced with elements of the weapons squad, a fourth vehicle carrying Brostrom and his platoon headquarters, and the last vehicle containing the TOW missile squad. Sergeant Brian Hissong remembered the HMMWVs being loaded "with as much food, water, ammo, and people as they could hold."[56] Staff Sergeant Benton recalled loading up his squad's HMMWV:

> A lot of the room was taken up by extra ammo and whatever defensive equipment we could find, sandbags and shovels, anything we could conjure up or snag that was just lying around. We also tried to pack as much water and food for two days. I don't remember the exact numbers but we kind of eyeballed it and were like "This is good." We'd done this before so we knew we could live off this much food and water for the next two days while doing hard work. We were prepared for at least two days of food and water. We had ammo out the ass and anything we could bring to defend our positions.[57]

The convoy arrived at Wanat before midnight.

Immediately the platoon established a vehicle laager in the open field just south of the mosque and hotel and west of the bazaar. The open field was the exact site identified by TF *Rock* for the proposed Wanat COP since June 2007. It was also the same location that First Lieutenant Andrew Glenn's engineers from the 3d Brigade, 10th Mountain Division, had used as a base in the fall of 2006 while they constructed bridges on the outskirts of the village. Shortly after they arrived, a drenching rainfall began and continued to fall for the remainder of the night. Hissong remembered it was "pitch black" and the rain flooded the northern part of the field. Stafford recalled, "We pulled in there, circled the HMMWVs, and then about that time it started dumping rain and a big thunderstorm."[58] With the heavy rain and darkness, little could be done except to establish local security until morning. Specialist Jeffrey Scantlin, manning the machine gun in the gunner's turret of Benton's HMMWV, recalled being absolutely drenched by the heavy rain, as he had packed his rain gear in his rucksack. At first light, the field was swept for mines and IEDs, the platoon leaders identified fighting positions, and entrenchment began. Lieutenant Brostrom and Sergeant Ryan Pitts, the platoon's forward observer (FO), began looking for the proper site for an OP on a ridge to the east.[59]

On the afternoon of 9 July, several Chinook helicopter flights delivered to Wanat the 2d Platoon Soldiers who had not been able to fit into the HMMWVs the night before. Other helicopter flights carried the mortars and crew to the site along with construction materials, such as HESCOs, hand excavation tools (shovels and picks), sandbags, and concertina wire. Most of this material along with supplementary ammunition, had been previously positioned at COP Bella and was transferred to Wanat.[60]

The 9 July Chinook sorties also inserted the 24 Afghan soldiers from the attached ANA platoon along with the three US Marine ETT members. Half came from Blessing in the morning, the remainder directly from Bella after dusk. The ANA company that provided the platoon to COP Kahler was a new ANA organization formed in January and February 2008. It had received initial unit training at Kabul and then been moved to the Pech/Korengal/Waygal Valley region in March 2008. The majority of the enlisted men were relatively young inexperienced recruits from northeastern Afghanistan, although operating out of the battalion's headquarters at Camp Blessing and not at Wanat. The *kandak's* operations sergeant major was an extremely experienced Safi Pashtun from the lower Waygal Valley and provided considerable local knowledge and familiarity. Three Marine ETT members, two of whom, the noncommissioned officer in charge (NCOIC) Staff Sergeant Luis Repreza and Corporal Jason Jones, had been in their positions since March 2008, advised the ANA platoon. Corporal Jason Oakes, who formerly had been performing administrative duties based on his finance military occupational specialty, joined the team and was slated to temporarily replace Repreza during his routine morale leave scheduled to begin 13 July. Oakes joined the ANA platoon on the ground at Camp Blessing on 9 July, just in time for the helicopter ride to Wanat. Lieutenant Colonel Kevin Anderson, a Marine reservist and the commander of the ETT, noted that the ANA company had been undergoing intensive training and had made considerable progress. Anderson specifically recalled that their level of training enabled the ANA to perform effective and independent dismounted local security patrols. The ANA's weaknesses were in logistics and communications and the Marine team provided the majority of these services. Unfortunately, the Afghan soldiers had not participated in 2d Platoon's planning for ROCK MOVE or precombat preparations before they arrived in Wanat.[61]

The six man engineer squad, led by Staff Sergeant Thomas Hodge, from C Company, 62d Engineer Battalion (Heavy), a unit that had just recently deployed to Afghanistan from Fort Hood, Texas, also arrived by Chinook helicopter on the morning of 9 July. Accompanying them was the Bobcat loader and a small CONEX shipping container filled with specialized engineer equipment. The engineers set up a large rubber fuel blivet for the Bobcat next to this CONEX, roughly located in the center of the field.[62]

Because five heavily laden HMMWVs could not transport the entirety of the platoon's needs, and to augment the air resupply shipments, TF *Rock* planned to send a convoy of civilian "jingle" trucks, large civilian cargo vehicles capable of navigating through the rutted roads of northeastern Afghanistan, with construction supplies and water. Since there were problems with the safety of movement of civilian vehicles on the road between Camp Blessing and Wanat, this convoy was slated to follow the TF *Bayonet* Route Clearance Package 8 (RCP 8) up the road on 9 July. RCP 8 was a special task organized force from the brigade engineer company designed to remove IEDs and clear ambushes from important routes in AO Rock. However, the RCP never cleared the road between Camp Blessing and Wanat after the execution of ROCK MOVE. On 8 July, while RCP 8 was clearing the main road through the Chawkay Valley (Destined Company sector), an operation which included members of the new RCP element from the relieving 3d Brigade Combat Team, 1st Infantry Division, the combined unit was involved in a TIC incident. The RCP convoy struck a command wire IED which destroyed a vehicle, killed one member of the new unit and wounded four other engineers. Due to a combination of the catastrophic effects of the detonation and the freshness of the unit which suffered the casualties, the RCP element's operations were disrupted for several days. This hindered both routine ground resupply to Wanat and Ostlund's scheduled visit to the new outpost on 10 July. Accordingly the jingle trucks never made it to the 2d Platoon's position. Myer later recalled that communication problems with the contractors further hampered the synchronization of the contractors' arrival in the first several days of operations at COP Kahler.[63]

However, as a backup and to provide routine resupply, Chosen Company had contracted five Afghan Toyota Hilux trucks from a local national in Nangalam. In the past, these small trucks had made numerous runs to COP Bella, merely requiring 24 hours notice to execute a mission. Consequently, after realizing that the jingle trucks would not make their scheduled delivery and after reprioritizing resupply requirements with Sergeant First Class Dzwik at Wanat, Company Executive Officer Captain Devin George arranged for the Hiluxes to deliver additional water and construction materials to COP Kahler. While these trucks also had security problems reaching Wanat, two did arrive at the outpost on 11 July, bringing about 15 cases of water.[64]

The Afghan civilians providing services to the Americans were naturally apprehensive. The AAF targeted anyone cooperating with the Coalition forces. In 2006, the insurgents destroyed some of the equipment of a Jalalabad construction company that was improving the road between Wanat and Bella. This incident would have been well known to Afghan firms in the region. Glenn suspected that local contractors may have even been "warned off" by other Afghans from going to Wanat. Therefore, traveling to Wanat without RCP protection was problematic. Nevertheless, the resourceful Nangalamis still managed to get several Hiluxes through to COP Kahler.[65]

With the arrival of the 120-mm mortar by helicopter on 9 July, all of the heavy weapons dedicated to support the new COP were in place. The mortar, smeared with mud, was immediately emplaced to fire. The mortar section was a combination of one of the company's two 60-mm mortar squads and a 120-mm mortar squad from the battalion mortar platoon. Staff Sergeant Erich Phillips led this ad hoc mortar section. Phillips was a very experienced NCO who had won the Distinguished Service Cross for valor during the Ranch House fight. The mortar section, engineers, and Afghan soldiers were the last reinforcements that would arrive at Wanat until the afternoon of 12 July when Myer finally arrived with Aass, his RTO, via Chinook helicopter. Myer brought supplies of water, rations, and replacement parts with him. Accordingly, on 13 July, there were 49 Americans and 24 Afghan soldiers at COP Kahler. In the plan for ROCK MOVE, Myer's company fire support officer (FSO), 1LT Erik Gonzalez, was supposed to accompany him to Wanat. However, Myer left him behind at Camp Blessing to conduct other duties as he felt that Sergeant Pitts, the 2d Platoon FO, was well able to supervise fire support activities for the unit there.[66]

The Terrain at Wanat and the Configuration of the COP

For COP Kahler to be effective, it had to be in close proximity to Wanat to allow the Americans to foster relations with the town's population and facilitate regular coordination with the district center and Afghan National Police (ANP). The site also had to be near the road from Camp Blessing to ease resupply. Of course, the COP had to be positioned and constructed so that its garrison could provide security for the community against the AAF that might seek to punish any within the community that cooperated with Coalition and Government of the Islamic Republic of Afghanistan (GIROA) forces.

To meet those criteria, COP Kahler had to be placed near the town. As with nearly every community in Konar and Nuristan, Wanat was located within a valley whose steep walls overlooked the settlement. Wanat was specifically located at the junction of the Wayskawdi Creek, which flowed generally from the east, and the larger Waygal River, which flowed south from the Hindu Kush through the valley and into the Pech River. The two bridges constructed by local labor and Glenn's engineers in the fall of 2006 had greatly improved the ability of Waygal Valley residents to travel to the Wanat area which in turn enhanced the town's standing as a commercial and political center in the valley. COP Kahler also had to be positioned to protect these two bridges as they were key terrain within the Waygal Valley.

In 2008, Wanat was a community of approximately 50 families (roughly 200 people) and it contained a mosque, hotel/restaurant, a large bazaar (market), and a district government center which included the district police headquarters from which a force of ANP operated. A local resident, "Ahmad" (not his real name), noted that the community had initially enjoyed good relationships with the US Army, "People were treated very good by US and Afghan Forces [in 2006] while building two bridges by US Forces. A lot of people were hired from Wanat and nearby villages and people from Wanat Village were and still are nice with US forces."[67] This statement referred to the fall 2006 project mounted by First Lieutenant Glenn. Ahmad further suggested that the town's population opposed the construction of an American base in their community primarily because it would be certain to attract attacks from the insurgents as the COPs at Ranch House and Bella had done. Ahmad noted, "The most important

Staff Sergeant Jesse Queck

Figure 10. View of Wanat COP looking west from mortar position with 2d Squad position, the bazaar and OP Topside's later location in the background, 9 July 2008.

reason I think, was that Wanat Villagers did not want their village to be a battlefield. They knew that if US Army build base there, militant will attack or fire rocket and villagers will be the most victim of fighting. That is why they were against the base. It was mentioned by villagers to the US Army in meetings."[68] Ahmad was referring to the dialogues between the Wanat elders and TF *Rock* officers during the two *shura*s held at Wanat on 26 May and 8 June 2008. American officers attending these meetings confirmed his statement.[69]

The location of COP Kahler was a large open field, which the Chosen Company troopers described as roughly the size of a football field, aligned lengthwise from north to south, and located generally south of and directly adjacent to the village of Wanat. The field was generally flat and level, declining slightly from north to south, with low terraces running east to west that were relatively easily negotiated. The center of the field was at an elevation of 3,350 feet and generally devoid of vegetation but contained numerous small rocks. As Wanat is surrounded by 10,000 foot ridges on all sides, the town is dominated by the high ground. For this reason, during the earlier brief American occupation of Wanat in 2006, the engineers attached to the 10th Mountain Division had established three OPs on high ground to provide overwatch for the American position.[70]

The Waygal River ran through a deep ravine on the immediate western side of the COP. The road from Camp Blessing to Wanat ran from south to north and defined the eastern periphery of COP Kahler. A large building with a prominent blue roof was located to the west of the COP and surrounded by a high stone wall. Due north was a smaller single story building that served as the Wanat mosque. The large district center was farther to the northwest of the mosque and located on a narrow isthmus between the river and the creek, immediately adjacent to and west of the road to Camp Blessing. It was relatively close to the COP, approximately 200 yards, but was located at a considerably lower elevation and could not be viewed from COP Kahler. A cluster of buildings existed to the northeast and east of the American position in the open field just across the road. This grouping included several multistory buildings that served as a hotel/restaurant/tea cafe and a long single story building to the east that served as the community bazaar or market.[71]

On the morning of 9 July, Brostrom established an OP on a ridge to the east of the main position, east of both the bazaar and the hotel/restaurant complex. In the spring, during visits to Wanat, Myer had directed Brostrom and Dzwik to place the OP on the high ground to the east of the bazaar. Myer had originally envisioned the OP to be located several hundred yards away from the COP. Once the platoon arrived, however, Brostrom chose a closer location among a group of large boulders and trees. Myer later recalled that after his arrival at Wanat, Brostrom explained to him that the protection afforded by the boulders made the OP site preferable to all others.[72]

This spot was on a prominent ridge located east of the Blessing-Wanat Road and southeast of the junction of Wayskawdi Creek and the Waygal River. This ridge was oblong and consisted of a large number of flattened agricultural terraces. The terrace walls were constructed of stone and were probably about 100 years old. The Americans noted that the terraces varied from waist to mid-chest in height. Overall, the ridge was of sufficient elevation to block completely all observation and fields of fire from the COP to the northeast and southeast. It also blocked visibility or control of the lower ground along the Wayskawdi Creek, which flowed through a large ravine to the north, northeast, and east of the ridge.

Thus placing an OP there provided some visibility of the terrain to the east that could serve as an AAF avenue of approach into Wanat and would otherwise have been masked from view of those at the COP. Also important was that the OP's location provided the paratroopers with visibility of the two bridges just north of the town. Specifically, the OP site was located on the western side of the ridge, approximately 60 yards east of the 2d Squad's position on the COP's perimeter. It was located below the topographical crest of the ridge, six terraces up (approximately 20 feet in elevation above the road and COP). The OP was separated by the long, single story market from the road and COP Kahler. It was relatively close to the COP but the climb up the terraces was steep and difficult, particularly given the weight of the individual body armor (IBA) and helmet that the paratroopers continually wore at Wanat.[73]

Pitts, the forward observer, noted that Brostrom had specifically positioned the OP with proximity to the COP in mind. Pitts recalled Brostrom saying "he didn't want the observation post to be too far out because we didn't really have a lot of people."[74] The platoon leader clearly wanted to be able to react to any problems at the OP quickly and was concerned about placing it in a position that was too far away from the COP. Any QRF required to assist the paratroopers at the OP had to be able to move on a route that was short and as safe as possible.

The OP site had one serious disadvantage. It offered poor to nonexistent lines of sight to the north because only ten yards to its north, the ground fell steeply into a tree filled ravine that contained the Wayskawdi Creek. Thus, to the immediate north, the OP site had considerable nearby dead space, an area that could not be seen or covered by direct fire weapons. That ravine could potentially serve as a covered and concealed route for an enemy intent on attacking the OP. In fact, careful use of this route could allow an insurgent force to approach within hand grenade range of the OP, as well as enter unobserved the hotel/restaurant complex of buildings.

The platoon called the OP "Topside" after a topographical feature on the island of Corregidor which the battalion had used as a drop zone on 16 February 1945 during the Battle of the Philippines in World War II. Topside was the most important drop zone in the history of the 503d Infantry. Albeit on a smaller scale, the ridge to the east of COP Kahler dominated the position just as Topside had dominated the topography of Corregidor.

There was a gap between the bazaar and the hotel/restaurant complex such that Soldiers could walk to the north of the bazaar from the COP to the OP. Just to the south of the bazaar, was a small separate building that served as the local public latrine for the market. To the south of this building, the 1st Squad set up a traffic control point (TCP) along the road to Camp Blessing. Although the troops could walk directly from the COP to the OP by taking a path north of the bazaar, they most frequently followed a less direct path that had been created through the 1st Squad's TCP. The TCP was located approximately 50 yards from the OP, although a number of vertical terraces had to be ascended to reach the OP.[75]

Within the open field was an unfinished (walls only) "C-shaped" building on the eastern side of the field with the open portion of the "C" facing to the northeast. The Americans did not occupy it. Dzwik recalled that they were not permitted to use the building which was an unfinished new bazaar. The building plans for the completed COP did not include this building within its limits. The road from Camp Blessing to Wanat ran between the existing bazaar and the C-shaped building.[76]

Agricultural terraces extended for a considerable distance to the south where the concertina wire perimeter fence was the only definition for the southern edge of the COP. Civilian compounds, consisting of multiple buildings, lookout towers, and potential enemy firing positions, were located on higher ground to the southwest and southeast of the COP and to the southeast and northeast of the OP. On the western side, COP Kahler abutted several Afghan compounds, behind which ran the Waygal River. On the other side of the river, the ground began to rise precipitously to form the valley wall.

Work on the COP had begun on 9 July with the rifle squads, mortar section, and TOW squad establishing their fighting positions. The engineers began surveying the field so that when the Afghan contractors arrived, they could assist with building the HESCO barriers. Dzwik recalled, "They were tracking that they were going to start building the FOB right away. They had marked off the guard towers and where the walls were going to go."[77]

The COP began to take shape over the next three days. The engineers used the Bobcat to fill a number of HESCO barriers around the three squad positions and to create a firing pit for the 120-mm mortar. The ANA platoon likewise established several squad positions. That platoon and its three-Marine ETT occupied the very northern tip of the COP, just a few yards from the mosque and the hotel complex. Slightly behind the ANA and oriented to the north, Brostrom set up his 3d Squad, led by Sergeant Israel Garcia, whose three-man fighting position consisted of several HESCOs and its HMMWV, equipped with a Mk-19 grenade launcher. On the eastern side of the COP, Brostrom placed his 2d Squad in a position reinforced with HESCOs. Staff Sergeant Benton and the six squad members oriented their HMMWV, mounting one Mk-19 grenade launcher, toward the east looking at the bazaar. The platoon command post; consisting of Brostrom, Dzwik, the RTO, and the medic, was protected by the platoon leader's HMMWV and several HESCOs and sat against the northwest wall of the

C-shaped building in the middle of the COP. As previously mentioned, the platoon's 1st Squad established a TCP just south of the bazaar on the Wanat-Camp Blessing Road. That control point roughly 30 yards to the southeast from 2d Platoon's position, consisted of the squad's HMMWV with its M2 .50-caliber machine gun oriented down the road to the south, several HESCO barriers, and a single strand of concertina wire stretched across the road as an obstacle. Squad leader Staff Sergeant Sean Samaroo had five paratroopers to man the TCP.[78]

The ANA platoon also established a TCP position along the road from Camp Blessing some yards south of the 1st Squad's TCP near the Wanat medical clinic. The double echeloning of TCPs was a security measure designed to minimize the effect of any vehicle borne IEDs. However, this redundancy could be construed as a luxury when viewed in the context of the lack of observation posts on higher ground around the COP.

To the south of the CP, Brostrom placed the three-man TOW missile squad and their HMMWV. Sergeant Justin Grimm, the squad leader, oriented the missile system to the south and west and used the ITAS to scan in those directions. Between 9 and 12 July, Grimm periodically moved the TOW HMMWV to other spots on the southern half of the COP. However, by 12 July the engineers had used the Bobcat to construct a ramp for the HMMWV to enhance its ability to observe and fire. The TOW HMMWV occupied this position just before dark on 12 July. The mortar crew set up the 60-mm mortar in the middle of the COP, approximately midway between the mortar pit and the command post. The crew did not regularly man that mortar and installed it in an incomplete firing position that offered virtually no protection.[79]

The platoon constructed specific positions within the COP using different configurations based on the terrain, resources, and time available. Dzwik specifically recalled that the soil at the COP was hard with a lot of rocks and that it was very difficult digging given the limited hand tools and entrenching tools that the platoon had. In his opinion, excavating more than a couple of feet down was not feasible. Scantlin called the excavation process "a labor intensive project to get nowhere."[80] Thus the positions were a mix of sandbags, vehicles, HESCOs, and other materials. The field latrine, for example, was a simple plywood structure constructed by the engineers and protected by approximately half a dozen HESCOs partially filled with dirt. The 120-mm mortar position was a C shaped bunker of HESCOs with the opening to the east (the interior of the COP). The bottom layer of HESCOs at this position was filled with dirt. On top of this layer, the mortarmen positioned a second tier of HESCOs. On both ends of the horseshoe-shaped wall of barriers, the mortarmen filled the

HESCOs with dirt excavated by the Bobcat. Because of a depression in the ground, the Bobcat could not reach the upper tier of HESCOs in the center of the mortar position Phillips filled these sections by hand, with a combination of dirt, empty ammo cans and miscellaneous debris located at the site. A weakness of the mortar position was its placement without any infantry security between it and the perimeter of the COP. Phillips did not anticipate enemy occupation of the nearby houses without some kind of warning. Ultimately the mortarmen depended on the HESCOS and barbed wire to protect themselves rather than the usual screen of infantry fighting positions.[81]

The infantry squads used HESCOs and other materials in the construction of their positions. The three ANA positions were excavated between 18 and 36 inches deep and had another two to three feet of double layered sandbags placed above the ground surface. Garcia's 3d Squad position was initially similar to the nearby ANA positions. The more experienced 2d Squad leader, Staff Sergeant Benton, looked at the position at Garcia's request and recommended that it be strengthened. Accordingly, by the evening of 12 July, Garcia's squad had improved it with six HESCOs in an "L" configuration to the north and west of the position with a strong sandbagged wall to the south. The HMMWV was positioned to the right (east) of the fighting position. Benton established a strong position for his 2d Squad that was approximately eight yards long and five yards wide, with a sandbag wall covering the north about five feet high, a three foot high rock wall on the east, the HMMWV serving as the western wall, and a three foot sandbag wall on the south side. Benton then created a smaller position made out of several four foot HESCOs to the north of his main squad position.[82]

The other positions on the main COP took shape as well. By 12 July, the 1st Squad's TCP was a substantial fighting position. Samaroo had improved the position with a three foot high triple wall of sandbags and two interlocked four foot HESCOs. To the east and at the control point's rear, there was a seven foot high terrace wall. The HMMWV was set up on the western side of the position. Finally, the squad hung camouflage netting over the position. The CP position too, was built up over the course of the position's occupation. Its site directly abutted the unfinished C-shaped building. Brostrom parked his HMMWV to the west. The CP position was excavated as a pair of long slit trenches with a sandbag wall to the north, a single HESCO to the south, and the building's wall to the east. The 60-mm mortar firing position was roughly in the center of the COP. It was excavated and the base plate had been settled but it was only protected by a few sandbags.[83]

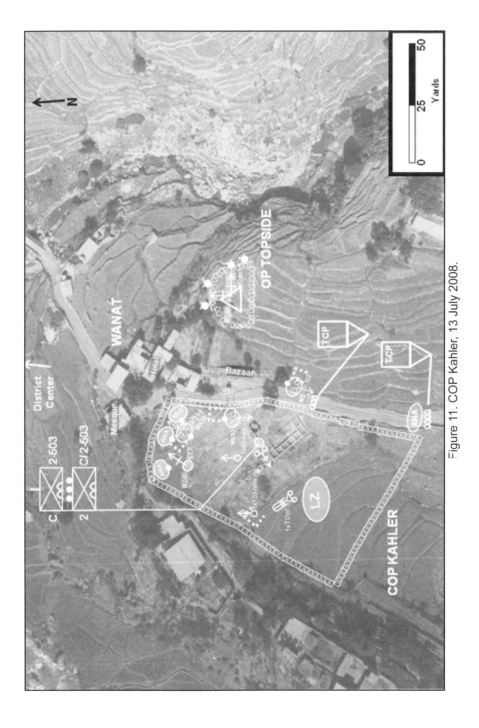

Figure 11. COP Kahler, 13 July 2008.

99

Because of the lack of available construction material, none of the positions had overhead cover. Such cover would protect against AAF mortar and rocket fires as well as from fragments from RPG rounds that could disintegrate in nearby foliage. Dzwik later noted that he had located some large wooden beams that could have been used for this purpose but they were piled by the unfinished bazaar and he did not want to take the wood without gaining the owner's permission and properly paying for it. Finally, by 12 July the paratroopers added an extra layer of protection to the COP by stringing a double layer of concertina wire around its periphery and partially anchoring that fence to the ground with the limited number of stakes they had brought. They made a small entryway in the wire on the eastern side of the COP, to the north of the 1st Squad's TCP and just south of the 2d Squad's position. This gap served as the entrance for any vehicles arriving from Camp Blessing.[84]

Figure 12. COP Kahler: Looking west towards the mortar pit after the battle.

Courtesy Colonel William Ostlund

The Configuration of OP Topside

By 12 July, the OP had become a complex of three interconnected fighting positions anchored by several large boulders that afforded an extra measure of protection. Brostrom emplaced the OP west of and several terraces below the top terrace at the pinnacle of the ridge. There was rising ground to the south and east and descending ground to the north and west. A large civilian compound stood about 100 yards to the southeast on

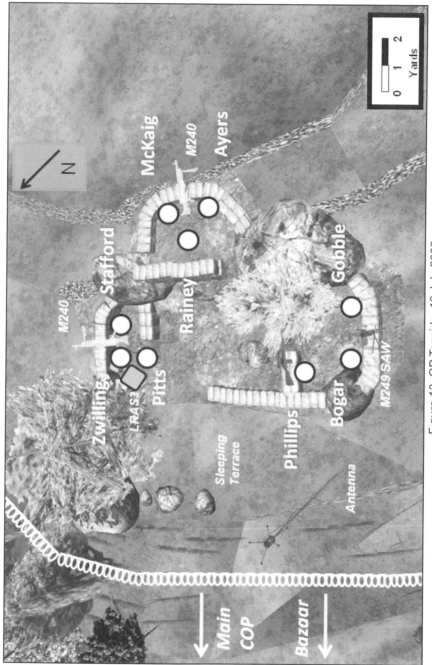

Figure 13. OP Topside, 13 July 2008.

higher ground. Following the 13 July engagement, reinforcing US troops would place an OP at this compound, as it was clearly key terrain. However, Brostrom did not feel that he had enough men available to defend a more remote and isolated OP location. The platoon leader considered a third position that provided better observation and fields of fire into the deep ravine to the north and east but this spot, east of where Topside was established, was much farther away from the COP and the ground between was particularly exposed to enemy observation and potential fire. Brostrom and Dzwik also considered establishing the OP in the two story hotel that dominated the mosque/hotel/bazaar complex of buildings within Wanat. However, an OP in the hotel would not have improved observation or obtained fields of fire to the east and would have required the Afghan residents of the hotel to be dislocated, thus potentially creating friction with the population.[85]

When Myer arrived on the afternoon of 12 July, he was not particularly enthusiastic about the location of OP Topside. He remembered, "I suggested moving it higher on the hill but all the paratroopers and the [platoon] leader said it would be more exposed on the hilltop and they would rather have the force protection of the rocks. I agreed we would move it when we had more force protection."[86] thus the OP stayed on the ridge just to the east of the COP. Perhaps its greatest advantage was that it was close to the COP. By placing it on the western military crest of the ridge, Brostrom assured access to the OP would be somewhat protected by the COP and TCP, although this location relinquished the ability to see into the nearby ravine to its north.

Brostrom and Dzwik created an ad hoc force to man OP Topside. They placed Sergeant Ryan Pitts, the platoon forward observer, in charge and gave him eight paratroopers. Two M240 machine gun teams, totaling five men from the platoon's weapons squad, occupied the OP along with the unit's dedicated marksman, a rifleman from 1st Squad, and a rifleman from 3d Squad. Brostrom also gave Pitts the LRAS3 to enable the observers at the OP to watch the high ground to their north, east, and southeast.[87]

As elsewhere on the COP, the Soldiers at OP Topside excavated and used sandbags to improve the natural protection afforded by the boulders. No HESCOs were used at OP Topside because the Bobcat could not ascend the terraces to fill them. OP Topside included a north facing fire team sized fighting position occupied by one of the M240 machine gun teams, an east facing fire team sized fighting position occupied by the second M240 team, and a southern facing fire team sized position with an M249 Squad Automatic Weapon (SAW) and an M203 40-mm grenade launcher. Both the north and south positions were rectangular and anchored on large boulders. The OP garrison constructed the southernmost fighting position at Specialist Jason Bogar's specific recommendation that the OP required more protection. The east facing fighting position was semicircular and dug into the next higher terrace to the east. Probably because it was the highest position at COP Kahler, it became known as the "Crow's Nest." The troops built a long strong sandbag wall along the western side of the OP which afforded protection for three individual fighting positions. They also constructed several short segments of sandbag walls within the interior of the position to prevent enfilading fire from sweeping the OP. Benton referred to the OP as a "little maze of sandbags" because of the various sandbag wall segments.[88] The paratroopers encircled the OP with a single strand of concertina wire. By 12 July, they had not staked down the concertina wire or otherwise secured it to the ground because the 2d Platoon had used all the available stakes and posts to install the double concertina fence around the main COP. At the OP, this barbed wire obstacle generally ran along the periphery of the agricultural terraces where the dead ground began roughly ten yards from the OP's fighting positions.[89]

Several large trees on the western periphery of the OP provided shade and some limited concealment. There was an area of dense brush and foliage immediately to the northwest. This vegetation partially obstructed fields of fire. The paratroopers did not possess adequate equipment such as axes or chain saws, to enable them to cut down the trees and brush, although the engineers had a limited capability to clear fields of fire. Brostrom decided to wait until adequate equipment and personnel arrived to clear the large trees to the west and this small copse of brush. Until this vegetation was cleared, it would limit the fields of fire and partially obscured the OP from the main COP below.[90]

To offer greater protection from close threats, the paratroopers at Topside emplaced four M18A1 Claymore command-detonated antipersonnel mines at the periphery of the dead ground to the east and the north where the tree filled ravine offered a particularly dangerous enemy avenue of approach. The operators positioned the mines after dark and recovered them at first light. The Claymores at OP Topside were not dug into the ground but simply placed on the ground inside the concertina wire and concealed with dirt and other debris. Stafford, who manned the machine gun in the northern part of the OP, specifically recalled testing the Claymores every night when he emplaced them and knew they were in working order. The paratroopers at the OP carried a large number of hand grenades up to the OP along with an M-203 40-mm grenade launcher mounted underneath an M16 5.56-mm rifle to assist in controlling the dead space. Pitts also established several target reference points in this dead ground to help defend the OP. On 12 July, Pitts registered 155-mm artillery fire on one of these targets and the mortar section fired both the 60-mm and 120-mm mortars to settle their base plates.[91]

The troopers at the OP used the terrace immediately to the west of (and below) the OP as their sleeping position with their individual tents located there. There were no fighting positions at the sleeping terrace because it was not intended to be defended. During hours of likely attack, such as dawn and dusk, the garrison was always awake and alert in the fighting positions at the OP. The Chosen paratroopers at the OP had constructed a short stretch of sandbags running east to west across the northern portion of the sleeping terrace to provide protection from the dead space to the north. The intention was eventually to extend this wall to provide protection to the entire sleeping terrace but by dusk on 12 July, only a short stretch of the north facing sandbag wall had been completed.[92]

Operations and Events at COP Kahler, 9-12 July

Between 8 and 12 July, the leaders of TF *Rock* were focused on a number of different actions. Ostlund was very busy during this period. From 8 to 10 July, he attended numerous previously scheduled *shuras* and meetings with key local leaders. As mentioned previously, the TF *Rock* commander had planned to visit Wanat on 10 July, a move that was cancelled due to the disruption of the RCP by an IED on 8 July. In addition, on 10 July, TF *Rock* suffered several enemy attacks, one each on the Pech River road and in the Korengal Valley. These attacks necessitated Ostlund's attention. In addition, the Chairman of the Joint Chiefs of Staff (CJCS), Admiral Michael Mullen, was scheduled to visit the Korengal area the next day. On 11 July, the 2-503d IN commander escorted Admiral Mullen on a tour of the TF *Rock* positions in that valley. Because of a variety of factors related to this visit, Ostlund ended up stranded overnight in the Korengal and did not return to Camp Blessing until early on 12 July. While Ostlund's staff was involved with the preliminary stages of the relief in place with the 1-26th IN, there was also additional enemy activity away from Wanat in the TF *Rock* AO that garnered their attention. In the Korengal Valley, seven separate incidents were recorded for this four day period. TF *Rock* Soldiers in the Pech Valley also came under enemy fire in four separate cases during the same period, including an instance of indirect fire aimed at Camp Blessing. D Company in the lower Konar and Chawkay Valleys reported four incidents.[93]

In the Waygal Valley, in contrast, the situation was relatively peaceful. Between 9 and 12 July, the 2d Platoon conducted a number of routine activities without any enemy interference. The US and Afghan Soldiers maintained local security, including the manning of the major weapon systems such as the TOW and the 120-mm mortar. Security operations also included the conduct of "stand-to" just before dusk and dawn on each day. Stand-to requires all unit Soldiers to be awake, alert, and ready to repel an enemy attack. It usually begins an hour before dawn at begin morning nautical twilight (BMNT) and an hour before dusk at end evening nautical twilight (EENT). The practice of stand-to was especially important in Afghanistan because insurgents in various parts of the country had displayed a tendency to attack Coalition forces before dawn.[94]

Brostrom and Dzwik carefully ensured that all weapons and supplementary weapons systems were positioned in overlapping fields of fire with formal range cards. Dzwik and Myer both recalled that Brostrom had drawn a detailed tactical diagram of the platoon defensive positions on a meal, ready to eat (MRE) box but this diagram could not be located following the 13 July battle. Pitts, the forward observer, pre-plotted target reference points for indirect fire (mortar and field artillery) all around the COP perimeter, paying particular attention to covering the dead space to the north and east of the OP. On 10 July, he forwarded an updated target plan to the battalion tactical operations center (TOC).[95]

In the opening days of ROCK MOVE, the force at Wanat also enjoyed a significant amount of ISR coverage. The operation had high priority at both CJTF and TF *Bayonet* levels. Thus, Wanat was to receive 24 hours of UAV and eight hours of SIGINT support in the 24 hour period beginning at 0730 on 8 July. In this period, the paratroopers at COP Kahler did get eight hours of SIGINT coverage but an imminent threat to Coalition troops elsewhere in RC-East directed the UAV away from Wanat, reducing the quantity of FMV coverage from 24 to 16.5 hours. In the next 24 hour period (9-10 July), Wanat again was to receive 24 hours of UAV and eight hours of SIGINT support. Another combat action outside of the TF *Rock* AO pulled the UAV away from Wanat, decreasing planned coverage to 16.5 hours. Other priorities also affected ISR support to Wanat in the next 24 hour period (10-11 July). TF *Bayonet* had apportioned 22 hours of UAV and seven hours of SIGINT coverage to COP Kahler. However, other combat operations in RC-East pulled the systems away from Wanat, resulting in 13 hours of FMV and seven and a half hours of SIGINT support over COP Kahler.[96]

Despite the reductions in ISR coverage, the Task Force *Rock* staff was satisfied with the support provided to COP Kahler. The staff directed the UAVs to look for insurgent movement on the hillsides surrounding Wanant as well as into the known insurgent "safehavens" in the area. First Lieutenant Matthew Colley, the assistant intelligence officer, recalled, "We were monitoring the area and everything was working great." According to a number of intelligence officers involved, including Colley and Lieutenant Colonel Gervais, the CJTF intelligence officer, none of these ISR systems detected any indications of a large number of insurgents gathering around Wanat in the period between 8 and 11 July.[97]

COP Kahler retained priority of fires within the battalion, meaning it had first call on the howitzers located at Camp Blessing and Asadabad. Manning these guns were a platoon from C Battery, 321st Field Artillery (the Cobras), 18th Fires [i.e. Field Artillery] Brigade, deployed out of Fort Bragg, North Carolina. Despite the relatively short straight line distance (8,750 yards or 4.97 miles) between Blessing and Wanat, because of the elevation of the intervening terrain, artillery had to be fired in a high angle trajectory. Due to the laws of physics and ballistics, the conditions within the Waygal Valley required a considerable probable error of range (PER), meaning that each round had a significant ballistic variation that could not be corrected by gunnery techniques. In other words, terrain conditions made field artillery (FA) fire less precise. At Wanat, because of the relatively short range, a reduced propellant charge had to be used, which meant that the PER or accuracy of FA fire at COP Kahler was between 32 and 65 yards, a still large but manageable variation. Accordingly, this required that field artillery fire had to be carefully observed and controlled by experienced forward observers such as Pitts. Without such careful control, it was dangerous to drop rounds near friendly troops. The firing conditions increased the possibility of fratricide if the gunners and observers did not use caution.[98]

As the platoon leadership focused on placing and adjusting weapon systems, the paratroopers continued to improve their positions. On 11 July, as noted earlier, the Bobcat ran out of fuel and could not refuel until the broken blivet pump was repaired. This mechanical failure, however, did not really affect construction, particularly the filling of HESCO barriers. The platoon used and filled all available sandbags and emplaced all the concertina wire on hand, using every picket available to partially secure the barbed wire around the COP.[99]

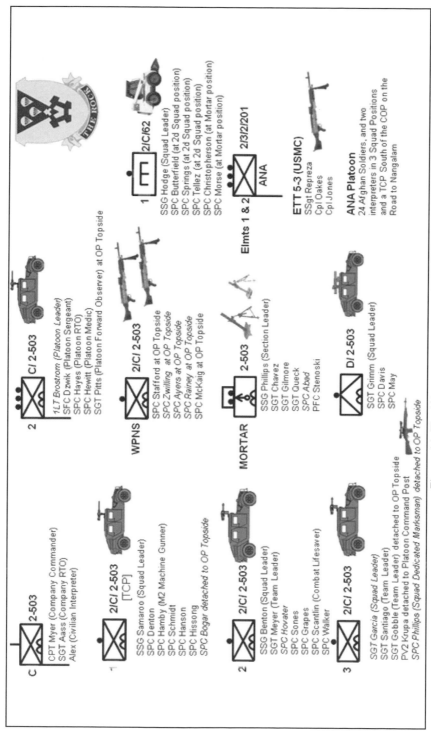

Figure 14. The Wanat garrison, 13 July 2008.

C 2-503
CPT Myer (Company Commander)
SGT Aass (Company RTO)
Alex (Civilian Interpreter)

2 2-503
1LT Brostrom (Platoon Leader)
SFC Dzwik (Platoon Sergeant)
SPC Hayes (Platoon RTO)
SPC Hewitt (Platoon Medic)
SGT Pitts (Platoon Forward Observer) at OP Topside

C/ 2-503

1 2/C/62
SSG Hodge (Squad Leader)
SPC Butterfield (at 2d Squad position)
SPC Springs (at 2d Squad position)
SPC Tellez (at 2d Squad position)
SPC Christopherson (at Mortar position)
SPC Morse (at Mortar position)

2/C/ 2-503 [TCP]
SSG Samaroo (Squad Leader)
SPC Denton
SPC Hamby (M2 Machine Gunner)
SPC Schmidt
SPC Hanson
SPC Hissong
SPC Bogar detached to OP Topside

WPNS 2/C/ 2-503
SPC Stafford at OP Topside
SPC Zwilling at OP Topside
SPC Ayers at OP Topside
SPC Rainey at OP Topside
SPC McKaig at OP Topside

Elmts 1 & 2 2/3/2/201 ANA

ETT 5-3 (USMC)
SSgt Repreza
Cpl Oakes
Cpl Jones

ANA Platoon
24 Afghan Soldiers, and two interpreters in 3 Squad Positions and a TCP South of the COP on the Road to Nangalam

2/C/ 2-503
SSG Benton (Squad Leader)
SGT Meyer (Team Leader)
SPC Hovater
SPC Sones
SPC Grapes
SPC Scantlin (Combat Lifesaver)
SPC Walker

MORTAR 2-503
SSG Phillips (Section Leader)
SGT Chavez
SGT Gilmore
SGT Queck
SPC Abad
PFC Stenoski

D/ 2-503
SGT Grimm (Squad Leader)
SPC Davis
SPC May

3 2/C/ 2-503
SGT Garcia (Squad Leader)
SGT Santiago (Team Leader)
SGT Gobble (Team Leader) detached to OP Topside
PV2 Krupa detached to Platoon Command Post
SPC Phillips (Squad Dedicated Marksman) detached to OP Topside

The hot weather hindered the platoon's efforts at constructing its defenses. At times, the heat rose to over 100 degrees Fahrenheit. Working or providing security in such weather increased water usage. As early as 9 July, the platoon leadership projected a water shortage. The ROCK MOVE plan called for a buildup of five days of water supply for the operation. At the operations briefing on 7 July, General Milley inquired about the ways in which the 2d Platoon would be supported logistically. He specifically recalled, "I would always ask up questions [on logistics] and I was briefed that [TF] *Rock* had plenty of it and that they had five days of supply and that there were no issues."[100] Accordingly, the 2d Platoon brought as much bottled water with them as they could carry. However, the Army's doctrinal manual for water supply posited a planning factor for troop water consumption in an arid climate of 5.9 gallons per man per day. For the 49 Americans at Wanat, this meant a total of 289.1 gallons a day for the Americans. Five days of supply would, therefore, total 1,445.5 gallons or the contents of four 400 gallon M149 water trailers or the equivalent of 5,472 one liter containers of bottled water. The troops could not carry such a large amount of water with them on their HMMWVs. In actuality the platoon brought what Dzwik, the platoon sergeant, estimated to be a two day supply with them. He felt that this was adequate until the first resupply missions arrived. The supply buildup for ROCK MOVE included water stockpiled at Camp Blessing. The battalion and company logisticians projected that these additional allocations would be brought forward via Chinook helicopters with vehicle shipment by an Afghan contractor as a backup plan. After the initial action of the operation, standard procedure was that resupply would be pushed forward based on unit requests. Accordingly, there was no fixed long term resupply schedule. The schedule constantly changed based on the tactical situation and the supply requirements of the supported unit.[101]

With resupply expected on the first day, Dzwik initially thought he had brought enough water to Wanat. Although he knew in advance that troop labor would be used to construct the first phase of the COP defenses, the unexpectedly high temperatures caused water to be consumed at a higher rate than Dzwik had originally estimated. He remembered, "The first couple days was just nothing but digging in hard ground, [in] which you could only get maybe a foot or two down. It was still the dead heat of Afghanistan, so during the hottest parts of the day in the afternoon, there was a lot less being done just because even working for 10 minutes, you're using up a lot of water."[102] On the first day at Wanat, Dzwik quickly realized that the platoon would need more water and recalled coordinating for a resupply. In the short term, however, Brostrom and his platoon sergeant decided to limit the hardest labor to cooler periods of the day to conserve water. Dzwik noted, "We tried to do as much as we could from first light at four o'clock in the morning [0400] until it got just too hot. Then we would rest up and then try to get some more stuff done when it started cooling down a little bit toward sundown."[103] Squad leader Benton recalled that the platoon leaders actually began discussing the rationing of water in the first few days of operations at Wanat.[104]

The 2d Platoon did have some alternatives to the strict rationing of their water supply and/or reduced labor. Local water sources in Wanat included the Waygal River and Wayskawdi Creek, both of which were flowing high because of recent rains, and a well located near the hotel just outside the perimeter of the COP. Dzwik stated that the platoon had water filtration equipment with them at Wanat but he felt that the labor required to create an adequate water supply from this equipment ruled out its use in the early days at Wanat. Additionally, the platoon medic carried several bottles of iodine tablets that could produce potable water. However, the iodine tablets took an hour to activate and a large number of tablets (40, practically an entire bottle) were required to decontaminate five gallons of water. In any event, Dzwik shied away from using the iodine tablets because he felt their use caused diarrhea among the Americans which would lead to additional dehydration. Platoon members did use the well on one occasion on 11 July to fill up a five gallon can which was then purified with iodine tablets. In contrast, the Marines had no qualms about using the iodine tablets and did so early.[105]

A helicopter shortage limited water resupply. This was initially considered not to be a problem since the troops had brought water with them. However, with the consumption rate higher than expected, water soon became an issue. A pallet of water arrived by Chinook on the 9th but this resupply only provided about three gallons (12 liters) per man, below the minimum daily requirement of 5.9 gallons. From the evening of the 9th on, Captain George, the company executive officer (XO) began coordination to push the contracted force of civilian Toyota Hi-Lux pickup trucks with water to Wanat. Since such an action required a 24 hour lead time, the earliest the trucks could go to Wanat was on the 11th. As previously recounted, several of these vehicles did, in fact, reach the outpost on that day, bringing about a day's supply of water. According to Sergeant Pitts this shipment contained approximately 15 cases of water. At this point, Dzwik later commented that, "By the 11th, water was no longer an issue."[106] The delivery was welcomed but the platoon leadership's decision to limit manual labor because of the limited supply of bottled water had already affected operations. To augment previous stockpiles, Captain Myer arrived by Chinook on the 12th with three or four additional pallets. During the days after the initial occupation of the Wanat site, through neither command nor logistical channels was the garrison there reported as being critically short ("black" in contemporary Army parlance) of water.[107]

Postbattle, some soldiers perceived the lack of heavy equipment (not organic to the infantry unit) and projected shortages of bottled water to be limiting factors in the development of the defense. One of the engineers stated, "We couldn't do much manual labor that day [10 July] because we ran out of water, or close to it, that morning."[108] An infantry sergeant noted the relative lack of unit equipment that allowed the men to dig and improve their own positions, "When we first started digging our foxhole we had to wait on shovels and pick axes not being used at the time. . . . I remember on the 10th, 11th we [were] down to less than a liter of [bottled] water per person and subsequently we did not dig or work to conserve our energy and water supply."[109] The additional barrier material that arrived on 11 July, however, included pickets that allowed the Soldiers to complete staking down the concertina wire around the COP.[110]

Despite these later misgivings, after four days of operations the 2d Platoon and its attached elements had made great progress towards the preparation of the defenses at the Wanat position. The OP, squad positions and the mortar area were virtually completed by the 12th. One squad leader was so impressed with his squad's work that he believed that his unit's position could withstand direct hits from the enemy's most lethal weapons. Similarly, the senior NCO at the OP felt that his men had "accomplished...a lot" in the short time they had been at Wanat.[111] Mortar section chief Phillips also felt satisfied with the position he and his men had constructed. When he arrived on the 12th, Myer noted that "they had a good amount built up."[112]

However, there were the untapped manpower assets available at Wanat of the ANA troops. The Marines advising the ANA platoon believed that the Afghan soldiers were fully competent and capable of performing dismounted local security patrols. In their opinion, the Afghans could have been utilized as additional manpower other than just manning three fighting positions in the COP and running a redundant TCP along the main road. However, only on 12 July did Brostrom plan the first patrol which was to depart on the morning of 13 July and include both US and ANA Soldiers. Some of the noncommissioned officers at the site were displeased with the decision to dispatch even this patrol. Sergeant Hissong noted, "I remember arguing with Staff Sergeant Samaroo about having to build a base and still do patrols with such a small amount of people."[113] The insurgent attack prevented this patrol from leaving the COP.[114]

Until Myer arrived, neither the ANA unit nor the 2d Platoon conducted *shuras* or meetings with the local elders, the district governor, or ANP officers. Brostrom did attempt to organize such meetings and the single patrol to the district center was to coordinate such gatherings but the local and district leadership in Wanat rebuffed his efforts. Scantlin remembered, "Lieutenant Brostrom tried to talk to people but never got anywhere."[115] The 2d Platoon did talk to some residents and, as noted below, these encounters did provide information. Nevertheless, in the first four days of operations at COP Kahler, interaction between the Wanat population and the US and Afghan Soldiers was minimal.

Because of Chosen Company's prior visits to Wanat, the AAF was well aware that the Americans intended to establish a COP in the large field immediately south of the village. As 2d Squad leader Benton, noted, "Every time we would set up any kind of base of operations once we got into Wanat, it was right where we ended up setting up [COP] Kahler."[116] This knowledge and their close relationship with at least some of the population in Wanat meant that the insurgents could make good use of the town and its people in preparing any attack on the Coalition base.

Many of the Americans at COP Kahler picked up indicators of the enemy's presence in Wanat before the attack. Corporal Oakes, a member of the Marine ETT, remembered the young Afghan men in civilian clothes who observed intently the paratroopers' activities:

> There were civilians who were watching us all through the day. There was nothing we could do to tell them, "You can't watch us digging in the ground here." They knew exactly where we were. You could do eye judgment 30, 40, 50 feet and then be in the city just walking around doing a pace count and there was nothing we could do. . . . You can't shoot somebody for walking around slowly.[117]

Stafford supported Oakes' comments, "A lot of guys would sit at the bazaar and just watch us really closely. They watched everything we did . . . military age males . . . we all kind of knew they were bad dudes but you can't do anything about it."[118] Hissong also noticed that they were under observation:

As it got later in the morning [9 July] we started to notice that there was a group of about 15 to 20 local men gathering in the bazaar. We later learned that the locals had told Captain Myer that they didn't want us there. As we built our fighting position, we noticed that small groups of men were gathering in the bazaar and appeared to be watching us work and talking about our base.[119]

Another platoon member echoed Hissong's comments, "The bazaar across the street from our fighting position had locals outside, around it everyday until the 13th. They all sat outside and watched us all day. Other than that, they really did not do much." [120]

Benton also believed he and his men were under close observation. He remembered, "We were a zoo. We were literally a caged in zoo. It was ridiculous and I was so nervous the entire time."[121] Benton was unnerved by the openness of this observation, "There was one shop that had at least five guys at a time every day just sitting there drinking chai tea. . . . They were distinctly and obviously watching us. It's not like they were facing each other having a conversation. They were just quiet, looking at us and watching us."[122] For Benton, the general absence of women and children in Wanat added to a growing sense of anxiety. He recalled, "Children were there [in Wanat] but not as prevalent as we'd seen before when we'd been to Wanat. There had been times when we went to Wanat and that bazaar was just full of people; men, women, and children. We knew the habits and we knew what it looked like before. It looked like a ghost town [after 9 July]."[123]

From these numerous accounts, it is clear that from the start the Americans were likely under continuous AAF observation. Photographs taken of COP Kahler from a helicopter landing at the landing zone at mid day on 9 July support the accounts that there were numerous military age males present in the town at the mosque, hotel, and bazaar watching the Americans. These observers would have been able to easily notice where each American and ANA fighting position was. Queck recalled that when the fighting began early on the morning of 13 July, "It's almost like they knew where everything was."[124] However, the location of the COP in lower ground and the minimal available concealment meant that the Coalition positions were all within plain eyesight of possible direct fire weapons positions and in the subsequent firefight, the AAF did not use indirect fire weapons, whose targeting would have been facilitated by exact measurements of locations on the COP. Direct fire weapons used at short and medium range would have been able to easily target the Coalition positions without the need for any specialized targeting equipment.

Another incident in this period heightened the paratroopers' concerns. When Myer arrived on the afternoon of 12 July, he went into the town to speak to the few local men who were standing around the bazaar. Sergeant Aass recalled that as Myer talked with these men, "One of our Soldiers, Specialist Denton, recognized one of the civilians hanging around as a former member of the Bella Afghan Security Guards (ASG). When confronted, he admitted freely that he was."[125] Aass further noted that by July 2008, many of the platoon members had become suspicious of the ASG, partly because of the fatal shooting of Sergeant Kahler at COP Bella in January 2008.

However, while Brostrom reported the local scrutiny to Myer, his company commander felt that such keen observation was par for the course. Myer later commented that, "The platoon was being observed, just as we expected them to be."[126] Since the activities of the local people around the new outpost were familiar to the experienced officers and had never previously resulted in a large attack, they were not viewed as an exceptional pattern of behavior.

Although it garnered minimal attention at the time, there was another possible indicator of impending enemy action revealed when, on the morning of 12 July, an irrigation ditch directly north of OP Topside suddenly began to fill with water. Although there had been considerable rainfall during the early morning hours of 9 July, both Sergeant Pitts and Specialist Stafford at the OP thought it was odd that an irrigation ditch would suddenly fill with rushing water. Pitts, who had spent most of the time at Wanat occupying the OP, believed the flooding of the irrigation ditch was very suspicious, contending the water flow "stopped halfway through the day and then it started again after only not flowing for approximately two hours. In hindsight it may have been done to help add noise allowing the AAF to sneak closer to our positions without being heard."[127] Stafford echoed Pitts' thought:

> The fields weren't being used and there were irrigation ditches that ran right in front of my position, on the other side of the sandbags, touching the sandbags. They had turned it on. At first Phillips had dug a ditch to divert it, a couple meters [two yards] in front of the OP but then it just kept running so we didn't think anything of it, really, other than we were all kind of joking like, "Wow, if somebody sneaks up on us, we can't hear them."[128]

Another event caught 2d Platoon by surprise. Early in the afternoon of 12 July, Brostrom heard that a *shura* was then taking place within the town between the community elders, the district governor, and the leaders of the district ANP. Brostrom was extremely angry that he had not been invited to this meeting because he had been trying to organize just such a meeting since the platoon's arrival at Wanat. Dzwik recalled, "The Wanat s*hura* gathered at the Wanat District Center without inviting any Coalition Forces. . . I was digging my fighting position when First Lieutenant Brostrom came over, quite upset and said they had a *shura* going. He was upset because we had spent the whole time trying to get a s*hura* together."[129]

In response to this news, Brostrom, Benton, the interpreter, and five other platoon members went immediately to the district center on the northeastern edge of the town. The ANA commander and a squad of ANA soldiers accompanied them. Under local cultural traditions, Brostrom had every right to be angry. As the senior American, he could be considered the elder or leader of the tribe of Americans that had just arrived in town. Deliberately excluding him (and thus the Americans) from a community or district *shura* could be interpreted as a considerable insult. Benton asserted that the Afghans at the district center were not happy to see the Americans and the ANA soldiers, recalling, "The reception was not warm at all. The ANP did not respond to any of our greetings and seemed very nervous that we were there."[130] Some of the platoon's Soldiers have speculated that the attack was actually being planned at this meeting. Dzwik was adamant about this suspicion, "It is my belief, due to the cold welcome and the events of the 13th that they were discussing an attack [on the COP]."[131] By inserting himself into this *shura* and expressing his displeasure, Brostrom was behaving appropriately within the local culture and he immediately reported the *shura* and his reception by the Wanat leaders up the chain of command, gaining the attention of both officers in the TF *Rock* intelligence section.[132]

Shortly after Brostrom's unsuccessful visit to the district center, a helicopter with Myer and his RTO, Sergeant Aass, landed at the COP. Myer and Aass had ridden on a resupply helicopter bringing the replacement pump for the fuel blivet so that the Bobcat could be refueled, along with water and MREs. The Chosen Company paratroopers were particularly pleased to receive the additional supplies onboard the helicopter. As previously noted, the plan for ROCK MOVE directed the Chosen Company commander's presence at the COP earlier but Myer had gone to Camp Blessing to participate in the investigation of the 4 July Apache attack. He also conducted various actions related to the impending relief by TF *Duke*.

After his arrival, Myer walked around the position and greeted his men. Then Brostrom briefed him on the defensive arrangements and fire support plan. They then conducted a joint inspection of the defenses. At some point, Myer walked past the bazaar and attempted to make contact with the local Afghans gathered there and in the process briefly spoke with Ibrahim, a Wanat elder well known to the Americans. Myer knew that Ibrahim was a strong advocate of the Afghan central government and the US forces. Also present was Ibrahim's son, Ishmael, who spoke fluent English and served as an interpreter with US forces at Jalalabad. Ibrahim invited Myer to dinner, although he specified it must be after dark.[133]

After nightfall, Myer and a small party walked to Ibrahim's house for the meal. Myer, Brostrom, Aass, and platoon RTO Specialist John Hayes attended from the American group, along with Ibrahim and one other senior member of the community. Ishmael translated throughout the dinner, according to Aass. Ibrahim told the Chosen Company leadership "if they saw any people up in the hills, we should shoot at them because they're bad. He pretty much said that everybody up in the hills was bad and that we should shoot at them . . . he said that there were bad people around."[134]

Despite the many warnings and the paratroopers' feeling of apprehension, Myer did not feel an attack was imminent. He fully expected the Americans to be under keen observation from the start. He and Brostrom had seen the absence of women and children before without an imminent attack. The officers had also routinely received attack warnings from Afghan civilians which did not pan out. In Myer's opinion, "The enemy was very deliberate and I expected them to recon, plan, and then use indirect fire or probing attacks to attack the position at Wanat. Nothing Lieutenant Brostrom communicated or that I saw led me to believe that a large attack was imminent."[135] Myer's greatest fear was an indirect fire or rocket attack on the troops at Wanat before their defenses, particularly overhead cover, were in place to provide adequate protection.

The Enemy, 9-12 July

As described earlier, TF *Rock* was well aware of significant enemy forces in the Waygal Valley and believed the leaders of these forces, especially Mullah Osman, intended to attack Coalition bases at both Bella and Wanat. However, enemy actions and decisions between 8 and 12 July are not clear. Osman himself was probably wounded during the Apache strike at Bella on 4 July. There is no precise indication of the size of the force that attacked on 13 July or its composition. Nor is there precise understanding of who planned and led the attack, although as noted earlier, an insurgent video of the assault on COP Kahler did identify another local insurgent leader, Mawlawi Sadiq Manibullah, as the actual leader of the attack. Pry, the TF *Rock* intelligence officer, had estimated enemy forces in the Waygal Valley to number between 130 and 150 but recognized that Mullah Osman had shown the ability to bring in other fighters for major operations. Pry and other American intelligence officers also knew that there was the possibility that foreign fighters associated with international terrorist groups could be operating in Konar and Nuristan. In fact, he had received reports in June 2008 of foreign fighters arriving in the Watapor Valley, located to the east of Waygal Valley. After the 13 July battle, one media report reinforced the idea that foreign fighters had played a significant role in the 13 July attack, claiming that the attacking force had an al-Qaeda combat element known as *Lashkar al Zil* or "the Shadow Army," at its core. Following the attack on COP Kahler, estimates of the insurgent force that may have included foreign fighters varied from 120 to 300.[136]

Given the nature of the subsequent assault on the COP, the leadership of the insurgent force and at least the core of the fighting force were most likely professional and experienced. The attack displayed considerable planning, effective intelligence, and accurate knowledge regarding the capabilities and effectiveness of American weapons systems and observation equipment. Benton's assessment was that the 13 July assault, "was not an uncoordinated attack by any means. You could tell rehearsals had been done, sand tables had been done, and planning had been done on this. They knew a year before we had even come out there that eventually we were going to come out there. They knew we wanted to do it. They knew we were planning to do it."[137] The significant amount of firepower employed for roughly two hours suggests that at least the core of the force was local fighters. That local connection would have been necessary to simply transport and supply the quantities of ammunition expended and successfully evacuate the casualties from the battlefield.

While the details of the enemy plan and intent are not available for this study, based on the actions of the enemy on 13 July, Pry was convinced that the enemy objective was to drive all Coalition forces out of Wanat. To do that, it is reasonable to assume that they intended to overrun COP Kahler and OP Topside. Chosen Company post battle accounts and reports consistently state that the entire COP and OP were surrounded by AAF who infiltrated into firing positions at extremely close range to the Americans. When the assault began early on 13 July, enemy fire came from the mosque, the hotel complex, and the bazaar, which were almost on top of the COP. Some paratroopers later reported receiving machine gun fire from the vicinity of the hotel or near the bazaar. US Soldiers also observed at least one RPG fired from an unfinished stall in the center of the bazaar.[138]

How did the insurgents move into their attack positions without alerting the Coalition forces at COP Kahler? It seems clear that at least some of the force had infiltrated the town between 9 and 12 July and constituted some of those who were closely watching operations at the COP. Other insurgents may have been among the town residents. Still, the large force that attacked COP Kahler on 13 July had to be partly composed of fighters from outside Wanat. Many likely began moving from nearby villages under cover of darkness on the nights leading up to the attack. The lack of Coalition radio message intercepts suggest that these insurgents were moving in small groups to avoid detection and were most likely practicing radio silence. To initiate their attack, the AAF leaders employed machine gun fire rather than depending on their radios. After regularly contesting ground with the 1st Battalion, 32d Infantry, and then TF *Rock* since April 2006, the AAF were well aware that their radio communications were monitored. Additionally, radios were typically a scarce commodity. On 13 July, indications are that the AAF avoided the use of radios before launching the attack. [139]

While the majority of the Americans except for the sentries, slept, those enemy insurgents who had not already infiltrated into the area began their movement from nearby villages into assault and fire support positions. In the aftermath of the battle, Pry determined, "They used the low ground with the water coming in from the east [the Wayskawdi Creek] as well as the [Waygal] river running north-south to conceal their movement, both visual and for sound as they walked over the shale and rocks in the area. We do know they had OPs up on the west."[140] TF *Rock* also later determined that the insurgents had established command and control positions on at least one of the mountain tops that offered excellent vantage points of Wanat.[141]

Whatever infiltration routes the insurgents took into Wanat the night before the battle, they employed a high degree of stealth and noise discipline. The Americans on guard that night detected nothing amiss. The sentinels were alert and active, one paratrooper even documented the 14 shooting stars he had observed in the early morning hours. Pitts specifically recalled walking to the edges of the terraces around OP Topside to monitor the dead space adjacent to them during his guard shift. Yet, not a single trooper reported seeing or hearing anything suspicious.

Specialist Christopher McKaig recalled, "It was very quiet just before we got attacked . . . no movement in our area."[142] The insurgents' ability to infiltrate without detection, although impressive, was a quality common among Afghan warriors. Attacks on a 10th Mountain patrol in Nuristan on 21 June 2006 and on TF *Rock* Soldiers at COP Ranch House on 22 August 2007 had demonstrated precisely the same capabilities.[143]

The Eve of the Attack

By 12 July, the Soldiers at COP Kahler had picked up some indications that they were not welcome in Wanat. Not only had they become aware of the observation by the many military age males inside the village but the ANP chief had directly told them they were not welcome in Wanat and openly failed to cooperate with them. A few Afghan citizens directly intimated to the US Soldiers or informed them indirectly through the ANA, that an attack was imminent. However, such warnings were routine and often proved to be false or exaggerated. After a year of operations in Afghanistan, the Chosen Soldiers were relatively inured to such reports. Still, the TF *Rock* staff had documented the presence of a relatively large insurgent force of at least several scores of fighters operating in the Waygal Valley and Pry had determined that many of these fighters would concentrate around Wanat once TF *Rock* had established the new COP in that town.

Still, the sum of these observations and concerns did not equate to a general fear of an immediate attack on the COP. The TF *Rock* S2 staff did receive reports of many of these indicators. Pry recalled that he received multiple reports from the 2d Platoon of young Afghan men in civilian garb watching the COP as well as the report of the nighttime observation of the five person group above Wanat just before the attack. Pry passed these reports up to TF *Bayonet* which Lieutenant Colonel Jimmy Hinton, the *Bayonet* S2, acknowledged. Hinton believed that the flow of intelligence from TF *Rock* was good.[144]

However, the intelligence reporting system that connected the brigade with the CJTF was based on requests for resources. Hinton would not normally have passed up the specific information about the reconnaissance of COP Kahler or the small groups of possible infiltrators. Instead, if he had thought that they constituted a major threat, he would have sent a request for more intelligence assets to collect information about the threat. Gervais, the CJTF intelligence officer, did not recall receiving any requests for resources to support COP Kahler. In the four days of the Wanat occupation when there was ISR support, neither the Predator UAV nor the aerial SIGINT collection platform detected any signs of imminent enemy action against the COP. Thus, the CJTF J2 saw no indicators of an impending attack at Wanat. Further, Milley, the CJTF-101 Deputy, recalled the information that reached his level about the operations at COP Kahler between 9 and 12 July unequivocally stated there was no enemy activity that would require further action or resources.[145]

The lack of indications that insurgent forces were massing and preparing to attack COP Kahler directly affected the amount of ISR support available to TF *Rock*. The amount of FMV and SIGINT available across Afghanistan decreased significantly after 10 July. In the 24 hour period beginning at 0730 on 11 July, the CJTF had only 12 hours of FMV and four hours of SIGINT support available for all of its units. In this environment of reduced assets, a small site like COP Kahler, which did not appear to be at risk, was not the focus of the CJTF's ISR effort. TF *Bayonet* received 6.5 hours of FMV and zero hours of SIGINT in this period. Wanat was supposed to receive some of this FMV support but after major combat actions near the city of Khowst and in the Tangi Valley became the CJTF priorities, COP Kahler received no ISR assets. In the following 24 hour period which ended on the morning of 13 July, the availability of ISR across Afghanistan decreased further as bad weather grounded most of the systems. TF *Bayonet* did receive four hours of SIGINT and this was allocated to Wanat. However, that support ended at 1630 on the afternoon of 12 July.[146]

Milley, the CJTF deputy commanding general, emphasized that the combat action near Khowst that pulled the Predator away from ROCK MOVE on 11 July was part of a larger operation in the Tangi Valley in eastern Afghanistan in early July 2008 that had become the top priority for the Coalition. During that operation, insurgents had launched a number of large attacks against Coalition convoys and briefly kidnapped an American Soldier. CJTF-101 accordingly attempted to focus as many ISR assets as possible in that region of the country.[147]

First Lieutenant Matthew Colley, the TF *Rock* assistant S2, recalled that he and Pry fiercely resisted the redirection of the ISR away from Wanat, stating, "We fought with [TF *Bayonet*] and [TF *Bayonet*] tried to get the assets reassigned to us but [CJTF-101] did not reallocate the assets to us."[148] Pry was furious. At the two ROCK MOVE briefings to TF *Bayonet* and CJTF-101, he believed CJTF-101 had given him a commitment that adequate ISR assets would be available to support ROCK MOVE. Nearly a full year after the engagement he recalled:

This was a major point of contention . . . between me and Colonel Hinton. I even got unprofessional with him the day before the attack happened because we were losing so many assets and had so little support. He was doing the best he could and in turn was doing the same thing to division. He was demanding the support we weren't getting but we weren't the priority anymore.[149]

Pry further remarked on the heated conversation he had with Hinton, "I think there were six people in the office and about once a minute one person was getting up and walking out because they didn't want to be witnessing the conversation." By the evening of 12 July, he fumed, "We had no support from brigade, division, or theater level assets at the time."[150]

Brigade S-2 Hinton was similarly frustrated with the problems related to managing a very limited number of ISR resources, especially in the case of ROCK MOVE. Hinton's thoughts on this issue are worth quoting at length:

The challenge for me and our headquarters was with collection assets. There were so many competing priorities for collection. CJTF-101 had a priority for intelligence, surveillance and reconnaissance (ISR) and those were approved by the assistant division commander for operations. We essentially did the same thing for ISR. There just wasn't enough collection to meet all the demands that were out there. At the same time we were getting this reporting at Wanat, we had daily mortar attacks against a position that, terrain wise, was even worse than Wanat and Bella up in northeast Nuristan. Our Shadows couldn't reach it either, so we were relying on Predator for full motion video support. It was an issue for us to provide adequate support and I kind of referenced that earlier when I said the battalion S2 was upset that he wasn't getting the level of support he thought he needed. He had guys that were building force protection on the ground and he didn't think they had the adequate overhead collection to mitigate that limited force protection. It was really challenging to provide ISR because there wasn't enough to go around to meet all the requirements that units had.[151]

Hinton concluded that the hard decisions that CJTF-101 and TF *Bayonet* made about the allocation of the scarce ISR assets that day, "will burn in me forever."[152]

As of the evening of 12 July, the 2d Platoon had not received any enemy fire. This fact is relevant because the key leaders in the 2d Platoon, Chosen Company, TF *Rock*, TF *Bayonet*, and CJTF-101, held certain assumptions about the way the enemy operated. As recounted earlier in this chapter, leaders at all of these levels believed that the insurgents would react with a series of increasingly escalating attacks that would begin with harassing small arms and indirect fire and perhaps culminate in a large scale assault like the attack on the Ranch House COP. Repetitive use of this pattern by the insurgents had convinced US Soldiers in Afghanistan that it had become an accepted and proven enemy tactic. Thus, these leaders expected the insurgents to initiate hostilities against COP Kahler with a few mortar rounds or sniper shots and only slowly escalate the attacks over days or weeks. This did not make the paratroopers of 2d Platoon, Chosen Company, and TF *Rock* complacent but it did have an effect on how they understood the evolving situation at COP Kahler.[153]

In the early hours of 13 July, the morning after the SIGINT and FMV assets had left the Waygal Valley, the COP and OP were coming to life. As do most US Army infantry units in combat, the 2d Platoon rigorously enforced a daily stand-to routine. The troops at COP Kahler and OP Topside were awakened for reveille between 0345 and 0350 and were at one hundred percent alert in their fighting positions at least one hour before dawn. Soldiers were dressed in "full battle rattle." Dzwik rigidly enforced stand-to. He had experiences that reinforced the value of the procedure:

> I was in the Ranch House attack back in August 2007 when they hit us at five o'clock in the morning, so I knew that was a time that they liked to hit. I'm a huge believer and a huge enforcer of stand-to. Everybody was ready, even a half hour before it got light. Everybody was up and in their armor, 100 percent security and not a lot of movement around. It's one thing I preach, you're down in your position scanning in your sector.[154]

The ANA and ETTs similarly participated in stand-to and COP Kahler and OP Topside were fully alert and ready for action at 0400 local time.[155]

While the platoon conducted stand-to, First Lieutenant Brostrom was organizing the joint US-ANA patrol of 13 Soldiers intended to find a potential OP site located on prominent high ground to the south. If the location proved to be acceptable, the ANA would subsequently occupy the site and TF *Rock* would airlift in CONEX containers with the necessary prepackaged materials to establish an OP. Brostrom's patrol assembled by the 2d Squad position and was scheduled to depart the COP at 0430.[156]

The Bobcat and the two engineers responsible for operating it were also busy at the mortar pit in the predawn darkness. Sometime during the night, a natural spring had opened up and poured water into the mortar pit. One of the engineers who had just completed his tour of nighttime guard duty discovered the flood when he dropped his body armor to the ground to get some sleep and it landed with a prominent splash. He awakened his fellow engineer and they began using the Bobcat to excavate a ditch around the mortar pit to divert the water. At the southern portion of the mortar pit, the water was boot-top to mid-shin deep. The water was only a couple of inches deep in the center and it was just wet and muddy to the north.[157]

Just before and during stand-to, several Soldiers inside the COP began to notice shadowy groups maneuvering in the hills around Wanat. On the previous day, random sightings of individuals in the high ground had occurred but they had not seemed threatening and thus were not engaged. For example, Sergeant Justin Grimm, the leader of the TOW squad recalled, "At dusk on the 12th we spotted one person to the west near a suspected fighting position 1,500 meters [1,600 yards] away high on the mountain . . . we were told not to engage."[158] The sightings during the early morning of the 13th were different. Sergeant Samaroo, the 1st Squad Leader, recalled that just before stand-to began, he received a report that the TOW section had identified a group of 7 to 10 individuals, possibly wearing packs and moving on the hillside south of Samaroo's TCP. At 0408, just after stand-to began, the TOW section spotted another small group of individuals on the hillside west of Wanat. In retrospect, these sightings were almost certainly members of the AAF assault force moving into position.[159]

After receiving the report of the group to the west, Captain Myer immediately recognized those individuals as a threat to the COP. Myer remembered that moment, stating, "Five shepherds aren't going to be together. Based on the terrorist videos that we've seen and things like that, a group of five to 10 guys in the mountains is commonly enemy personnel."[160] Myer immediately began to coordinate an integrated attack using the TOW missile and the 120-mm mortar. At OP Topside, Sergeant Pitts shifted the LRAS3 towards the group on the hillside in order to obtain precise grid coordinates on the location. He was preparing to radio the coordinates to the command post when the action started. Staff Sergeant Phillips, the mortar squad leader, had his crew lay the mortar on the target, and Sergeant Grimm at the TOW recalled, "We had the back of the turret dropped ready to fire."[161]

It was just over an hour before dawn and the ground remained entirely dark, although dark blue light was beginning to streak the sky. Twelve minutes passed as the platoon prepared to launch the TOW and fire the mortar rounds. Just to the southeast at the 1st Squad's TCP, Sergeant Hissong was talking to Staff Sergeant Samaroo regarding the TOW team's observation of personnel moving around them in the hills. Concerned with the delay in launching the strike, Hissong growled, "We better...kill these guys before we get hit."[162] Samaroo's reply was interrupted by two bursts from an insurgent's RPD machine gun and then, "about a thousand RPGs at once."[163]

Notes

1. Captain Matthew Myer, e-mail to Dr. Donald P. Wright, Combat Studies Institute, Fort Leavenworth, KS, 18 November 2009; Brigadier General Mark Milley, interview by Douglas R. Cubbison and Dr. William G. Robertson, Combat Studies Institute, Fort Leavenworth, KS, 18 and 20 August 2009, 18.

2. TF *Rock*, "CONOP ROCK MOVE, 2/3 ANA, C/2-503 IN (ABN) and 2-17 CAV, Level 1 CONOP, 8–9 July 2008" Briefing, slide 11.

3. TF *Rock*, "CONOP ROCK MOVE", Briefing, slide 12.

4. "CONOP ROCK MOVE", Briefing, slides 9, 10, 14, 18, 23; TF *Bayonet* only had four Chinooks normally available for operations and these were generally divided into day and night shifts, although additional CH-47s associated with regularly scheduled supply runs and redeployment activities were often used by the brigade out of division assets based at Bagram Air Base. See Exhibit 21b (LTC, Brigade XO, 173d ABCT, interview) to US Central Command (CENTCOM), "Re-investigation into the Combat Action at Wanat Village, Wygal District, Nuristan Province, Afghanistan, on 13 July 2008 (Redacted), 8, 9; and Exhibit 28b (CPT, Assistant S-3, 2-503d IN, interview) to US Central Command (CENTCOM), "Re-investigation into the Combat Action at Wanat Village, Wygal District, Nuristan Province, Afghanistan, on 13 July 2008 (Redacted), 13, 23-4.

5. "CONOP ROCK MOVE"., Briefing, slides 9, 14.

6. "CONOP ROCK MOVE", Briefing slides 14, 22, 23; Exhibit 21b (LTC, Brigade XO, 173d ABCT, interview) to US Central Command (CENTCOM), "Re-investigation into the Combat Action at Wanat Village, Wygal District, Nuristan Province, Afghanistan, on 13 July 2008 (Redacted), 9; Exhibit 14b (MAJ, BN XO, 2-503d IN, interview) to US Central Command (CENTCOM), "Re-investigation into the Combat Action at Wanat Village, Wygal District, Nuristan Province, Afghanistan, on 13 July 2008 (Redacted), 18; Exhibit 12a (COL, Commander, 101st Aviation Brigade, interview) to US Central Command (CENTCOM), "Re-investigation into the Combat Action at Wanat Village, Wygal District, Nuristan Province, Afghanistan, on 13 July 2008 (Redacted), 67.

7. Colonel William Ostlund, e-mail to Donald P. Wright, Combat Studies Institute, Fort Leavenworth, KS, 3 December 2009; Captain Matthew Myer, e-mail to Dr. Donald P. Wright, Combat Studies Institute, Fort Leavenworth, KS, 5 December 2009; Exhibit 6a (Operations Officer, 2-503d IN, interview) to US Central Command (CENTCOM), "Re-investigation into the Combat Action at Wanat Village, Wygal District, Nuristan Province, Afghanistan, on 13 July 2008 (Redacted), 16; Exhibit 6b (Operations Officer, 2-503d IN, statement) to US Central Command (CENTCOM), "Re-investigation into the Combat Action at Wanat Village, Wygal District, Nuristan Province, Afghanistan, on 13 July 2008 (Redacted), 3; Exhibit 22b (Brigade Engineer, 173d Airborne Brigade Combat Team, interview) to US Central Command (CENTCOM), "Re-investigation into the Combat Action at Wanat Village, Wygal District, Nuristan Province,

Afghanistan, on 13 July 2008 (Redacted), 13; Exhibit 27b (Battalion S4, 2-503d IN, statement) to US Central Command (CENTCOM), "Re-investigation into the Combat Action at Wanat Village, Wygal District, Nuristan Province, Afghanistan, on 13 July 2008 (Redacted), 1; Exhibit 50a (Forward Support Company Commander, F Company, 2-503d IN, interview) to US Central Command (CENTCOM), "Re-investigation into the Combat Action at Wanat Village, Wygal District, Nuristan Province, Afghanistan, on 13 July 2008 (Redacted), 2-3.

8. TF *Rock*, "CONOP ROCK MOVE" Briefing, slide 3; Daniel D. Desjardins and James C. Byrd, "Air Vehicle Displays in the Operational Environment, PowerPoint briefing, Air Force Research Laboratory, Aeronautical Systems Center, 19 August 2007, slide 14, www.sidchapters.org/greaterdayton/Desjardins_ Byrd_SPIE07.pdf (accessed on 17 August 2010); Exhibit 12a (COL, Commander, 101st Aviation Brigade, interview) to US Central Command (CENTCOM), "Re-Investigation into the Combat Action at Wanat Village, Wygal District, Nuristan Province, Afghanistan, on 13 July 2008 (Redacted), 8-9.

9. Exhibit 6b (Operations Officer, 2-503d IN, statement) to US Central Command (CENTCOM), "Re-investigation into the Combat Action at Wanat Village, Wygal District, Nuristan Province, Afghanistan, on 13 July 2008 (Redacted), 2; TF *Rock*, "CONOP ROCK MOVE" Briefing, slide 3; Exhibit 11a (COL, Brigade Commander, 173d ABCT, interview) to US Central Command (CENTCOM), "Re-Investigation into the Combat Action at Wanat Village, Wygal District, Nuristan Province, Afghanistan, on 13 July 2008 (Redacted), 9, 12; Colonel William Ostlund, email to Donald P. Wright, Combat Studies Institute, Fort Leavenworth, KS, 10 September 2010.

10. Ostlund, e-mail, 3 December 2009; Myer, e-mail, 5 December 2009.

11. TF *Rock*, "CONOP ROCK MOVE" Briefing, slides 4–6; For video, see Jim Sciutto, "'Relax, Brother': Exclusive Video Shows Taliban Attack That Killed 9 U.S. Soldiers at Afghan Post July 2008 Incident Shown From Taliban Viewpoint: 'We Attacked From 4 Sides,'" 12 November 2009, http://abcnews. go.com/WN/Afghanistan/exclusive-video-shows-taliban-attack-killed-us-soldiers/story?id=9068156 (accessed 7 December 2009).

12. Pry, interview, 6 May 2009, 6.

13. TF *Rock*, "CONOP ROCK MOVE" Briefing, slides 4 and 5.

14. TF *Rock*, "CONOP ROCK MOVE" Briefing, slide 6; Pry, interview, 6 May 2009, 6.

15. TF *Rock*, "CONOP ROCK MOVE" Briefing, slide 7.

16. Captain Matthew Myer, interview by Matt Matthews, Combat Studies Institute, Fort Leavenworth, KS, 1 December 2008, 8.

17. Sergeant First Class David Dzwik Statement, CJTF-101, "Army Regulation 15-6 Investigation into Battle of Wanat (Redacted, Unclassified Version)" (Bagram Air Base, Afghanistan, 21 October 2008).

18. Schloesser, interview, 5 August 2009, 6, 9; Colonel William Ostlund, e-mail to Dr. Donald P. Wright, Combat Studies Institute, Fort Leavenworth, KS, 19 November 2009; Lieutenant Colonel Pierre Gervais, the CJTF-101 *G2* emphasizes the role of this pattern in assessing enemy courses of action at Wanat in July 2008. *See* Lieutenant Colonel Pierre Gervais, interview by Douglas R. Cubbison, Combat Studies Institute, Fort Leavenworth, KS, 19 June 2009, 3.

19. The discussion of rifle platoon organization is based on Department of the Army, *Field Manual (FM) 3-21.8 (Fm 7-8), The Infantry Rifle Platoon and Squad* (Headquarters, Department of the Army: Washington, DC: 2007), 1-11 to 1-21; For mention of the Javelin, see Specialist Tyler M. Stafford, interview by Douglas R. Cubbison, Combat Studies Institute, Fort Leavenworth, KS, 10 February 2009, 16. The 2d Platoon was short of its TOE strength because it had about a squad's worth of men to reinforce COP Michigan.

20. Department of the Army, *Field Manual (FM) 3-21.8*, page 1-18.

21. TF *Rock*, "CONOP ROCK MOVE" Briefing, slides 22, 23; Exhibit 38a (Sergeant, USMC, ETT 5-3, interview) to US Central Command (CENTCOM), "Re-investigation into the Combat Action at Wanat Village, Wygal District, Nuristan Province, Afghanistan, on 13 July 2008 (Redacted), 25. In The ROCK MOVE plan, the ANA force, including ETT members, was projected to be 30. When the plan was executed, however, the number was actually 27.

22. Major Brian T. Beckno, interview by Douglas R. Cubbison, Combat Studies Institute, Fort Leavenworth, KS, 2 July 2009, 6.

23. Myer, e-mail, 18 November 2009. For operations in northeastern Afghanistan, the battalion mortar platoon and company mortar sections had been consolidated then broken up into smaller sections to provide support for each of the platoon-size outposts in the TF *Rock* area of operations. Although by organizational structure the battalion mortar platoon was equipped with both 81-mm and 120-mm mortars, the battalion only used the 120-mm tubes in Afghanistan. The mortarmen received additional 120-mm mortars from theater stocks upon deployment and each company in the battalion provided augmentees to reinforce the platoon. For a discussion of TF *Rock* mortar operations in Afghanistan in 2008 see Sergeant First Class Jason Levy, "Battalion Mortar Platoon Operations in Afghanistan," *Infantry* (July 2009): 23-32.

24. Lieutenant Colonel John Lynch, interview by Douglas R. Cubbison, Combat Studies Institute, Fort Leavenworth, KS, 12 May 2009, 11; Exhibit 7b (Battalion Commander, 2-503d IN, interview) to US Central Command (CENTCOM), "Re-investigation into the Combat Action at Wanat Village, Wygal District, Nuristan Province, Afghanistan, on 13 July 2008 (Redacted), 4.

25. Sergeant First Class David Dzwik, interview by Douglas R. Cubbison, Combat Studies Institute, Fort Leavenworth, KS, 2 April 2009, 3. Two of the six engineers were slated to supervise the Afghan equipment operators.

26. Milley, interview, 18 and 20 August 2009, 24.

27. Major Scott Himes, interview by Douglas R. Cubbison, Combat Studies Institute, Fort Leavenworth, KS, 25 April 2009, 6, 11; Exhibit 27a (Battalion S4, 2-503d IN, interview) to US Central Command (CENTCOM), "Re-investigation into the Combat Action at Wanat Village, Wygal District, Nuristan Province, Afghanistan, on 13 July 2008 (Redacted), 9; Exhibit 77 (Contracts) to US Central Command (CENTCOM), "Re-investigation into the Combat Action at Wanat Village, Wygal District, Nuristan Province, Afghanistan, on 13 July 2008 (Redacted). Exhibit 16a (Company Commander, C Co, 2-503d IN, interview) to US Central Command (CENTCOM), "Re-investigation into the Combat Action at Wanat Village, Wygal District, Nuristan Province, Afghanistan, on 13 July 2008 (Redacted), 43-4; The stone wall contract was still pending because the chain of command initially rejected it. But Ostlund pushed for it and it was approved eventually. See Exhibit 27a (Battalion S4, 2-503d IN, interview) to US Central Command (CENTCOM), "Re-investigation into the Combat Action at Wanat Village, Wygal District, Nuristan Province, Afghanistan, on 13 July 2008 (Redacted), 6-7; and Exhibit 27b (Battalion S4, 2-503d IN, statement) to US Central Command (CENTCOM), "Re-investigation into the Combat Action at Wanat Village, Wygal District, Nuristan Province, Afghanistan, on 13 July 2008 (Redacted), 2. Myer recollected that the stone wall contract had been awarded to a local national in the Wanat area. See Exhibit 16a, 45.

28. The two LRAS3s were not TOE items in the airborne infantry battalion, but rather an augmentation equipment item given to the unit in theater. Exhibit 16a (Company Commander, C Co, 2-503d IN, interview) to US Central Command (CENTCOM), "Re-investigation into the Combat Action at Wanat Village, Wygal District, Nuristan Province, Afghanistan, on 13 July 2008 (Redacted), 32-3.

29. TF *Rock*, "CONOP ROCK MOVE" Briefing, slides 8, 9; Exhibit 16a (Company Commander, C Co, 2-503d IN, interview) to US Central Command (CENTCOM), "Re-investigation into the Combat Action at Wanat Village, Wygal District, Nuristan Province, Afghanistan, on 13 July 2008 (Redacted), 36; Exhibit 20a (First Lieutenant, Assistant BN S2, 2-503d IN, interview) to US Central Command (CENTCOM), "Re-investigation into the Combat Action at Wanat Village, Wygal District, Nuristan Province, Afghanistan, on 13 July 2008 (Redacted), 4.

30. Exhibit 59a (LTC, G2 Officer, RC-East, interview) to US Central Command (CENTCOM), "Re-investigation into the Combat Action at Wanat Village, Wygal District, Nuristan Province, Afghanistan, on 13 July 2008 (Redacted), 24.

31. Chief Warrant Officer 3 Chuck Whitbeck, e-mail to Douglas R. Cubbison, Combat Studies Institute, Fort Leavenworth, KS, 20 February 2009; Exhibit 8a (Captain, Battalion S2 Officer, 2-503d IN, interview) to US Central Command (CENTCOM), "Re-investigation into the Combat Action at Wanat Village, Wygal District, Nuristan Province, Afghanistan, on 13 July 2008 (Redacted), 12; TF *Rock*, "CONOP ROCK MOVE" Briefing, slide 8.

32. First Lieutenant Matthew A. Colley, e-mail interview by Douglas R. Cubbison, Combat Studies Institute, Fort Leavenworth, KS, 25 March 2009, 4; Exhibit 39 (First Lieutenant, Assistant S2, 2-503d IN, statement) to US Central Command (CENTCOM), "Re-investigation into the Combat Action at Wanat Village, Wygal District, Nuristan Province, Afghanistan, on 13 July 2008 (Redacted), 4; Sergeant Erick J. Rodas, e-mail to Douglas R. Cubbison, Combat Studies Institute, Fort Leavenworth, KS, 27 February 2009; and Himes, interview, 25 April 2009, 6. A dual failure of Raven UAVs is documented to have occurred at the Battle of Fallujah, Iraq, in 2004. Matt M. Matthews, *Operation AL FAJR: A Study in Army and Marine Corps Joint Operations* (Fort Leavenworth, KS: Combat Studies Institute Press, 2006), 42.

33. Milley, interview, 18 and 20 August 2009, 28; TF *Rock*, "CONOP ROCK MOVE" Briefing, slide 8; Exhibit 8a (Captain, S2 Officer, 2-503d IN, statement) to US Central Command (CENTCOM), "Re-investigation into the Combat Action at Wanat Village, Wygal District, Nuristan Province, Afghanistan, on 13 July 2008 (Redacted), 13.

34. Exhibit 8a (Captain, S2 Officer, 2-503d IN, statement) to US Central Command (CENTCOM), "Re-investigation into the Combat Action at Wanat Village, Wygal District, Nuristan Province, Afghanistan, on 13 July 2008 (Redacted), 13; Brigadier General Mark Milley, interview by Douglas Cubbison, Combat Studies Institute, Fort Leavenworth, KS, 18 August 2009, 42-44.

35. TF *Rock*, "CONOP ROCK MOVE" Briefing, slides 8, 9; Exhibit 16a (Company Commander, C Co, 2-503d IN, interview) to US Central Command (CENTCOM), "Re-investigation into the Combat Action at Wanat Village, Wygal District, Nuristan Province, Afghanistan, on 13 July 2008 (Redacted), 36; Exhibit 20a (First Lieutenant, Assistant BN S2, 2-503d IN, interview) to US Central Command (CENTCOM), "Re-investigation into the Combat Action at Wanat Village, Wygal District, Nuristan Province, Afghanistan, on 13 July 2008 (Redacted), 4; Milley, interview, 18 and 20 August 2009, 46-48; TF *Rock*, "CONOP ROCK MOVE" Briefing, slide 8; Exhibit 8a (Captain, S2 Officer, 2-503d IN, statement) to US Central Command (CENTCOM), "Re-investigation into the Combat Action at Wanat Village, Wygal District, Nuristan Province, Afghanistan, on 13 July 2008 (Redacted), 11-14, 16, 32-3; Exhibit 62a (Sergeant, Brigade Collections Manager, HHC, 173d Airborne BCT, interview) to US Central Command (CENTCOM), "Re-investigation into the Combat Action at Wanat Village, Wygal District, Nuristan Province, Afghanistan, on 13 July 2008 (Redacted), 18-19, 21.

36. Dzwik, interview, 2 April 2009, 1-2.

37. Dzwik, interview.

38. Myer, e-mail, 18 November 2009; Major Himes, the TF *Rock* S3 operations officer, also recognized that after a year in Afghanistan, the orders process in the TF was not always formal. *See* Himes, interview, 25 April 2009, 7; See also TF *Rock*, "CONOP ROCK MOVE" Briefing, 7 July 2008; Exhibit

7a (LTC, Battalion Commander, 2-503d IN, interview) to US Central Command (CENTCOM), "Re-investigation into the Combat Action at Wanat Village, Wygal District, Nuristan Province, Afghanistan, on 13 July 2008 (Redacted), 82.

39. Dzwik, interview, 2 April 2009, 1-3.

40. Staff Sergeant Jonathan Benton, interview by Douglas R. Cubbison, Combat Studies Institute, Fort Leavenworth, KS, 4 August 2009, 5.

41. Benton, 4.

42. Stafford interview, 10 February 2009, 5.

43. Sergeant Jesse L. Queck, e-mail to Matt Matthews, Combat Studies Institute, Fort Leavenworth, KS, 6 February 2009.

44. Sergeant First Class David Dzwik, e-mail to Douglas R. Cubbison, Combat Studies Institute, Fort Leavenworth, KS, 15 June 2009.

45. Exhibit 110 (1LT, A/2-503d IN, statement) "Army Regulation 15-6 Investigation into Battle of Wanat (Redacted, Unclassified Version)" (Vincenza, Italy, 4 August 2008), 1.

46. Captain Amanda Wilson, "Personal Statement re: 1LT Jonathan Brostrom," Memorandum, 25 November 2008.

47. "Army Regulation 15-6 Investigation into Battle of Wanat (Redacted, Unclassified Version), 1.

48. Captain Matthew Myer, e-mail to Dr. Donald P. Wright, Combat Studies Institute, Fort Leavenworth, KS, 17 December 2009.

49. "Army Regulation 15-6 Investigation into Battle of Wanat (Redacted, Unclassified Version), 1.

50. Dzwik, interview, 2 April 2009, 2–3.

51. Myer, interview, 1 December 2008, 4–5; Exhibit 16a (Company Commander, C Co, 2-503d IN, interview) to US Central Command (CENTCOM), "Re-investigation into the Combat Action at Wanat Village, Wygal District, Nuristan Province, Afghanistan, on 13 July 2008 (Redacted), 87

52. Exhibit 16a (Company Commander, C Co, 2-503d IN, interview) to US Central Command (CENTCOM), "Re-investigation into the Combat Action at Wanat Village, Wygal District, Nuristan Province, Afghanistan, on 13 July 2008 (Redacted), 25-7, 31, 87. In his statements, Myer both claimed to have left Bella on 8 July and to be on the last helicopter out of Bella. However, it is clear from the ROCK MOVE Operations Order Briefing and statements from the ETT personnel and Myer's RTO that this had to have been 9 July as the ETTs and half of the ANA platoon left Bella and flew directly to the newly established Wanat outpost after dark on the evening of 9 July. The two outposts briefly coexisted on 8-9 July. See TF *Rock*, "CONOP ROCK MOVE" Briefing, slide 23; Exhibit 16a (Company Commander, C Co, 2-503d IN, interview) to US Central Command (CENTCOM), "Re-investigation into the Combat Action at Wanat Village, Wygal District,

Nuristan Province, Afghanistan, on 13 July 2008 (Redacted), 31-2; Exhibit 41a (ETT OIC, ETT 5-3, interview) to US Central Command (CENTCOM), "Re-investigation into the Combat Action at Wanat Village, Wygal District, Nuristan Province, Afghanistan, on 13 July 2008 (Redacted), 1; Exhibit 41b (ETT OIC, ETT 5-3, statement) to US Central Command (CENTCOM), "Re-investigation into the Combat Action at Wanat Village, Wygal District, Nuristan Province, Afghanistan, on 13 July 2008 (Redacted), 15; Sergeant Erik Aass, interview by Matt Matthews, Combat Studies Institute, Fort Leavenworth, KS, 13 January 2009, 1-3; Exhibit 7a (LTC, Battalion Commander, 2-503d IN, interview) to US Central Command (CENTCOM), "Re-investigation into the Combat Action at Wanat Village, Wygal District, Nuristan Province, Afghanistan, on 13 July 2008 (Redacted), 7.

53. Aass interview, 2.

54. Exhibit 16a (Company Commander, C Co, 2-503d IN, interview) to US Central Command (CENTCOM), "Re-investigation into the Combat Action at Wanat Village, Wygal District, Nuristan Province, Afghanistan, on 13 July 2008 (Redacted), 31.

55. Colonel Charles Preysler, e-mails to Douglas R. Cubbison, Combat Studies Institute, Fort Leavenworth, KS, 5 May 2009, 8 May 2009, and 19 May 2009; Beckno, interview, 2 July 2009, 7, 11–12; Myer, interview, 1 December 2008, 5-6; Exhibit 16a (Company Commander, C Co, 2-503d IN, interview) to US Central Command (CENTCOM), "Re-investigation into the Combat Action at Wanat Village, Wygal District, Nuristan Province, Afghanistan, on 13 July 2008 (Redacted), 25.

56. Sergeant Brian C. Hissong, personal statement, "Combat Outpost Kahler, July 8–15," (not dated), 1. The final garrison figures for Wanat were, therefore 44 US Army personnel from 2d Platoon, and the mortar, TOW and engineer elements, 2 members of Myer's party, 3 US Marine ETT advisors, and 24 ANA troops. This total of 73 was one less that ROCK MOVE's projection of 74 because Myer left his FSO behind.

57. Benton, interview, 4 August 2009, 5.

58. Stafford, interview, 10 February 2009, 6.

59. Stafford, interview, 4; Dzwik, interview, 2 April 2009, 1–3; Glenn, 3–4; Hissong, personal statement, 1; Sergeant Jeffrey Scantlin, interview by Douglas R. Cubbison, Combat Studies Institute, Fort Leavenworth, KS, 20 August 2009, 2.

60. Sergeant Hector Chavez, interview by Douglas R. Cubbison, Combat Studies Institute, Fort Leavenworth, KS, 19 March 2009, 4; Dzwik, interview, 2 April 2009, 3; Aass, interview, 13 January 2009, 3–4.

61. Lieutenant Colonel Kevin J. Anderson, interview by Douglas R. Cubbison, Combat Studies Institute, Fort Leavenworth, KS, 2 April 2009, 3–4; Exhibit 41b (ETT OIC, ETT 5-3, statement) to US Central Command (CENTCOM), "Re-investigation into the Combat Action at Wanat Village, Wygal District, Nuristan

Province, Afghanistan, on 13 July 2008 (Redacted), 12; Exhibit 38a (ETT NCO, ETT 5-3, statement) to US Central Command (CENTCOM), "Re-investigation into the Combat Action at Wanat Village, Wygal District, Nuristan Province, Afghanistan, on 13 July 2008 (Redacted), 2. The name of the ANA operations sergeant major was Qiamudin Safi.

62. Exhibit 42, (SSG, C/62d Eng Bn, statement), CJTF-101, "Army Regulation 15-6 Investigation into Battle of Wanat (Redacted, Unclassified Version)" (Camp Blessing, Afghanistan, 16 July 2008), 1.

63. Captain Devin George, e-mail to Douglas R. Cubbison, Combat Studies Institute, Fort Leavenworth, KS, 22 April 2009; Beckno, interview, 2 July 2009, 8; Myer, e-mail, 17 December 2009; Exhibit 17a (CPT, Company XO, C/2-503d IN, statement) to US Central Command (CENTCOM), "Re-investigation into the Combat Action at Wanat Village, Wygal District, Nuristan Province, Afghanistan, on 13 July 2008 (Redacted), 3-4; Exhibit 17b (CPT, Company XO, C/2-503d IN, interview) to US Central Command (CENTCOM), "Re-investigation into the Combat Action at Wanat Village, Wygal District, Nuristan Province, Afghanistan, on 13 July 2008 (Redacted), 9-10; TF *Bayonet*, "09 July 2008 Bayonet CUB [Combat Update Brief] to CJTF-101," 9 July 2008; TF *Rock*, "Rock Daily Snapshot-Thursday, July 10, 2008;" TF *Rock*, "TIC Asset Tracker" Spreadsheet, 22 July 2008. The engineer killed on 8 July 2008 was Sergeant Douglas J. Bull, Company A, Special Troops Battalion, 3d Brigade Combat Team, 1st Infantry Division. Prior to the transition, RCP 8 was composed of members of Company A, Special Troops Battalion, 173d Airborne Brigade Combat Team.

64. Exhibit 17a (CPT, Company XO, C/2-503d IN, statement) to US Central Command (CENTCOM), "Re-investigation into the Combat Action at Wanat Village, Wygal District, Nuristan Province, Afghanistan, on 13 July 2008 (Redacted), 3-4; Exhibit 63 (SGT, C / 2-503d IN), CJTF-101, "Army Regulation 15-6 Investigation into Battle of Wanat (Redacted, Unclassified Version)" (Landstuhl Regional Medical Center, Germany, 17 July 2008), 3. George remarked that "the AAF were watching the road. See George, e-mail, 22 April 2009.

65. Glenn, interview, 2 April 2009, 5.

66. Dzwik, interview, 2 April 2009, 3-4; TF *Rock*, "CONOP ROCK MOVE" Briefing, 7 July 2008, slide 23. The FO assigned to Chosen Company's 1st Platoon had been wounded at the Bella OP on 2 July 2008. This factor may have been one of Myer's considerations in leaving Gonzalez behind at Blessing, where the 1st Platoon was then stationed. See Task Force Bayonet, "Memorandum, Subject: AR 15-6 Investigation (Findings and Recommendations) __COP Bella Allegation of Non-Combatant Casualties, 4 July 2008," 26 July 2008, 4.

67. "Ahmad," e-mail to Matt Matthews, Combat Studies Institute, Fort Leavenworth, KS, 13 November 2008; "Ahmad," e-mail to Douglas R. Cubbison, Combat Studies Institute, Fort Leavenworth, KS, 2 March 2009. Note: Because of security considerations, "Ahmad" has requested that his true name not be revealed.

68. "Ahmad," e-mails, 13 November 2008 and 2 March 2009.

69. Himes, interview, 25 April 2009, 4-5; Lieutenant Colonel William Ostlund, "Battle of Wanat Storyboard and Brief" Briefing, 16 July 2008, slides 1 and 2.

70. Captain Andrew Glenn, e-mail to Douglas R. Cubbison, Combat Studies Institute, Fort Leavenworth, KS, 20 August 2009.

71. Sergeant First Class David Dzwik, e-mail to Douglas R. Cubbison, Combat Studies Institute, Fort Leavenworth, KS, 24 August 2009.

72. Exhibit 25, (SFC, C/2-503d IN, statement), CJTF-101, "Army Regulation 15-6 Investigation into Battle of Wanat (Redacted, Unclassified Version)" (Bagram Air Base, Afghanistan, 25 July 2008), 1; Exhibit 63 (SGT, C / 2-503 IN), CJTF-101, "Army Regulation 15-6 Investigation into Battle of Wanat ," 2; Myer, e-mail, 17 December 2009; Exhibit 55 (CPT, C/2-503d IN, statement), CJTF-101, "Army Regulation 15-6 Investigation into Battle of Wanat (Redacted, Unclassified Version)"(Camp Blessing, Afghanistan, 16 July 2008), 1. TF *Rock* planners had long looked to this ridge to the east of the main position for an OP location, although its general site was farther to the south and the east at a higher point along the ridge. See Task Force *Pacemaker*, "Recon Results Brief, Proposed Wanat COP," 10 April 2008.

73. Dzwik, e-mail, 24 August 2009.

74. Sergeant Ryan Pitts, interview by Matt Matthews, Combat Studies Institute, Fort Leavenworth, KS, 14 January 2009, 4.

75. Dzwik, e-mail, 24 August 2009.

76. Dzwik, interview, 2 April 2009. 4.

77. Dzwik, interview, 2 April 2009, 4.

78. Exhibit 42, CJTF-101, "Army Regulation 15-6 Investigation into Battle of Wanat, 1; Dzwik, interview, 2 April 2009, 8.

79. Dzwik, interview, 2 April 2009, 8; Exhibit 34 (SSG, 1st Plt, D/2-503d IN, statement), CJTF-101, "Army Regulation 15-6 Investigation into Battle of Wanat (Redacted, Unclassified Version)" (Camp Blessing, Afghanistan, 16 October 2008), 1.

80. Scantlin, interview, 20 August 2009, 2.

81. Dzwik, interview, 2 April 2009, 6; Exhibit 43a (SSG, Mortar Section Leader, C/2-503d IN, interview) to US Central Command (CENTCOM), "Re-Investigation into the Combat Action at Wanat Village, Wygal District, Nuristan Province, Afghanistan, on 13 July 2008 (Redacted), 5-6.

82. Benton, interview, 4 August 2009, 4-6; Exhibit 13 (SSG, C/2-503d IN, statement), CJTF-101, "Army Regulation 15-6 Investigation into Battle of Wanat (Redacted, Unclassified Version)" (Camp Blessing, Afghanistan, 16 July 2008), 1-2.

83. Exhibit 17 (SGT, C/2-503d IN, statement), CJTF-101, "Army Regulation 15-6 Investigation into Battle of Wanat (Redacted, Unclassified Version)" (Camp Blessing, Afghanistan, 16 July 2008), 2.

84. Dzwik, interview, 2 April 2009, 4.

85. Dzwik, interview, 2 April 2009, 2–5; Pitts, interview, 14 January 2009, 3–4.

86. Exhibit 55, CJTF-101, "AR 15-6 Investigation into Battle of Wanat," 1.

87. Pitts, interview, 14 January 2009, 4-7; Stafford, interview, 10 February 2009, 10. The designated marksman was a squad member who received special training and was equipped with an optically-enhanced personal weapon. His mission was "to improve the squad's precision engagement capabilities at short and medium ranges." See Department of the Army, *Field Manual (FM) 3-21.8 (FM 7-8), The Infantry Rifle Platoon and Squad* (Washington, DC: Department of the Army, 2007), p. 1-18.

88. Pitts, interview, 14 January 2009, 13; Benton, interview, 4 August 2009, 12.

89. Stafford, interview, 10 February 2009, 7; Pitts, interview, 14 January 2009, 6; Specialist Chris McKaig, interview by Matt Matthews, Combat Studies Institute, Fort Leavenworth, KS, 19 November 2008, 2; Exhibit 38a (Sergeant, USMC ETT Team 5-3, interview) to US Central Command (CENTCOM), "Re-investigation into the Combat Action at Wanat Village, Wygal District, Nuristan Province, Afghanistan, on 13 July 2008 (Redacted), 16.

90. Dzwik, interview, 2 April 2009, 6.

91. US forces have been under an antipersonnel mine moratorium since 1997. For more information see *Landmine Monitor Report 2009* (Ottawa: International Campaign to Ban Landmines, 2009), 101, 206, 1130-1138. This report is available online at http://www.the-monitor.org/index.php/publications/display?url=lm/2009/(accessed on 25 July 2010); Stafford, interview, 10 February 2009, 12; Captain James Fisher and Captain (P) Ryan Berdiner, interview by Douglas R. Cubbison, Combat Studies Institute, Fort Leavenworth, KS, 16 July 2009, 2; Chavez, interview, 19 March 2009, 5; Dzwik, interview, 2 April 2009, 11.

92. Stafford, interview, 10 February 2009, 7; Pitts, interview, 14 January 2009, 6-7.

93. TF *Rock*, "TIC Asset Tracker" Spreadsheet, 22 July 2008; General Charles Campbell, "Memorandum, Subject: Army Action on the Re-Investigation into the Combat Action at Wanat Village, Wygal District, Nuristan Province, Afghanistan, on 13 July 2008, 13 May 2010, 8-9, 11; TF *Rock*, "Rock Daily Snapshot-Thursday, July 10, 2008."

94. TF *Rock*, "TIC Asset Tracker" Spreadsheet, 22 July 2008.

95. Exhibit 25, CJTF-101, "Army Regulation 15-6 Investigation into Battle of Wanat," 2-3; Exhibit 58, (CPT, C/2-503d IN, statement), CJTF-101, "Army Regulation 15-6 Investigation into Battle of Wanat (Redacted, Unclassified Version)"(Camp Blessing, Afghanistan, 23 July 2008), 1.

96. US Central Command (CENTCOM), "Re-Investigation into the Combat Action at Wanat Village, Wygal District, Nuristan Province, Afghanistan, on 13 July 2008 (Redacted), 43-45.

97. Exhibit 20c (CPT, Assistant S2, 2-503d IN, statement) to US Central Command (CENTCOM), "Re-Investigation into the Combat Action at Wanat Village, Wygal District, Nuristan Province, Afghanistan, on 13 July 2008 (Redacted), 2; Exhibit 59a (LTC, RC-East G2 Officer, interview) to US Central Command (CENTCOM), "Re-Investigation into the Combat Action at Wanat Village, Wygal District, Nuristan Province, Afghanistan, on 13 July 2008 (Redacted), 26; Exhibit 20c (1LT, Assistant S2, 2-503d IN, statement) to US Central Command (CENTCOM), "Re-Investigation into the Combat Action at Wanat Village, Wygal District, Nuristan Province, Afghanistan, on 13 July 2008 (Redacted)."

98. Fisher and Berdiner, interview, 16 July 2009, 1–3; Lieutenant Colonel Stephen J. Maranian, "Field Artillery Fires in the Mountains of Afghanistan," *Fires* (July–September 2008): 35–36. Captain Berdiner noted, "Every fire mission during our 14 months was shot at high angle."

99. Exhibit 18 (SPC, C/62d Eng Bn, statement), CJTF-101, "Army Regulation 15-6 Investigation into Battle of Wanat (Redacted, Unclassified Version)"(Camp Blessing, Afghanistan, 16 July 2008), 1-3; Exhibit 43a (SSG, Mortar Section Leader, C/2-503d IN, interview) to US Central Command (CENTCOM), "Re-Investigation into the Combat Action at Wanat Village, Wygal District, Nuristan Province, Afghanistan, on 13 July 2008 (Redacted), 10.

100. Milley, interview, 18 and 20 August 2009, 25.

101. Dzwik, interview, 2 April 2009, 6; Exhibit 33b (SFC, Platoon Sergeant, 2d Platoon, C/2-503d IN, interview) to US Central Command (CENTCOM), "Re-Investigation into the Combat Action at Wanat Village, Wygal District, Nuristan Province, Afghanistan, on 13 July 2008 (Redacted), 39-40; Captain Devin George, e-mail to Douglas R. Cubbison, Combat Studies Institute, Fort Leavenworth, KS, 23 April 2009; TF *Rock*, "CONOP ROCK MOVE" Briefing, 7 July 2008, slide 33; Department of the Army, *Field Manual (FM) 10-52, Water Supply in Theaters of Operation* (Washington, DC: Department of the Army, 1990), p. 3-5; TF *Rock*, "CONOP ROCK MOVE" Briefing, 7 July 2008, slide 33. Exhibit 17b (CPT, Company XO, C/2-503d IN, interview) to US Central Command (CENTCOM), "Re-Investigation into the Combat Action at Wanat Village, Wygal District, Nuristan Province, Afghanistan, on 13 July 2008 (Redacted), 22; Exhibit 28b (CPT, BN S-3 Air, 2-503d IN, interview) to US Central Command (CENTCOM), "Re-Investigation into the Combat Action at Wanat Village, Wygal District, Nuristan Province, Afghanistan, on 13 July 2008 (Redacted), 26, 28;

Exhibit 27a (CPT, Battalion S4, 2-503d IN, interview) to US Central Command (CENTCOM), "Re-Investigation into the Combat Action at Wanat Village, Wygal District, Nuristan Province, Afghanistan, on 13 July 2008 (Redacted), 3, 22. The ANA platoon used the local sources for their water needs.

102. Sergeant First Class David Dzwik, interview by Matt Matthews, Combat Studies Institute, Fort Leavenworth, KS, 21 October 2008, 2.

103. Dzwik, interview, 21 October 2008, 2.

104. Dzwik, interview, 2 April 2009, 6–7; Benton, interview, 4 August 2009, 8; Exhibit 33b (SFC, Platoon Sergeant, 2d Platoon, C/2-503d IN, interview) to US Central Command (CENTCOM), "Re-Investigation into the Combat Action at Wanat Village, Wygal District, Nuristan Province, Afghanistan, on 13 July 2008 (Redacted), 39-40-1 .

105. Dzwik's comment regarding filters made to Colonel William Ostlund. Ostlund, e-mail, 19 November 2009; Dzwik, interview, 2 April 2009, 6–7; Exhibit 33b (SFC, Platoon Sergeant, 2d Platoon, C/2-503d IN, interview) to US Central Command (CENTCOM), "Re-Investigation into the Combat Action at Wanat Village, Wygal District, Nuristan Province, Afghanistan, on 13 July 2008 (Redacted), 43-44; Exhibit 16a (CPT, Company Commander, C/2-503d IN, interview) to US Central Command (CENTCOM), "Re-Investigation into the Combat Action at Wanat Village, Wygal District, Nuristan Province, Afghanistan, on 13 July 2008 (Redacted), 39-40; Exhibit 7a (LTC, Battalion Commander, 2-503d IN, interview) to US Central Command (CENTCOM), "Re-Investigation into the Combat Action at Wanat Village, Wygal District, Nuristan Province, Afghanistan, on 13 July 2008 (Redacted), 50-2, 99; Exhibit 25b (1SG, First Sergeant, C/2-503d IN, interview) to US Central Command (CENTCOM), "Re-Investigation into the Combat Action at Wanat Village, Wygal District, Nuristan Province, Afghanistan, on 13 July 2008 (Redacted), 8; Exhibit 17b (CPT, Company XO, C/2-503d IN, interview) to US Central Command (CENTCOM), "Re-Investigation into the Combat Action at Wanat Village, Wygal District, Nuristan Province, Afghanistan, on 13 July 2008 (Redacted),46, 53-4; Exhibit 27a (CPT, Battalion S4, 2-503d IN, interview) to US Central Command (CENTCOM), "Re-Investigation into the Combat Action at Wanat Village, Wygal District, Nuristan Province, Afghanistan, on 13 July 2008 (Redacted), 14; Exhibit 33a (SFC, Platoon Sergeant, 2d Platoon, C/2-503d IN, statement) to US Central Command (CENTCOM), "Re-Investigation into the Combat Action at Wanat Village, Wygal District, Nuristan Province, Afghanistan, on 13 July 2008 (Redacted), 4.

106. Exhibit 33b (SFC, Platoon Sergeant, 2d Platoon, C/2-503d IN, interview) to US Central Command (CENTCOM), "Re-Investigation into the Combat Action at Wanat Village, Wygal District, Nuristan Province, Afghanistan, on 13 July 2008 (Redacted), 46.

107. Dzwik, interview, 2 April 2009, 6; Beckno, interview, 2 July 2009, 5; Exhibit 17a (CPT, Company XO, C/2-503d IN, statement) to US Central Command (CENTCOM), "Re-Investigation into the Combat Action at Wanat Village,

Wygal District, Nuristan Province, Afghanistan, on 13 July 2008 (Redacted), 5; Exhibit 33a (SFC, Platoon Sergeant, 2d Platoon, C/2-503d IN, statement) to US Central Command (CENTCOM), "Re-Investigation into the Combat Action at Wanat Village, Wygal District, Nuristan Province, Afghanistan, on 13 July 2008 (Redacted), 4; Exhibit 33b (SFC, Platoon Sergeant, 2d Platoon, C/2-503d IN, interview) to US Central Command (CENTCOM), "Re-Investigation into the Combat Action at Wanat Village, Wygal District, Nuristan Province, Afghanistan, on 13 July 2008 (Redacted), 42-4; Exhibit 17b (CPT, Company XO, C/2-503d IN, interview) to US Central Command (CENTCOM), "Re-Investigation into the Combat Action at Wanat Village, Wygal District, Nuristan Province, Afghanistan, on 13 July 2008 (Redacted),45-6; Exhibit 33a (SFC, Platoon Sergeant, 2d Platoon, C/2-503d IN, statement) to US Central Command (CENTCOM), "Re-Investigation into the Combat Action at Wanat Village, Wygal District, Nuristan Province, Afghanistan, on 13 July 2008 (Redacted), 4. SFC Dwzik states that he "let [the company XO] know [that the platoon] was black on water." See Exhibit 33b (SFC, Platoon Sergeant, 2d Platoon, C/2-503d IN, interview) to US Central Command (CENTCOM), "Re-Investigation into the Combat Action at Wanat Village, Wygal District, Nuristan Province, Afghanistan, on 13 July 2008 (Redacted), 43. However this statement is disputed by multiple witnesses. See Exhibit 17b (CPT, Company XO, C/2-503d IN, interview) to US Central Command (CENTCOM), "Re-Investigation into the Combat Action at Wanat Village, Wygal District, Nuristan Province, Afghanistan, on 13 July 2008 (Redacted), 11-12); Exhibit 28b (CPT, BN S-3 Air, 2-503d IN, interview) to US Central Command (CENTCOM), "Re-Investigation into the Combat Action at Wanat Village, Wygal District, Nuristan Province, Afghanistan, on 13 July 2008 (Redacted), 26, 28; Exhibit 27a (CPT, BN S-4, 2-503d IN, interview) to US Central Command (CENTCOM), "Re-Investigation into the Combat Action at Wanat Village, Wygal District, Nuristan Province, Afghanistan, on 13 July 2008 (Redacted), 14, 30; and Exhibit 16a (CPT, Company Commander, C/2-503d IN, statement) to US Central Command (CENTCOM), "Re-Investigation into the Combat Action at Wanat Village, Wygal District, Nuristan Province, Afghanistan, on 13 July 2008 (Redacted), 2; Exhibit 63, CJTF-101, "Army Regulation 15-6 Investigation into Battle of Wanat, " 3.

108. Exhibit 15 (SPC, C/62 Eng Bn, statement), CJTF-101, "Army Regulation 15-6 Investigation into Battle of Wanat (Redacted, Unclassified Version)"(Camp Blessing, Afghanistan, 16 July 2008), 1.

109. Exhibit 69 (SGT, C/2-503d IN, statement), CJTF-101, "Army Regulation 15-6 Investigation into Battle of Wanat (Redacted, Unclassified Version)" (Camp Blessing, Afghanistan, 16 July 2008), 1-2.

110. Exhibit 64 (SSG, C/2-503d IN, statement), CJTF-101, "Army Regulation 15-6 Investigation into Battle of Wanat (Redacted, Unclassified Version)" (Landstuhl Regional Medical Center, Germany, 17 July 2008), 3.

111. Exhibit 67 (SSG, C/2-503d IN, statement), CJTF-101, "Army Regulation 15-6 Investigation into Battle of Wanat (Redacted, Unclassified Version)" (Landstuhl Regional Medical Center, Germany, 17 July 2008), 2.

112. Myer, interview, 1 December 2008, 7; Exhibit 43a (SSG, Mortar Section Leader, C/2-503d IN, interview) to US Central Command (CENTCOM), "Re-Investigation into the Combat Action at Wanat Village, Wygal District, Nuristan Province, Afghanistan, on 13 July 2008 (Redacted), 24.

113. Hissong, personal statement, 3.

114. Staff Sergeant Luis Repreza, interview by Douglas R. Cubbison, Combat Studies Institute, Fort Leavenworth, KS, 23 February 2009. 14. *See also,* Anderson, interview, 2 April 2009, 3–4; Scantlin, interview, 20 August 2009, 2; Sergeant Jason T. Oakes, interview by Douglas R. Cubbison, Combat Studies Institute, Fort Leavenworth, KS, 18 February 2009, 6.

115. Scantlin, interview, 20 August 2009, 2.

116. Benton, interview, 4 August 2009, 16.

117. Oakes, interview, 18 February 2009, 6.

118. Stafford, interview, 10 February 2009, 5.

119. Hissong, personal statement, 1.

120. Exhibit 15, CJTF-101, "Army Regulation 15-6 Investigation into Battle of Wanat," 1-2.

Redacted Soldier Statements, CJTF-101, "Army Regulation 15-6 Investigation into Battle of Wanat."

121. Benton, interview, 4 August 2009, 7.

122. Benton, interview.

123. Benton, interview.

124. Kate Wiltrout, "Soldier from Eastern Shore Recounts Deadly Battle in Afghanistan, SSG Jesse L. Queck," *Hampton Roads Virginian-Pilot,* 19 July 2008, http://hamptonroads.com/2008/07/soldier-eastern-shore-recounts-deadly-battle-afghanistan (accessed 2 February 2009).

125. Aass, interview, 13 January 2009, 4.

126. Exhibit 16b (CPT, Company Commander, C/2-503d IN, statement) to US Central Command (CENTCOM), "Re-Investigation into the Combat Action at Wanat Village, Wygal District, Nuristan Province, Afghanistan, on 13 July 2008 (Redacted), 3; Exhibit 16a (CPT, Company Commander, C/2-503d IN, interview) to US Central Command (CENTCOM), "Re-Investigation into the Combat Action at Wanat Village, Wygal District, Nuristan Province, Afghanistan, on 13 July 2008 (Redacted), 62-4.

127. Exhibit 63, CJTF-101, "Army Regulation 15-6 Investigation into Battle of Wanat, " 3.

128. Stafford, interview, 10 February 2009, 9.

129. Exhibit 23 (SFC, C/2-503d IN, statement), CJTF-101, "Army Regulation 15-6 Investigation into Battle of Wanat (Redacted, Unclassified Version)" (Bagram Air Base, Afghanistan, 25 July 2008), 1;

130. Exhibit 13, CJTF-101, "Army Regulation 15-6 Investigation into Battle of Wanat," 2.

131. Exhibit 23, CJTF-101, "Army Regulation 15-6 Investigation into Battle of Wanat," 1.

132. First Lieutenant Matthew Colley, e-mail to Douglas Cubbison, Combat Studies Institute, Fort Leavenworth, 14 May 2009; Pry, interview, 6 May 2009, 8–9.

133. Aass, interview, 13 January 2009, 3; Myer, interview, 1 December 2008, 6.

134. Aass, interview, 13 January 2009, 4; Exhibit 16a (CPT, Company Commander, C/2-503d IN, interview) to US Central Command (CENTCOM), "Re-Investigation into the Combat Action at Wanat Village, Wygal District, Nuristan Province, Afghanistan, on 13 July 2008 (Redacted), 60-62.

135. Exhibit 16b (CPT, Company Commander, C/2-503d IN, statement) to US Central Command (CENTCOM), "Re-Investigation into the Combat Action at Wanat Village, Wygal District, Nuristan Province, Afghanistan, on 13 July 2008 (Redacted), 3.

136. *See* Sciutto, "'Relax, Brother': Exclusive Video Shows Taliban Attack That Killed 9 U.S. Soldiers at Afghan Post July 2008 Incident Shown From Taliban Viewpoint: 'We Attacked From 4 Sides,'" 12 November 2009; Pry, interview, 6 May 2009, 6; Bill Roggio, "Al Qaeda's Paramilitary 'Shadow Army,'" (9 February 2009), http://www.longwarjournal.org/archives/2009/02/al_qaedas_ paramilita.php (accessed 9 March 2009); The official TF *Rock* briefing completed after the battle in July 2008 estimated 300 insurgents in the attacking force. See Ostlund, "Battle of Wanat Storyboard and Brief," 16 July 2008. After the battle, Captain Pry stated that the initial attack element contained about 120 fighters, and reinforcements from local Nuristan villages that poured into the engagement area the day of the battle increased the size of the attacking force to 200 fighters.

137. Benton, interview, 4 August 2009, 16.

138. Pry, interview, 6 May 2009, 10; Oakes, interview, 18 February 2009, 8.

139 Gervais, interview, 19 June 2009, 5; Milley, interview, 18 and 20 August 2009, 29.

140. Pry, interview, 6 May 2009, 10.

141. Pry, interview.

142. Specialist Chris McKaig, e-mail to Matt Matthews, Combat Studies Institute, Fort Leavenworth, KS, 22 January 2009.

143. Exhibit 18, CJTF-101, "Army Regulation 15-6 Investigation into Battle of Wanat," 2; Pitts, interview, 14 January 2009, 8.

144. Lieutenant Colonel Pierre Gervais, interview by Douglas R. Cubbison, Combat Studies Institute, Fort Leavenworth, KS, 9 June 2009, 6; Milley, interview, 18 and 20 August 2009, 30–32; Pry, interview, 6 May 2009, 8-9; Lieutenant Colonel Jimmy Hinton, interview by Douglas Cubbison, Combat Studies Institute, Fort Leavenworth, KS, 18 March 2009, 8-9.

145. US Central Command (CENTCOM), "Re-Investigation into the Combat Action at Wanat Village, Wygal District, Nuristan Province, Afghanistan, on 13 July 2008 (Redacted), 44-5.

146. Gervais, interview, 19 June 2009, 5; Milley, interview, 18 and 20 August 2009, 36–37.

147. Milley, interview, 18 August 2009, 42-44.

148. Pry, interview, 6 May 2009, 12; Colley e-mail interview, 25 March 2008, 8.

149. Pry, interview, 12.

150. Pry, interview, 12.

151. Hinton, interview, 18 March 2009, 9.

152. Exhibit 16a (CPT, Company Commander, C/2-503d IN, interview) to US Central Command (CENTCOM), "Re-Investigation into the Combat Action at Wanat Village, Wygal District, Nuristan Province, Afghanistan, on 13 July 2008 (Redacted), 60-3, 68-9; Exhibit 11a (COL, Brigade Commander, 173d ABCT, interview) to US Central Command (CENTCOM), "Re-Investigation into the Combat Action at Wanat Village, Wygal District, Nuristan Province, Afghanistan, on 13 July 2008 (Redacted), 17-19; Exhibit 7a (LTC, Battalion Commander, 2-503d IN, interview) to US Central Command (CENTCOM), "Re-Investigation into the Combat Action at Wanat Village, Wygal District, Nuristan Province, Afghanistan, on 13 July 2008 (Redacted), 23, 50-1, 54-5; Exhibit 9a (MG, CJTF-101 Commander, 101st Airborne Division, interview) to US Central Command (CENTCOM), "Re-Investigation into the Combat Action at Wanat Village, Wygal District, Nuristan Province, Afghanistan, on 13 July 2008 (Redacted), 26, 29-30; Milley interview, 18 and 20 August 2009, 22-3.

153. Dzwik, interview, 21 October 2008, 3–4.

154. Dzwik, interview, 2 April 2009, 12, 167.

155. Benton, interview, 4 August 2009, 9, Scanlin, interview, 20 August 2009, 2; Sergeant John Hayes, interview by Douglas R. Cubbison, Combat Studies Institute, Fort Leavenworth, KS, 21 April 2009, 9. All three Soldiers were scheduled to participate in this patrol.

156. Chavez, interview, 19 March 2009, 8; Dzwik, interview, 2 April 2009, 12–13.

157. Exhibit 18, CJTF-101, "Army Regulation 15-6 Investigation into Battle of Wanat," 2.

158. Exhibit 34, CJTF-101, "Army Regulation 15-6 Investigation into Battle of Wanat (Redacted, Unclassified Version)", 1.

159. Exhibit 36 (Timeline to Battle of Wanat Army Regulation 15-6 Investigation Storyboard) to US Central Command (CENTCOM), "Re-Investigation into the Combat Action at Wanat Village, Wygal District, Nuristan Province, Afghanistan, on 13 July 2008 (Redacted); Exhibit 67 (SSG, C/2-503d IN, interview), CJTF-101, "Army Regulation 15-6 Investigation into Battle of Wanat (Redacted, Unclassified Version)" (Landstuhl Regional Medical Center, Germany, 17 July 2008), 3-4.

160. Myer, interview, 1 December 2008, 8–9.

161. Exhibit 34, CJTF-101, "Army Regulation 15-6 Investigation into Battle of Wanat," 1-2; Exhibit 37b (SGT, Team Leader, C/2-503d IN, statement) to US Central Command (CENTCOM), "Re-Investigation into the Combat Action at Wanat Village, Wygal District, Nuristan Province, Afghanistan, on 13 July 2008 (Redacted), 2.

162. Sergeant Brian Hissong, "Combat Outpost Kahler, July 8-15," Unpublished manuscript, 3.

163. Specialist Tyler Hanson, interview by Matt Matthews, Combat Studies Institute, Fort Leavenworth, KS, 19 November 2008, 3. Several Chosen Company members, including Queck and Samaroo related that they heard that the gunner on the ITAS had sighted a moving force of unknown individuals to the south of the main COP prior to the attack. See Exhibit 64 (SSG, Mortar Section, C/2-503d IN, statement), CJTF-101, "Army Regulation 15-6 Investigation into Battle of Wanat (Redacted, Unclassified Version)" (Landstuhl Regional Medical Center, Germany, 16 July 2008), 3-4; and Exhibit 67 (SSG C/2-503d IN, statement), CJTF-101, "Army Regulation 15-6 Investigation into Battle of Wanat (Redacted, Unclassified Version)" (Landstuhl Regional Medical Center, Germany, 17 October 2008), 3.

Chapter 3

The Fight at Wanat, 13 July 2008

The Attack on COP Kahler

At 0420 local time, two long bursts of RPD machine gun fire echoed through the valley at Wanat. Immediately after this signal, insurgents opened up with intense and continuous volleys of machine gun and rocket-propelled grenade (RPG) fire from hidden locations on all sides of the American/ANA position. This initial volley started an intense firefight that lasted for over three and a half hours. For the most part, the battle of Wanat was primarily a contest to obtain and maintain fire superiority with each side laying down intense fire. The AAF fire, particularly the opening salvo, was accurate and came equally from nearby positions within the village of Wanat and the surrounding hillsides. Firing locations in the village itself included the mosque, hotel, and bazaar buildings, all of which were within several yards of the American perimeter.[1]

The AAF fire was not only intense but also almost continuous. Grimm, the TOW missile squad leader, noted that the RPG fire that day was very rapid, in quick and methodic succession and relatively accurate. Specialist John Hayes, the 2d Platoon radio operator, found the number of RPGs fired at the Americans staggering, "The enemy engaged with RPGs. Lots and lots and lots of RPGs. It seemed like they went on forever. They must have had someone running resupply or a major cache of RPGs."[2] Sergeant First Class David Barbaret, the platoon sergeant from the quick reaction force (QRF) platoon that arrived late in the battle, observed the results of enemy fire after the engagement, noting that a post battle analysis "showed that the AAF had made use of all available dead space and buildings surrounding the area where COP Kahler was established and the high ground on all sides."[3] The insurgent fire, a deadly combination of machine gun rounds and RPG rockets, seemed endless, without lulls for resupply.[4]

The proximity of the enemy positions made OP Topside particularly vulnerable. Barbaret stated, "the OP was open to fires from the high ground on its north and west sides which was evident by the RPG tail fins found inside of the position on the south and east walls."[5] The crescendo of fire from positions within the village itself, including the bazaar and the hotel complex, effectively isolated the OP from the main position. Aside from gaining fire superiority, reinforcing and maintaining contact with the OP became Myer and Brostrom's main priority during the fight.

The AAF opening volley was particularly devastating as it targeted the crew-served weapons at both the OP and on the main COP. These included the truck mounted TOW missile system, the ground mounted machine guns at the OP, the ground mounted mortars at the main position, and the vehicle mounted heavy machine guns and automatic grenade launchers. Initial enemy success included the destruction of the TOW and the suppression of the mortars and one of the machine guns at the OP. The vehicle mounted machine guns and grenade launchers, although under intense fire, survived the initial volley and provided the basis for the American defense in the early phases of the battle.

As previously mentioned, to the enemy the most dangerous of the American weapons was the TOW antitank missile launcher. The TOW was mounted on a high mobility multipurpose wheeled vehicle (HMMWV) located in the middle of the main COP in a position between the command post (CP) and the 120-mm mortar pit. At the start of the fight, a crossfire of three RPG rounds, fired from nearby positions on both sides of the COP, struck the TOW HMMWV, destroying the vehicle and setting it on fire. Although the TOW squad had been preparing to fire its weapon at the five insurgents seen on high ground to the west, the eruption of enemy fire interrupted their action. While the RPG rounds did not hurt any of the squad members, the destruction of their vehicle forced squad leader Grimm to evacuate his men to the CP area. The TOW vehicle burned throughout the remainder of the action.[6]

At the time of the initial enemy volley, Phillips' six man mortar section was manning its single 120-mm mortar at its firing position just west of the TOW HMMWV. The mortarmen were about to fire at the five insurgents on the high ground to the west when the enemy struck. The section was also responsible for the single 60-mm mortar, which was left unmanned in a partially completed sandbagged firing position in the center of the COP. As previously noted, an eight foot HESCO barrier surrounded the 120-mm mortar facing to the west. Beyond this barrier were the perimeter concertina fence and a row of trees that separated the open area of the COP from houses in the southern end of the village of Wanat. The trees loomed over the mortar position.[7]

When the AAF opened fire, the mortar pit became a prime target. Insurgents were firing from the roofs of nearby buildings and from the trees adjacent to the perimeter wire. The mortarmen responded with grenades and small arms fire. One of them, Sergeant Hector Chavez, fired at the insurgents high up in the trees, possibly killing three or four of the attackers. While the rest of his men engaged the enemy with small arms

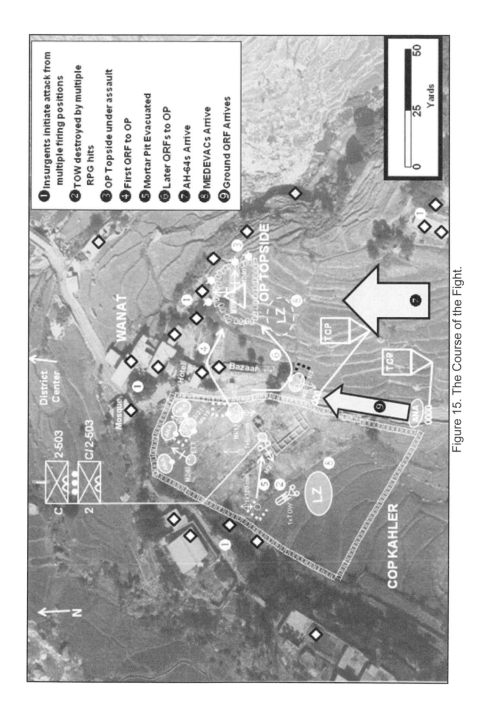

Figure 15. The Course of the Fight.

143

and grenades, Phillips and Private First Class Scott Stenoski managed to fire four high-explosive (HE) mortar rounds using the settings aimed at the individuals on the hillside to the west. After this, enemy fire was too intense to permit further firing and a close RPG hit forced Phillips and Stenoski away from the weapon. Then machine gun rounds began ricocheting off the mortar tube and the RPG fire became more accurate. An insurgent managed to aim an RPG round through an opening in the HESCO barrier at its southwest corner. The rocket flew between Phillips and Stenoski and continued across the COP to strike the bazaar, which at the time was being used by the AAF as a firing position. The impact of the round set a section of the bazaar structure on fire, a blaze that continued to burn throughout the firefight. One of the defenders recalled that, "during the firing, RPGs and rounds were hitting the [mortar] pit constantly."[8]

When the action began, the two engineers who were operating the Bobcat next to the mortar area reinforced Phillips' men in the mortar pit. There, the defenders used whatever weapons were available to them, firing personal weapons furiously into the nearby trees and aiming 40-mm grenades at more distant enemy positions. Without any machine guns of their own, the mortarmen had to use M4 assault rifles firing at the maximum rate of fire simply to suppress the enemy in order to survive. In this way, Phillips burned out a series of three M4s. He then picked up an M249 SAW belonging to the engineers and tried to fire it but it failed to shoot. Mortarman Queck had previously tried to fire the SAW but it was jammed. Another trooper later fired it successfully after changing its barrel. Queck instead fired an AT-4 rocket launcher he found at one of the buildings from which enemy fire was coming. Soldiers nearby followed up Queck's effort with hand grenades.[9]

Despite the heavy enemy fire, no one in the mortar pit had been wounded yet. Platoon sergeant Dzwik commented on the paradox of enemy fire:

> There was a lot of small arms, a lot of AK, definitely a lot of PKM [light machine gun] and RPK [a 7.62-mm Soviet model light machine gun, essentially a light machine gun version of the AK rifle] [fire] from their fire support positions. There was a lot of that raining in. The RPGs were pretty heavy. When I was down at that mortar pit, there was a guy shooting either in a tree or from behind a tree and luckily enough he wasn't smart enough to realize that when he shot the RPG, it would come out, the fins would pop out, they'd catch the branches and it would send that RPG off in a different direction. He did

that multiple times and he had a good eyes-on into the center of the pit, so it was pretty fortunate that he wasn't intelligent enough to figure out that he had to move to a better position.[10]

Eventually such fire had to hit something and shrapnel from an RPG impact seriously wounded Specialist Sergio Abad, one of the mortarmen, in the legs and shoulders. After he received first aid, Abad's condition did not at first seem critical because he was still able to hand ammunition to Chavez.[11]

During this firefight, Phillips, Stenoski, Chavez, and Queck periodically tried to reach the 60-mm mortar position to put that weapon into action. Enemy fire sweeping through the interior of the COP made it suicidal to remain in open areas for any extended period of time. The mortar crewmen simply could not reach the mortar. The 60-mm mortar would not be fired during the entire engagement.[12]

After an RPG round exploded near the ammunition supply point (ASP) containing a stockpile of mortar rounds in the corner of the mortar pit, Phillips realized the mortar pit had to be evacuated. One of the engineers recalled, "An RPG hit in the east corner of the ASP and hit the stack of 120-mm mortar rounds. Staff Sergeant [Phillips] fell over because of the concussion and when he got back up, I looked around, the cases were sparking and he yelled to all of us, 'get the [hell]out of here.'"[13]

In response to Phillips' order, the mortarmen and engineers left the shelter of the HESCOs and ran across the short but open distance to the CP area. Chavez and engineer Specialist Joshua Morse dragged Abad across this space through heavy enemy fire. During this evacuation, Chavez was shot through both legs, collapsing to the ground. Able only to crawl, he nevertheless attempted to pull Abad along. Luckily, other Soldiers, including company radio-telephone operator Aass and Queck came to Morse's aid and succeeded in getting both wounded men into the shelter of the CP position.[14]

At the CP, the 2d Platoon's medic, Private First Class William Hewitt, had been wounded in the arm and taken out of action when he attempted to accompany the first reinforcements headed for OP Topside. However, Specialist Jeffrey Scantlin, a SAW gunner from the 2d Squad, was trained as a combat lifesaver. Scantlin handed off his SAW and filled in for Hewitt. Throughout the action, Scantlin skillfully treated the casualties on the main COP, including Abad and Chavez. Ultimately, all the wounded on the COP were successfully evacuated except Abad, whose situation soon began to deteriorate. His wounds were more serious than they originally appeared to be and Scantlin went to work desperately trying to save Abad's life, as a medical evacuation (MEDEVAC) at the time was impossible given the tactical situation. Nevertheless, after repeated attempts at decompressing Abad's chest and CPR, the mortarman died from the effects of his wounds. In the midst of the battle, Abad's death was a shock to the men at the CP. He was the only fatality within the main COP during the battle of Wanat.[15]

There could be no pause for mourning as the action continued at a furious pace. Shortly after the evacuation of the mortar pit, the burning TOW vehicle finally exploded, scattering flames and smoldering TOW missiles in all directions. The fireball caught and severely burned one unfortunate ANA soldier. Two of the Marine ETT members, Corporal Jason Jones and Corporal Jason Oakes, sprinted from their position to assist the ANA soldier, moved him to cover, and began medical treatment. The explosion knocked out the tactical satellite (TACSAT) radio antenna and with it all TACSAT radio backup communications. Two unexpended TOW missile rounds landed directly in the CP, with one having its missile motor running.

Phillips, arriving at the CP from the mortar pit, responded with characteristic energy, grabbing the hot missile using a pair of empty sandbags as expedient gloves, then carrying the round out of the CP into the middle of the open area through heavy enemy small arms fire. Miraculously, Phillips returned to safety unhurt. Myer, the company commander, also responded rapidly to the threat of the missiles, scooping up the other missile and heaving it over the side of the sandbag wall. To add to the confusion, a small pile of fabric debris remaining from the HESCOs that had been cut down and piled by the engineer CONEX container caught fire from the TOW explosion. The HESCO fabric smoldered, adding to the considerable quantities of thick black smoke emanating from the burning HMMWV and bazaar that slightly hindered the arrival of the medical evacuation helicopters later in the fight.[16]

Myer was otherwise busy trying to manage fire support assets and dispatching reinforcements. When the enemy opened fire, he immediately reported the contact to the battalion tactical operations center (TOC) at Camp Blessing. Myer announced the first volley of RPGs to the battalion in unmistakable terms, "This is a Ranch House style attack."[17] The battalion staff listening at the TOC could clearly hear the sounds of machine gun fire and RPGs exploding in the background of the radio transmission. Myer had two FM radios with him, one on the 2d Platoon's internal network and the other on the TF *Rock* battalion command net. He also had TACSAT as a backup until the TOW explosion destroyed the antenna. Hayes, the

2d Platoon RTO, and Aass assisted Myer with his radio coordination until Aass later departed to reinforce OP Topside. Having unfortunately left his fire support officer (FSO) at Camp Blessing, as he had done on 4 July at Bella, Myer focused his efforts on obtaining and coordinating fire support.

The TF *Rock* TOC recorded the initial contact report from Wanat at 0423, the time the first field artillery fire mission was executed. This was an immediate suppression mission aimed at a target approximately 550 yards to the northwest of the COP, danger close (less than 650 yards from friendly positions) for 155-mm field artillery, and about as close to friendly positions as high angle artillery could be safely fired in the mountainous terrain. TF *Rock* commander Ostlund briefly delayed the execution of the fires while he confirmed with Myer that all the Chosen Company defenders were within the perimeter, as he knew that a patrol was scheduled to depart the COP at around the same time. Within six minutes of the start of the action, the first rounds impacted. Myer initially focused the artillery on the southern and western sides of the COP. However, since most of the insurgent positions were much closer than 650 yards to friendly positions, the field artillery fire could not be directed against many enemy positions. The two gun trucks equipped with the Mk-19 grenade launcher had similar restrictions. The grenades fired by these weapon systems had a minimum arming distance and the insurgents were so close to the Coalition positions that if fired by the launchers at these most threatening targets, the projectiles would not be effective.[18]

While Myer had left his company FSO behind at Camp Blessing, the 2d Platoon's forward observer, Sergeant Ryan Pitts, was also unavailable. When the battle started, Pitts had been at OP Topside and was soon wounded and isolated there. This left Myer and the 2d Platoon leader, First Lieutenant Brostrom, with no trained field artillery fire support personnel at the CP. Making things more difficult were the communications difficulties caused by the mountainous terrain which was exacerbated by the destruction of the TACSAT antenna. To support their comrades, the artillerymen at Camp Blessing were forced to fire from a preplanned target list, engaging each target with four rounds of HE, armed with a "delay" fuse. Although using fuse delay reduced the effectiveness of the rounds, the howitzer crews at Camp Blessing deliberately employed the technique because it provided increased safety for friendly forces in the event that a shell inadvertently fell short.[19]

For the first half hour of the engagement, the only fire support that COP Kahler received was this relatively ineffectual and distant field artillery fire. Between 0429 and 0505, the 155-mm platoon at Camp Blessing fired five missions, a total of 52 HE projectiles. This rate of fire, less than two rounds per minute per cannon, was far below the standard sustained rate of fire of four rounds per minute. The time consuming need to elevate the gun tubes to a nearly vertical position to fire and then lower them to reload greatly slowed the gunners' work. Because the missions were danger close, the artillerymen also had to visually recheck the gun sights before each round was shot. Given the conditions, the artillerymen were firing the guns as rapidly as possible.[20]

Apart from the field artillery, Myer expected support from various fixed and rotary wing aircraft, although these assets by their nature were less immediately responsive than the artillery. Generally, close air support in the initial stage of the engagement was not used to provide direct support to the troops under fire. Rather, practice in Afghanistan had developed to the point where these powerful aerial weapons were used to limit access to the battlefield and to prevent AAF insurgents from transiting to and from the battlefield (referred to by the aviators as "air interdiction"). Accordingly, the first CAS mission to arrive on station over Wanat at 0458, a B-1 bomber, callsign "Bone", dropped two bombs to the north to isolate the battlefield. The absence of qualified air control personnel on the ground at Wanat also served as an obstacle to the use of CAS against enemy positions near the COP.[21]

As Myer and his radio operators worked feverishly to get support, the enemy maintained heavy fire on the CP area and the rest of the COP. The Americans marveled at the insurgents' ability to sustain this pressure. RTO Aass remembered that the "RPG fire was like machine gun fire."[22] Queck, now fighting from the CP, recalled, "Every time, it seemed, I would poke my head up from behind the sand bags, I would hear bullets whizzing by my head."[23]

With the TOW HMMWV now destroyed, there were three vehicles with heavy weapons still available to fire from the main COP position. These included the two squad HMMWVs on the northern segment of the perimeter, both armed with Mk-19 automatic grenade launchers, and the platoon headquarters HMMWV, mounting an M2 .50-caliber machine gun at the CP. On the ground, the Marine ETT also had an M240 7.62-mm medium machine gun manned by Corporal Jones. This gun's importance increased because both of the 2d Platoon's organic M240 machine guns were at OP Topside and therefore unable to support the main position. The AAF fire was so devastating that the 3d Squad's grenade launcher was quickly disabled when struck with a bullet through its feed tray. The 2d Squad's Mk-19 initially jammed, a common malfunction, but later was brought back into operation. Thus, as the initial AAF onslaught continued, the American and Afghan defenders at the main COP had only the .50-caliber machine gun at the CP, the Marine M240 machine gun, and their own small arms to repel the assault. It is to the credit of the C Company paratroopers that they maintained at least fire parity with the insurgents at COP Kahler.[24]

To achieve this effect with the available weapons, the 2d Platoon paratroopers were forced to fire their small arms at the maximum cyclic rate. The initial fight at the mortar pit, described earlier in this chapter, illustrated this. In other positions as well, the SAWs and, in particular, the M4s, experienced difficulty maintaining such a rate after the barrels got excessively hot. When that occurred, the weapons would jam, as happened to Phillips. Without heavier weapons, the enemy fire forced the Americans to return an equal volume of fire or risk the enemy overrunning the position. One young platoon member later complained, "I ran through my ammo 'til my SAW would not work anymore despite the 'Febreze' bottle of CLP [lubricant] I dumped into it."[25]

Soldiers were, on occasion, able to bring back into action previously jammed weapons. As mentioned above, the engineers' SAW that failed to work in the mortar pit fight was later used in another location after its barrel was replaced. In the midst of intense enemy fire, one paratrooper described how he "grabbed the engineer's weapon that was left at our position and which was a SAW and . . . started laying down about 800-1,000 rounds at the bazaar and wood line around the mosque."[26] The .50-caliber machine gun mounted on the platoon headquarters HMMWV also remained in action. Its gunner was Private William Krupa, who was detached from the 3d Squad for this duty and had joined the platoon only two months earlier. Krupa acquitted himself well in his first firefight. Aass later commented in admiration, "Private Krupa . . . was up in the turret, taking direct fire from multiple locations and he was literally standing ankle deep in .50-cal casings from all the rounds that he'd fired. I was worried that after he shot off his first can of ammo he wasn't going to know what to do next but under fire he changed maybe a dozen cans of ammo."[27] Krupa recounted:

RPGs were coming in constantly from the west. I remember at one point I had to slow my fire down because the barrel was red hot and there was a debate on how much ammo was left. By this time I had shot about ten .50-cal 100 round ammo cans. . .I would wait for the tree leaves to kick up so I knew where the enemy were at. Immediately after they would fire, I would fire at their positions.[28]

The insurgents did not spare the 1st Squad's traffic control point (TCP) position, located south of the CP across the road from the main COP. The TCP's main weapon was an M2 .50-caliber machine gun mounted in the turret of the squad HMMWV. One of the squad's fire team leaders, Sergeant Brian Hissong, watched Specialist Adam Hamby firing the M2 to the south, "The truck was taking very heavy fire, I've never seen a truck take so many hits as it was right then."[29] Hamby fired a 100 round belt of ammunition at the enemy position from which an RPG had been fired, recalling, "an RPG came sailing [in]. . . . It left a very definitive trail from the point of origin. I then dumped what was left [of my ammunition] in that location."[30] Incredibly, the volume of insurgent fire actually increased. Hamby continued, "I went down into the truck and grabbed a can of .50-cal ammo to reload. As I was reloading, the turret I was in became overwhelmed with gunfire."[31] Hissong was alarmed, "When he ducked down to reload, it was like the turret of the truck exploded from all of the bullets hitting it and RPG's impacting around it."[32] As Hamby attempted to get the machine gun back into action under this heavy fire, an enemy 7.62-mm round struck the gun directly in the top of its feed tray cover, which Hamby had raised for reloading. This hit permanently disabled the gun. Hamby's squad leader, Staff Sergeant Sean Samaroo, believed that the .50-caliber was knocked out within five minutes of the start of the engagement. The 1st Squad fought on without its heavy machine gun. To combat the incessant AAF fire, Hissong fired an AT-4 rocket against the large house on a high hill to the southeast of the TCP. Although the rocket destroyed the position, insurgent fire from other positions remained ferocious.[33]

To most Americans in Afghanistan, the enemy remained a shadowy figure who fired mortar rounds, emplaced improvised explosive devices (IEDs), or sprung small arms ambushes at a distance but for C Company, 2-503d IN, the experience was different. At both the Ranch House fight and the Bella ambush, the enemy was nearby. So it was at Wanat on 13 July 2008. The insurgents were so close and so aggressive in pushing their attack that the Americans regularly observed and engaged them as individuals. Many of the defenders recalled the appearance of the AAF. While some individual fighters wore masks over their faces, other wore on their heads. For uniforms they wore a combination of camouflaged BDUs [battle dress uniforms] and traditional *shalwar kameez*, the latter often referred to by the American troops as "man jammies".[34]

The ANA platoon defended its portion of the perimeter from its fighting positions in the northern sector. For the most part, the Afghan troops remained in their three fighting positions along the northern perimeter of the COP and at the TCP from which they directed fire against the insurgents. Numerous Chosen Company paratroopers complained of their inactivity. Dzwik was ambivalent about their performance:

> They never got out of their holes. They only had four wounded, which tells me that the enemy directed their fire at the Americans, not the Afghans. The Afghans sprayed and prayed. That's about it. To be honest, though, it was more than I expected. The other numerous occasions I've been on with Afghan soldiers as our backup, they ran.[35]

Sergeant Hissong summed up what most of the 2d Platoon Soldiers felt about the Afghan soldiers, "They were still pretty much totally useless."[36]

These sentiments, however, do not reflect actual ANA performance at Wanat. The ANA platoon did contribute to the defense of the COP to the best of its abilities. No ANA areas were overrun, occupied, or seized. The Marines who were directly responsible for observing the ANA platoon felt that the Afghan soldiers covered their assigned sectors responsibly and effectively while controlling their rates of fire. Such fire control was a step forward for the ANA, whose prior reputation was that of shooting blindly in the general direction of the enemy until all ammunition was expended. Four ANA troops were wounded and required evacuation in the action, a figure which matches almost exactly the American casualties on the main COP (one killed in action [KIA], four wounded), even though the ANA element was half the size of the American contingent.[37]

The major difference in overall casualties was that no ANA troops fought at OP Topside or were sent to reinforce it. Most of the American casualties and all but one of the KIAs would be inflicted at OP Topside. Neither the Marine advisors nor the Army officers shifted the Afghans around during the heat of battle because of language difficulties and a fear of fratricide. While troops of the 2d Platoon may have looked at the ANA with a jaundiced eye based on previous experience with the less well trained and unprofessional Afghan Security Guard (ASG) at the Ranch House and Bella, at Wanat the ANA seemed to have pulled their own weight.[38]

The Initial Defense of OP Topside[39]

Enemy intentions at Wanat are unknown and any analysis is thus speculative. Pry, the TF *Rock* S2 officer, believed that the AAF objective was the ejection of American forces from the area by overrunning the new outpost. Whatever the insurgents' goal was prior to the start of the battle, it was soon evident that American firepower on the main COP precluded a successful direct assault there. Things were, however, different at the isolated OP position:[40]

The TOW squad leader, Grimm, reflected on the insurgents' objectives:

They [the enemy] infiltrated a couple of days before. Fire [was] initiated from multiple locations at once, from covered and concealed positions, engaging heavy weapons first. They fired on the [COP] to keep us pinned down in the low ground so that they could isolate and overwhelm the OP. It felt like they were not trying to come inside the perimeter at the low ground, only at the OP.[41]

Grimm recalled, "There was a heavy volume of fire on us but I did not see AAF attempting to enter the main COP perimeter."[42]

The OP's position in the overall defensive scheme made its location especially vulnerable. The insurgents had infiltrated the bazaar which lay between the main American forces and the observation post. This hindered communication with Topside once the firefight started and made movement from the main position to the OP difficult. Nevertheless, American fire kept the enemy at bay to such an extent that Myer and Brostrom retained the freedom to maneuver and shift their forces around the defensive perimeter. This ability proved to be decisive as it allowed the company and platoon leaders to periodically reinforce the OP at critical times. Still, throughout the action, the defenders of OP Topside found themselves under great enemy pressure.

At the start of the fight, nine C Company paratroopers manned the three connected fighting positions at OP Topside. Specialist Tyler Stafford (gunner) and Specialist Gunnar Zwilling (assistant gunner) fought out of the northern M240 machine gun position. The platoon forward observer, Pitts, was also in this position with his radio. Corporal Jonathan R. Ayers, Specialist Christopher McKaig, and Specialist Pruitt Rainey were in the other M240 machine gun position in the middle fighting position called the Crow's Nest. There were three men in the southernmost fighting position, Specialists Jason Bogar and Mathew Phillips and Sergeant Matthew Gobble. Phillips was the platoon's designated marksman and had a designated fighting position on the sleeping terrace behind the short stretch of the double sandbagged wall facing the north. He was not manning this position when the attack started. As previously mentioned, Brostrom had placed the LRAS3 at the OP. It was located in the northern fighting position. FO Pitts usually operated the system.[43]

At 0420 on the morning of the attack, Stafford had been manning the LRAS3. He began moving the short distance back to his machine gun position for stand-to when the enemy opened fire. A wave of RPG rounds almost immediately engulfed the OP. This first round of explosions was devastatingly accurate. Everybody in the OP was immediately killed, wounded, or stunned. Stafford remembered:

> I yelled to Zwilling, then we got hit and I got blown out of that position back into the middle of the OP. I could feel all the shrapnel. It was burning pretty badly in my legs and my stomach was burning really bad and my arm. I thought I was on fire because it burned so bad, so I started rolling around screaming that I was on fire and then I just woke up from that. I regained my senses from that and sat up looking back toward the west. I could see Zwilling, who was just a couple feet from me, and he had the same look I would have on my face after getting hit in the face by Mike Tyson, probably. Then there was another explosion that happened right behind me. I'm not sure if it was a hand grenade or an RPG but that threw me down onto the terrace where we slept.[44]

Surprisingly, Stafford remained conscious, recalling that the grenade had "blown my helmet off but that one really didn't hurt me because I think my interceptor body armor caught most of that."[45] Still, he recognized he was badly hurt.

Stafford looked around to assess the damage. Zwilling had disappeared. Pitts lay in the bottom of the position wounded. Nearby, Phillips appeared unhurt. Stafford described what happened next:

> I looked up and saw Phillips and he was kind of hunkered down on his knees below that sandbag position. He was just popping his head up over the sandbags. I called to him, "Hey, Phillips, man, I'm hit, I'm hit. I need help." He just looked at me and nodded his head yes and just gave me a Phillips smile like he was saying, "I'll get you, man. Hold on but I need to kill these guys first." He had a grenade so he pulled the pin on his grenade and he stood up and threw it. Right as he threw

it, an RPG either hit the sandbags right in front of me or the boulder that was right behind me that was protecting us from the west. The RPG, once it exploded, the tail [fins] ricocheted and hit me in the helmet. I put my head down and it smacked me right on the top of my helmet. There was a big imprint in my helmet and everything . . . I looked up after that, after the dust settled, and I could see Phillips who was slumped over like he was sitting on his knees. He was slumped over with his chest on his knees and his hands all awkwardly beside him, turned backwards. I screamed at him four or five times, "Phillips! Phillips!"[46]

Pitts told a similar story, "The next thing I knew, things just started exploding inside our fighting positions. Multiple RPGs were shot at us, along with hand grenades. . . I was shell-shocked for a couple of seconds and I had been hit immediately."[47] Zwilling and Phillips had been killed almost immediately. Gobble was wounded so badly that he was effectively knocked out of the fight and every one of the remaining six Soldiers in the OP had sustained wounds of varying degrees and severity.

Stafford crawled back to the protection of the southern part of the OP. There he watched Bogar single handedly put up a heroic defense. Although badly wounded and at times barely conscious, Stafford recalled, "Bogar had just set his SAW on top of the sandbags and he was just kind of spraying, going through SAW rounds pretty quick. I remember him loading and spraying, loading and spraying."[48] Stafford noted Bogar had fired about 600 rounds at the cyclic rate of fire when his "SAW jammed, basically it just got way overheated because he opened the feed tray cover and I remember him trying to get it open and it just looked like the bolt had welded itself inside the chamber. His barrel was just white hot."[49]

Above Bogar in the Crow's Nest, Ayers was firing complete bursts with the M240 machine gun. Stafford was impressed with his volume of fire, "I could also hear the 240 going off above me in the Crow's Nest because Ayers was just ripping them apart. I could hear Rainey screaming at Ayers not to melt the barrel on the 240 and to control his fires."[50] Eventually, Ayers ran out of machine gun ammunition. In the heat of battle, he did not realize that ammunition for Stafford's now unmanned M240 lay nearby.

McKaig remembered the continuing action from his perspective in the middle position, "We had to fire constantly just to get the upper hand . . . they were coming from the southeast about 50 to 75 meters [82 yards]

Figure 16. OP Topside from the east following the engagement, providing the enemy perspective of the position.

away. They were all different ranges coming from all different directions. We had to stay low because the fire they were putting down on us was extremely effective."[51] At least one of the RPG rockets that exploded at the OP also set aflame material located around the fighting positions. McKaig was appalled, "Me and Ayers also had a fire from an explosion that caught some of our equipment on fire. I remember engaging the enemy and trying to kick out the fire at the same time. I remember telling myself 'The Army never trained me for this kind of situation.'"[52]

With their M240 effectively out of action, Ayers and McKaig continued the fight at the Crow's Nest with two M4 carbines. Their technique was to pop up together at intervals, fire six to nine rounds at the muzzle flashes ringing the OP, then drop down before the enemy could respond. Although scared, the pair continued this maneuver until enemy return fire struck and killed Ayers, who collapsed over his weapon. Now alone in the position, McKaig began to experience problems with his M4. "My weapon was overheating. I had shot about 12 magazines by this point already and it had only been about a half hour or so into the fight. I couldn't charge my weapon and put another round in because it was too hot, so I got mad and threw my weapon down."[53] When he tried to use Ayers' rifle, he discovered that an AK-47 round had disabled it in the same volley that had killed his squad mate.

Out of weapons, McKaig remembered that he still had two Claymore antipersonnel mines emplaced just outside the OP. A quick glance revealed that at least one insurgent had exploited the lapse in gunfire and emerged from the dead ground to the southeast to breach the concertina obstacle and assault the OP. Without hesitation, McKaig detonated both mines, remembering, "The first one killed an insurgent that was in our wire. Sparks flew out of him, I don't know if he had ammo or whatever on him, and it killed him instantly."[54] Now also in the southern position as the result of the concussive effects of numerous RPG blasts, Pitts was virtually incapacitated by multiple wounds to his arms and legs. He looked so bad that Bogar had paused briefly during his fight to put a tourniquet on the FO's right leg.

Meanwhile, a badly wounded Stafford crawled back into the northern firing position and emptied the magazine of his 9-mm pistol over the sandbag wall. Then Stafford reached for his two Claymores, recalling, "I grabbed one clacker and I brought it down, took the safety off, and I started clacking and there was nothing. I clacked it probably 10 times and nothing went off." The Claymore's wires lay on top of the ground and almost certainly one of the many RPG blasts had severed them. Stafford continued, "Then I saw the other one and so I grabbed it and clacked it. I don't know, the reports say [the] insurgents had turned them around and stuff like that, so I don't know if they had come in and turned them around, if they were that ballsy, or if all the RPG blasts had made them fall down but when I clacked, it blew up and back at us."[55] Startled, Stafford grabbed an M4 carbine that was in the position (either Pitts or Zwilling's) and began firing it. However, he recalled being hit almost immediately by enemy fire, "I probably got off four or five rounds before another RPG hit right in front of that wall and tore my hands up really bad. So I dropped the rifle and I was hurting really bad at this point . . . I'm bleeding out of both legs, arms, hands, stomach."[56] Stafford crawled back to the southern position where the other OP survivors had at this moment clustered. Bogar's earlier suggestion that the troops at the OP build the southern position had almost certainly saved the lives of those who remained at Topside.[57]

Stafford told Pitts that Phillips was dead and that he thought Zwilling was likely gone as well.[58] Despite his wounds, Pitts became furious on hearing this and returned to the now vacant northern firing position to reenter the fight. Pitts remembered, "I threw six or seven hand grenades into the dead space into the riverbed . . . I was cooking them off for about three or four seconds so they would blow up as soon as they got over the concertina wire and landed on the other side."[59] In between lobbing grenades, he radioed the CP, described the situation at the OP, and requested urgent help. While he waited for assistance, Pitts tried to fire Stafford's M240. His severe wounds, however, prevented him from aiming the machine gun effectively.[60]

Reinforcing OP Topside

Pitts did not have to wait long for help to arrive. The first reinforcements soon appeared from the main COP. This party consisted of the platoon leader, Brostrom and Specialist Jason Hovater. Recognizing that the OP had become the critical sector of the defense, and with Myer present to run the fight from the CP, Brostrom felt his place was at Topside. He told Myer, "We need to get up there." Myer responded, "Okay, go ahead."[61] Although vegetation obscured a direct view of the OP from the CP area, the salvos of RPGs bursting around Topside were clearly visible from the main COP. With heavy fire also sweeping the open fields of the main position, Myer feared weakening the COP until he knew what was going on at the OP. Accordingly, he allowed Brostrom to move out with a small party. The platoon leader then ran to the nearby 2d Squad position to gather a force to accompany him. Following a short conversation with the squad leader, Staff Sergeant Jonathan Benton, Brostrom took the platoon medic, Hewitt, and Hovater with him. Hewitt was to treat the wounded known to be at the OP.[62]

The three paratroopers stepped out of the shelter of the 2d Squad fighting position to move to the OP but, as previously recounted, Hewitt only took a few steps before he was shot through the arm, receiving a wound serious enough that it knocked him out of the rest of the battle. Undaunted, Brostrom and Hovater continued forward, sprinting together through intense fire, moving between the bazaar and the hotel complex, and then scrambling up the terraces to the OP. Standing on the sleeping terrace, Brostrom shouted urgently to Pitts in the northern position to hand over the machine gun and ammunition, formerly manned by Zwilling and Stafford, which Pitts himself was too badly wounded to fire. Rainey then joined Brostrom and Hovater on the sleeping terrace. Pitts was the last to see any of them alive. Although it remains unclear exactly what happened next and what Brostrom's intentions were, it appears that he wanted to place Rainey and Hovater with the M240 machine gun on the sleeping terrace at the sandbag wall where Phillips position had been. However, this position had no view of the bazaar/hotel area. Presumably, such a position could cover the movement of reinforcements to the OP and the evacuation of the wounded by suppressing the enemy in the bazaar and hotel areas.[63]

However, insurgent activity interrupted Brostrom's plans. Stafford distinctly recalled the ensuing engagement on the sleeping terrace:

> I heard First Lieutenant Brostrom up at the OP talking. He was screaming at Rainey and I could hear them shouting back and forth together and I don't remember who said it, but they said, "They're inside the wire" and then I heard a bunch of gunfire and Rainey screaming, "He's right behind the...sandbag! He's right behind the...sandbag!" I don't know if they were grenades or RPGs but there was a whole bunch of fire down on the sleeping terrace where we slept. Then all fire from the OP went quiet like there was no outgoing fire anymore.[64]

McKaig remembered the incident in nearly identical terms, stating, "There was an insurgent right on the other side of a rock near our sleeping area. I remember hearing people screaming and yelling that he was right over there. I don't know if it was that insurgent or another insurgent that killed Brostrom and Hovater but shortly afterwards I couldn't hear them anymore and they were probably killed."[65]

While exactly what happened may never be known, Brostrom and Rainey were likely placing the M240 into action, while Hovater provided security, when they were surprised by insurgent small arms fire from near the large rock on Topside's northwest corner. Brostrom was shot from the front as was Hovater, who was apparently reloading his weapon. Hovater had stayed and fought with Brostrom to the very end. Rainey was probably also killed at this time.[66]

The destruction of Brostrom's team showed how close the enemy was to overrunning the OP. Immediately afterwards, Gobble, although seriously wounded, was still able to fight. He saw an enemy soldier "inside the wire. I quickly shot at him but he dove behind a large rock."[67] At the same time, several RPG rounds exploded nearly on top of Stafford. Meanwhile, Bogar was firing hundreds of rounds from his SAW directly above Stafford's head. The insurgents were so close that Stafford could hear the recoil and cycling of their weapons as they were being fired. He would recall, "It sounded to me like they were right up on top of the hill, on top of the hill from the OP. That's how close they sounded to me."[68] Enemy logistical difficulties may have saved the OP survivors. The AAF attackers may have run out of ammunition. McKaig recalled, "The insurgents then started throwing a whole bunch of rocks at us. They apparently mixed some fragmentary grenades in with them as well. As soon as it fell into my hole, my first reaction was to grab it and throw it out, or to jump out.

Once I saw that they were rocks, though, I started yelling, "They're rocks! They're rocks!" They were trying to get us to jump out."[69] Whether this was a ruse to force the paratroopers out into the open or a desperate enemy attempt to keep fighting without grenades or ammunition is unclear. What is clear is that a new wave of fully armed attackers was soon present near the OP.

In addition to the threat posed by the insurgents literally yards away, the men at OP Topside were receiving fire from the buildings near their position. Specialist Bogar, known in the platoon as being utterly fearless, apparently attempted to suppress this incoming fire and began to engage insurgents in the bazaar and the hotel. McKaig and Pitts, aware of his courage, were not surprised to see him jump up and leave the OP to get closer to his targets. Although they did not know it at the time, Bogar was soon after killed by enemy fire outside the OP position.[70]

The situation at the OP remained perilous. Pitts had an M203 grenade launcher and an M4 carbine with him in his northern fighting position. Stafford's M240 machine gun now lay on the sleeping terrace with no one to fire it. Phillips' M21 sniper rifle lay twisted into a pretzel by his side on the sleeping terrace. At the Crow's Nest, Ayers' M240 was thought to be out of ammunition, Bogar's SAW was jammed and needed a barrel change. One M4 carbine was destroyed and another irreparably jammed. With Gobble, Stafford, and Pitts badly wounded, only McKaig, armed with an M4, remained able to fight. He recalled:

> I only had two magazines left and I knew I needed to save them in case the insurgents jumped over the sandbags. We could hear their voices and they were still throwing rocks at us. I had hand grenades up in my position so I went back up there and threw two hand grenades to the southeast, then I threw another two to the northeast into the dead space where we were taking fire from.[71]

He then made a timely discovery:

> I slid back down to where Sergeant Gobble and Stafford were, and by some miracle there was a LAW [light antitank weapon] rocket hanging in a tree nearby. We were taking fire about 40 meters [43 yards] to our southeast from these little mud huts that were there. I saw a bunch of muzzle flashes and movement over there, so I opened up the LAW and tried to fire it. It wouldn't fire. Sergeant Gobble came to and told me to pull harder on the safety, so I pulled as hard as I could on

the safety and then leaned out and fired the LAW rocket. I hit dead center where those guys were.[72]

This shot had an immediate effect on the enemy. McKaig remembered, "The shooting stopped after that for what seemed like an eternity but it was only about six seconds."[73]

Gobble and McKaig decided that they had no choice but to abandon the OP. When Pitts did not respond to their shouts, they believed he had died of his wounds. Stafford had lost a lot of blood and desperately needed evacuation. Gobble pushed the rear (west) double wall of sandbags over and the three paratroopers began working their way through this gap and down to the sleeping terrace. Gobble checked on the three men lying still on the sleeping terrace but quickly realized they were dead. While doing this, an insurgent shot him at close range from behind a large rock inside the OP perimeter. Weaponless he was unable to return fire. Despite the wound, Gobble was able to move with the group that was evacuating the OP. Rather than follow the direct route that would take them close to insurgent positions in the bazaar, the three survivors veered to the southwest toward the 1st Squad's TCP. This movement was not easy for the wounded men. Stafford, in particular, had a difficult time getting through the concertina, briefly becoming entangled in the wire. Exhausted, he thought, "I was pretty sure I was going to die right there."[74] Stafford finally got through the obstacle and descended, rolling down the terraces, and practically fell into Samaroo's arms. "Sergeant Sam shouted, 'What the hell's going on in the OP?'" Specialist Stafford gasped out, "They're all dead, Sergeant."[75] Samaroo moved the wounded men back to the protection of the TCP and began treating their wounds.[76]

What the OP survivors at the TCP did not realize was that Pitts was still alive at the position. Rainey had left his M203 grenade launcher with Pitts when he took the M240. Despite his wounds, Pitts immediately brought this weapon into action, recalling, "I started shooting [40-mm grenades] straight up into the air so they'd drop in as close as they could on one side. I was putting them right where I put the grenades and hoped the arc would bring them down into the riverbed."[77] After he threw all his hand grenades and fired all 40-mm rounds he had, Pitts noticed "It was quiet and nobody was shooting but me."[78] He soon realized he was alone at the OP. Fortunately as the FO, he had a radio and it still worked. Pitts remembered that he "got on the radio and told them that everybody was either dead or gone except for me and that if they didn't send anyone up here, the position was going to fall. I let them know that the enemy was really close."[79] The insurgents were, in fact, so close that Pitts could plainly hear them talking outside the OP perimeter. From his squad's position, Benton remembered hearing Pitts' call over the platoon radio net, "Sergeant [Pitts] said in a hushed tone that he was hit, laying down behind cover, and could hear [insurgents] walking within 10 meters (11 yards) of his position."[80] Pitts prepared to make a last stand with an M4 carbine.

The 2d Platoon, by standard operating procedure, routinely designated a platoon QRF to reinforce whatever position required assistance in the event of an attack. With the OP situation unclear and the problems at the mortar pit and TOW position, Myer and Dzwik had not yet activated the QRF when the OP went quiet. However, when Samaroo noticed the lack of firing at the OP from his position, he decided on his own initiative to send reinforcements to the OP. Taking two squad members with him, Specialist Tyler Hanson and Specialist Adam Hamby, he began moving towards Topside. However, he almost immediately encountered the three evacuees from the OP: Gobble, McKaig, and Stafford who he promptly brought back down to the TCP position.[81]

With the wounded trio being treated, Samaroo then organized a new force from paratroopers who had begun assembling at the TCP to assist the OP. The new group consisted of Samaroo himself, Specialist Michael Denton from his 1st Squad, Sergeant Israel Garcia of the 3d Squad, and Private First Class Jacob Sones from the 2d Squad. The latter two had sprinted from the main position to the TCP when they heard about the desperate situation of the OP. Before moving across the open terraces to the OP, Samaroo carefully scanned the hillside where the OP was located for any enemy activity. He recalled, "That's when I engaged a man, shot him, he was directly on top of the OP shooting over a large boulder into the OP."[82] Samaroo and his three men then ascended the hill. Their vigorous counterattack drove away the AAF who had entered OP Topside's perimeter, regained control of the position, and permanently secured it in American hands.

For a brief period, Pitts had been alone at the OP. At this time, except where Pitts remained in the northern fighting position requesting assistance, the AAF controlled the OP but this control was tenuous at best. Throughout, Pitts remained capable of fighting. Nearby lay two M240 machine guns, the LRAS3, a number of rifles, a radio antenna, and considerable personal gear. When Samaroo's force arrived, those weapons remained undisturbed on the ground of the position, suggesting that any enemy occupation of the OP had been temporary at best.

The scene that Samaroo's group found at Topside was "chaotic". The 1st Squad leader reacted quickly, finding Pitts and putting Ayers' M240 back into action at the Crow's Nest. Samaroo's men quickly determined that, other than Pitts, the five casualties present at the OP (Phillips, Rainey, Ayers, Hovater, and Brostrom), were all killed in action. Samaroo's force had arrived just in time. The enemy had regrouped and apparently, rearmed. The AAF once again began to place heavy fire on the OP. One of Samaroo's paratroopers remembered being engaged "from all four cardinal directions. They used mortars, recoilless rifles, RPGs, RPKs, PKMs, AKs, and anything they could get a hold of. I can't even tell you how many RPGs hit, there were so many of them."[83] Soon, another wave of RPG rockets struck. Denton recalled:

> That's when my position was hit by, I believe, two RPGs with a third hitting inside the actual OP. . . . The blast blew me outside of my bunker, causing me to land on my head and neck, then the rest of my body hit the ground. I lost my weapon in the process. After that, I started crawling to get away from the position by a few feet and I could hear everyone screaming, including my squad leader [Staff Sergeant Samaroo], that he had been hit.[84]

Pitts remembered the exact moment when the renewed attack began:

> [Sergeant] Garcia was pulling security in the middle area and keeping a lookout. Sones was treating me against the north wall. I was sitting down and he was bandaging me up. That's when another volley of RPGs and hand grenades came in. I was hit again, as was Sones. That's when Garcia took a direct hit from an RPG. I thought he was dead from his wounds. I knew Samaroo and Denton were wounded and I could hear Samaroo screaming that he was hit. I don't remember much after that. I do know that I crawled over to Garcia and talked to him some. Sones and I crawled into the southern position and Samaroo and Denton jumped in as well. I told them that Garcia was messed up. I don't remember who did it but one of them dragged Garcia into our position. Samaroo needed a radio so I got a multiband inter/intra team radio (MBITR) up so we could talk [to the COP]. He told them we needed more people and that they were wounded.[85]

Pitts, saw that, despite the arrival of reinforcements, the state of affairs at the OP was still dire. All the defenders who were still able to fight were now wounded. He observed that, "Denton started pulling security to the east, despite being hurt and Samaroo was doing the same toward the north and west. Sones was pretty shell-shocked and Denton's hand was pretty messed up."[86]

162

The situation became even worse. The wounded Denton recalled, "I started looking for a weapon for myself and found one. I couldn't fire with my right hand, it was hard to stand because both my legs had been hit, but I could stand to pull security to the east where we were still taking fire from the most, where they had snuck up on us, and tried to run us over from."[87] As Pitts had observed, an RPG had struck Garcia directly in the abdomen, below his body armor. His wounds were fatal, although he remained conscious for a few moments. Pitts crawled over to him and held his hand until Garcia died.[88]

When Garcia was hit, he fell onto his radio mike, fixing it in the on position and accidentally jamming the platoon frequency. This caused a "hot mike" situation which hindered platoon communications for a few minutes until the problem rectified itself. At the CP, Dzwik was confused by the jamming of the radio signal during such a critical time and recognized that he did not have an accurate picture of where his men were located. He quickly decided personally to lead a fourth force to the OP, first gathering Phillips (the mortar section chief) and Benton (the 2d Squad leader) as his subordinate leaders. To this force he quickly added Aass (the company RTO), Queck (mortars), Scantlin (2d Squad, acting as the platoon medic), Grimm (TOW squad), and Specialist Aaron Davis (TOW squad), and Marines Oakes and Jones, who brought along their M240 machine gun.[89]

Dzwik's force took the less direct route through the 1st Squad's TCP that provided greater cover and concealment from enemy fire. From the TCP, Specialist Reid Grapes, knowledgeable of the exact enemy situation at the time, guided Dzwik the rest of the way to the OP, avoiding known enemy positions and fields of fire. To obscure enemy observation, Grapes threw a yellow smoke grenade into the open area near the hotel that had to be crossed. As this group ascended the terraces toward the OP, Apache attack helicopters appeared overhead.

Arrival of Attack Helicopter Support

About an hour into the fight, two AH-64 Apache attack helicopters arrived over Wanat and immediately went into action under Myer's direction. The Apache with the callsign "Hedgerow 50" executed its first 30-mm gun run at 0523 against the north side of the brushy area immediately adjoining OP Topside. As the gunships approached the OP, the gunner in the lead Apache remarked, "There is a guy right on the other side of the trees."[90] The aviators immediately fired their cannon at the insurgent. Although he was concealed from normal view, the Apache's thermal sights clearly saw him within the brush.[91] This attack was very close to the OP. First Lieutenant Michael Moad, who would arrive at the OP later in the day as part of a larger QRF, remarked on the proximity of this fire to the 2d Platoon members at the OP, "I observed the 30-mm cannon strafe marks in the ground just one-two meters outside the OP itself just in front of the sandbag defensive wall, which was ultimately inside the wire about 10 meters from the sandbags."[92] The trailing AH-64, "Hedgerow 53," followed its leader and oriented on a green smoke grenade thrown by Samaroo's force, placed about 50 HE cannon rounds into the dead ground 50 yards to the east of the OP, an area from which Denton remembered most of the enemy firing coming at the time. These initial gun runs against the enemy positions around OP Topside came just over one hour after Captain Myer's first radio call to the TF *Rock* TOC requesting support.[93]

Hedgerow 50 and Hedgerow 53 were assigned to 2d Squadron, 17th Cavalry (2-17th Cav), part of TF *Out Front* based out of Forward Operating Base (FOB) Fenty at Jalalabad. The squadron provided aviation support to TF *Bayonet*. Squadron commander Lieutenant Colonel John Lynch, a highly experienced OH-58 pilot, commented:

> My task force at that time consisted of 14 Kiowa Warriors, which was one of my organic troops, as well as a platoon out of 2d Troop. I had an Apache company-minus with six AH-64s [Apache Attack helicopters]. I had a Chinook platoon with four CH-47s, a MEDEVAC detachment with three forward support medical teams, three UH-60 air ambulances, a Black Hawk assault platoon with six UH-60L, and an unmanned aerial vehicle detachment with four Hunter UAVs. I also had a Pathfinder detachment.[94]

Similar to many other Army units in Afghanistan, TF *Out Front* was stretched thin. The squadron had to cover the entire TF *Bayonet* battle space that consisted of four provinces. The rugged terrain of northeast Afghanistan also constrained operations. The OH-58D Kiowa Warriors could only operate below 6,000 feet, which severely limited their use in Nuristan. To support TF *Rock*, they were primarily used in the river valleys in Konar Province. For contingencies, the six AH-64 Apaches provided a continuous 24 hour QRF of two gunships, to which Hedgerows 50 and 53 belonged on the morning of 13 July. The Apache company also provided a two gunship escort for any cargo helicopters flying into certain areas, including the Waygal and Korengal Valleys. Battle damage and the inevitable mechanical breakdowns exacerbated the limitations derived from operating only six gunships over an immense geographic area. When mission, maintenance, and flight crew constraints permitted, the Apaches were employed on deterrence and direct attack missions.

As mentioned above, on the night of 12-13 July, 2-17th Cav had a two helicopter Apache QRF ready at Jalalabad. This QRF was in direct support of TF *Bayonet* and the positioning of the Apaches at Jalalabad was routine and reflected the general situation as perceived by both the TF *Bayonet* and TF *Rock* chains of command. There were two UH-60 Blackhawks also on call as MEDEVACs. Accordingly, at the time of the attack on Wanat, the closest AH-64 helicopters to Wanat—in the air or on the ground—were at FOB Fenty in Jalalabad, approximately 40 miles away, or roughly 30 minutes flight time under normal conditions.[95]

At 0430, 2-17th Cav was performing a routine QRF shift change at FOB Fenty when the alert for the Wanat support mission was received. This alert came only five minutes after Myer's first call to the TF *Rock* TOC. The Apache shift change was normally scheduled so that the helicopters would be ready to respond to any incidents at dawn, the most common time of day for the AAF to launch an attack. Within 23 minutes after receiving the alert, the two Apaches were warmed up and in the air. During that time interval, TF *Rock* reported that the force at Wanat had sustained three wounded, and TF *Out Front* immediately alerted the two MEDEVAC helicopters. At 0453, the flight surgeon recorded the departure of the MEDEVAC helicopters with the Apaches. The shift change caused no delay in response by the Apaches. In fact, two sets of aircrew were available for the mission. The Apaches, however, required time to warm up their engines and prepare for the mission. The attack helicopters also had to escort the MEDEVAC Blackhawks to the Camp Blessing area.[96]

Once they departed the Jalalabad area, the helicopters made the flight to the Waygal Valley in 29 minutes, close to the usual flight time of 30 minutes. However, the attack helicopters had to wait for the completion on an ongoing field artillery mission in the same airspace before proceeding to Wanat. The tight confines of the Waygal Valley forced approaching helicopters to fly directly over Camp Blessing from where the artillery was firing. Once the airspace was clear, the Apaches flew directly to the battlefield, while the two MEDEVAC helicopters remained at Camp Blessing until the Apaches cleared the way.[97]

The arrival of the Apaches had an immediate and decisive impact on the situation at OP Topside. Their cannon fire into the dead space to the north and east of the OP suppressed or destroyed insurgent forces there. The pressure on Samaroo's defenders quickly slackened. Still, the fight continued with the stubborn enemy. Insurgent fire now came from a greater distance and became, accordingly, far less accurate. Because of this, the AAF adopted the tactic of aiming their RPGs at the trees near the OP from their firing positions several hundred yards away. Aass noted, "I remember somebody saying they were shooting the RPGs up into the trees. I think they were trying to have the RPGs explode over us and rain down shrapnel on top of us."[98] Despite the effectiveness of the Apache gun runs, the OP position remained a dangerous place for the troops fighting there. RPG shrapnel badly wounded Davis. Dzwik received a minor wound in his arm from another RPG. Marine Oakes also received a shrapnel wound. The AAF gunners were determined and would remain in their firing positions for at least two hours after the beginning of the attack, until intense attack helicopter and CAS strikes finally drove them away.[99]

Shortly after the appearance of the Apaches, Myer went to the OP, running up past the bazaar. He wanted to get a firsthand look at the situation at the OP, particularly the number of casualties requiring evacuation. Communications between the OP and the CP was still poor. When he arrived with one of the QRFs, Aass had found multiple hand mikes out of operation, all riddled with bullet holes. At the OP, Myer quickly grasped the urgency of the situation and requested the immediate dispatch of the MEDEVAC flights. While at Topside, the company commander realized how close the fighting there had been when he came across a grenade that hadn't exploded. He recalled, "I reached down and threw it about 20 meters out of the pit. I remember seeing the spoon sticking out of it."[100]

Indirect fires, CAS, and Apache gun runs had now effectively suppressed the insurgent fire at the main position, freeing more troops to help at the OP. Specialist Scantlin, the substitute medic, made the climb and began treating the wounded. McKaig also got back into the fight and began carrying boxes of machine gun ammunition up to the OP. The most desperate fighting at Topside had ended by 0630, a little over two hours after the opening shots and one hour after the arrival of the Apaches.[101] By this time, the bodies of the nine paratroopers killed in action had been recovered. One of the Apache helicopter pilots expressed the sentiments of every American on the ground and in the air when the grim call came over the radio frequency, "We will have additional fallen hero missions to follow. I have a total of nine KIA."[102] The pilot then swore, "GOD-DAMN-IT!!!"[103]

Arrival of the 1st Platoon Quick Reaction Force

On 13 July 2008 Chosen Company's 1st Platoon at Camp Blessing was the designated TF *Rock* QRF, the unit selected to react to any tactical situation in the *Rock* area of operations that required reinforcement. At 0430, the TF *Rock* TOC alerted the platoon for immediate movement to Wanat. Led by First Lieutenant Aaron R. Thurman and his platoon sergeant, Sergeant First Class William S. Stockard, the platoon left Camp Blessing at 0515 in four HMMWVs. One vehicle was armed with an M2 .50-caliber machine gun, two others had Mk-19 grenade launchers, and the fourth an M240 machine gun. First Sergeant Scott Beeson, the senior noncommissioned officer (NCO) in Chosen Company, accompanied the QRF. The platoon's departure was delayed by the need to load additional ammunition into the HMMWVs. Stockard noted, "The sun was starting to come up so it wasn't too dark. We didn't have NODs (night observation devices) mounted or anything. We could see fine."[104] The QRF moved up the road from Camp Blessing as quickly as was prudent, expecting ambushes and IEDs along the way. The platoon used its heavy weapons systems to fire into every ravine and draw along the way, as well as other known or suspected ambush positions. There was no enemy contact and the platoon made it to Wanat in about 45 minutes, arriving at the American perimeter at 0601. They had made it in half the usual time required to get from Camp Blessing to Wanat.[105]

Upon arrival the 1st Platoon found an extremely confused situation. Fires burned at the site of the TOW HMMWV, the HESCO pile, and in the stall in the bazaar. The smoke from these various fires drifted to the east and pooled over the COP and road, obscuring visibility. OP Topside was still under heavy fire and the Apache helicopter pilots observed weapons flashes all around the valley.[106] Communications between the QRF and Myer at COP Kahler were spotty at best, obscured by both the terrain and the combat action that the main COP was still experiencing. Heavy enemy fire continued to pour into the COP from the bazaar, hotel complex, and mosque. As the QRF approached the COP, only a few paratroopers remained at the 1st Squad TCP as most of them had moved to reinforce OP Topside. The four HMMWVs stopped briefly at the TCP. A wave of small arms and RPG fire welcomed the lead QRF truck to Wanat.[107]

In response to this fire, the QRF went immediately into action. Staff Sergeant Kyle Silvernale, one of the 1st Platoon squad leaders, asked for a situation update from Hissong who was manning the TCP. Hissong recalled that his report was less than helpful:

When they arrived, I ran from my position to link up with them. The first person I saw was Staff Sergeant Silvernale. I don't remember the conversation but he later told me that when I got to him, he asked me where the enemies were. He said I just looked around and didn't really answer him so he asked me again and I said, "I didn't know." He said "What do you mean you don't know" and my response was ". . . they're everywhere man."[108]

The 1st Squad's HMMWV blocked the road and had to be moved for the convoy to proceed. To augment the depleted manpower at the TCP, 1st Platoon dropped two men there. Additionally, the 1st Platoon medic who had accompanied the QRF climbed out of his HMMWV and immediately ran to the casualty collection point (CCP) located at the CP to assist with the casualties being evacuated to that site. Beeson, accompanied by an RTO, also exited his HMMWV and went to the CP to check in with Myer to ascertain where his services were most needed. After a quick shouted conversation, Beeson, his RTO, and the medic immediately turned around and sprinted toward OP Topside.[109]

Back on the road, the platoon leader, Thurman, in his first combat action, acted quickly. He split his small force into two squads, one under his personal direction that he immediately led toward the bazaar, and a second ad hoc squad under Stockard that followed Beeson up to OP Topside. Two of the HMMWVs remained at the TCP as a reserve, while the other two, under Thurman's personal leadership, advanced up to the center of Wanat. By this time, the firing at the TCP was nowhere near as severe as it had been just a few minutes earlier but several times it swelled and the fighting again became furious. One of the new arrivals at the TCP described receiving fire from a compound on the west side of the town and the reaction of the ANA troops:

As I was pulling security . . . I heard incoming small arms whizzing by. Specialist [not identified] yelled to me that the fire was coming from the compound to the west. He informed me of tracers coming out of the compound, so I traversed my turret and returned fire once I recognized the source of the fire. Ten meters to our north on the west side of the road was an ANA bunker. Four ANA were inside. They were shooting and taking fire from the same compound. As I fired into the windows, the ANA would fire an RPG into that same spot. Contact [enemy fire] with the compound was over in roughly 10 minutes.[110]

The other 1st Platoon member at the TCP related a nearly identical story about the soldiers at the ANA TCP, "We began taking small arms fire from a compound to the west. Corporal [not identified] returned fire with the M240B into the compound. Four ANA soldiers were also at the checkpoint and began firing with RPGs and PKM[s] into the compound. After about 10 minutes of continuous fire into the compound, we stopped receiving small arms [fire]."[111]

The other two HMMWVs drove aggressively forward, stopping just north of the bazaar close to the mosque and hotel/restaurant complex. While passing through the area on the way to the OP, Beeson noticed that the forceful movement by the two heavily armed HMMWVs caught the insurgents in the nearby buildings off guard. To capitalize on the enemy confusion, Thurman ordered an immediate assault. Supported by the firepower of the trucks, he led a dismounted charge into the bazaar. The driver of the lead truck, which mounted a Mk-19, described what occurred as he drove his vehicle past the bazaar:

> I drove my truck through the bazaar on the road to the north, past the hotel and mosque. I parked the truck using a rock wall as cover and blocked the road with the truck. Specialist [unknown] shot a round with his M4 at the building to northeast doing a recon by fire. Immediately after his shot the truck came under PKM fire, Specialist [unknown] shot the Mk-19 at the house and then a LAW when the ammo can was empty . . . I opened up with my M249 at the house and received effective SAF [small arms fire] from the house. Sergeant [unknown] handed me an AT-4 [antiarmor weapon] to shoot and took my M249 [SAW]. I got down off the road onto a lower terrace and shot the AT-4 at the house and hit the bottom floor. Specialist [unknown] then handed me another AT-4 he had in the turret for me to shoot, I went to the side of the truck and shot again at the house and knocked out a bottom floor window, at that point we stopped taking fire from the house.[112]

Despite this heavy fire suppression, the squad continued to receive sporadic fire from other insurgent locations near the hotel and on the eastern outskirts of the town. The HMMWVs were highly effective in supporting the assault. Dismounted enemy infantry could not stand up to the American firepower. As one Soldier recalled, "We engaged [the enemy] heavily with [the vehicle-mounted] M240 and .50-cal. After about 30 to 40 rounds I [could] no longer see any [enemy] trying to maneuver in the alley."[113] At first, the enemy tried to mount a defense with volleys of RPG rockets. Hissong at the TCP observed Thurman's assault, "1st Platoon returned [the enemy fire] with a massive amount of fire from their machine guns. It seemed like they drove the enemy out of the bazaar by the COP."[114] Thurman's assault was a huge success. Aass watched the fight from the OP, "I remember [Staff] Sergeant Silvernale from 1st Platoon getting on the radio and announcing that he was going to clear the hotel. I made sure nobody was firing at the hotel and he went in there with two or three other guys and cleared the hotel."[115]

Silvernale participated in the clearing operations as part of Thurman's assault force. While waiting to move into the bazaar, he was wounded by an RPG explosion. Nevertheless he still led his men into the bazaar and the hotel:

> Moving to the northern end of the bazaar behind the second truck, I noticed a fresh blood trail leading through an overhang between the hotel and the building just north of the hotel. Pushing past the building just north of the hotel my element came into heavy enemy contact once again. We started taking effective direct small arms fire from the north and east. Multiple enemy positions to the east of our position, one directly behind the hotel. . . . I moved into the bazaar and started clearance operations throughout the bazaar. Starting at the 2d floor northeast corner of the hotel, clearing a foot hold, I moved through the northeastern most room to the window in order to throw [fragmentary grenades] down on the enemy position in a flanking maneuver.[116]

Silvernale remembered that while moving through the hotel, he and his squad came across an ax. They used it and a shotgun they had brought to break down doors. This group successfully cleared the building of insurgents.[117]

While the fight in the bazaar and hotel was going on, Stockard led the other half of the QRF up to reinforce OP Topside. By this time the OP was still receiving heavy enemy fire from a distance but was no longer under the threat of a direct ground assault. The insurgents continued to place small arms and RPG fire in the vicinity of the American position from at least three overlooking hilltops. Closer to the OP, additional enemy forces remained in various hidden folds of terrain surrounding the site. The nearest such hilltop was a house approximately 100 to 150 yards to the southeast and above the OP, the next closest one was a large compound across the Wayskawdi Creek ravine 300 yards to the northeast, and a third was a large compound to the south of the TCP and COP. Beeson was now at OP Topside:

> We just continued to hold our position under fire. We then took an RPG right above my head that hit the rock and a tree and forced me to the ground. Right after that, either an RPG or a grenade landed in the CP area and blew up cutting the LRAS3 in two pieces and wounding [three men].[118]

To help eliminate the insurgents that remained close by, Stockard threw a number of fragmentation grenades to his front. The enemy fire at the OP died down shortly thereafter.

While the insurgents kept pressure on the OP, Thurman's group continued to fight a determined enemy. The driver of one of the HMMWVs remembered:

> I was going to turn the truck around in case we needed to move quickly. As soon as I turned the truck around a volley of RPGs started hitting inside the wire [just to the west of the road]. First Lieutenant Thurman jumped back in the truck. I looked to my left and saw an RPG explode about five meters from my truck. I told First Lieutenant Thurman, "Sir, those RPGs are RIGHT here!" He said, "I know, drive!"[119]

The driver had vivid memories of the intensity of the enemy fire, "A bunch of RPGs started blowing up to our 9 o'clock. Maybe 10 to 15 RPGs. I've never seen that many RPGs hit at once before. It literally took my breath away to see."[120] In addition to the RPG rockets, enemy small arms fire also remained intense. One of the vehicle gunners called out that he had identified insurgents between the TCP and OP Topside. The vehicle driver remembered, "We engaged that area with small arms, frags [fragmentation hand grenades], and Mk-19. We just couldn't seem to kill all of them."[121]

After Silvernale's squad had cleared the hotel and bazaar complex, the remaining insurgents were out in the open. Thurman directed Silvernale to throw yellow smoke grenades onto identified enemy positions to mark them for attacks by the Apaches. The attack helicopters responded quickly with multiple gun runs, which came within several yards of the friendly positions. However, the Apache gunners took advantage of the targeting capabilities of their cannon system to provide precision fires that avoided hitting the Americans. The attack helicopters followed up the effects of this fire by shooting Hellfire missiles into the buildings within the village of Wanat from which the insurgents had been firing. Then they shifted their

171

fires towards the enemy positions that had been threatening OP Topside. At 0639 the Apaches fired their first Hellfire missile into the large compound to the northeast of the COP across the stream valley. Although fire poured out of the building, the insurgents continued to use it. Accordingly, at 0820 in response to the terse exasperated command from the ground, "level the buildings," an Apache fired a second Hellfire into the ruined structure which finished the job.[122]

The wave of nearly continuous Apache gun and missile runs began to slowly but perceptibly weaken the insurgent resistance. Within four hours of the battle's start, the insurgents began to disengage. The balance in the fight had initially been tipped in favor of the beleaguered 2d Platoon when the two Hedgerow Apaches had arrived one hour after the battle began. By 0830, after the arrival of the 1st Platoon QRF, the Coalition forces had clearly regained the initiative.

The MEDEVACs at Wanat

The first of the two MEDEVAC helicopters, which had been waiting at Camp Blessing, landed at Wanat between 0552 and 0605. The MEDEVACs used two landing zones (LZs) at Wanat. The first was the designated LZ at the southern end of the open field at COP Kahler, the second was an impromptu LZ set up on a terrace to the south of OP Topside. The Blackhawk with the callsign Dustoff 35 went to the LZ at COP Kahler and Dustoff 36 landed near the OP.[123]

Dustoffs 35 and 36 were from the 1st Platoon, C Company, 6th Battalion, 101st Aviation Regiment, stationed at FOB Fenty at Jalalabad Airfield. Chief Warrant Officer 3 Christopher Hill commanded Dustoff 35 and Chief Warrant Officer 2 Wayne McDonald commanded Dustoff 36. A flight surgeon, Captain Justin Madill, was also on Dustoff 36. As previously mentioned, the two Blackhawks accompanied the Apaches from Jalalabad as far as Camp Blessing. After the situation stabilized a little at Wanat, the two aircraft proceeded up the Waygal Valley to the battlefield.

Normally a flight surgeon would not be onboard a MEDEVAC flight but Madill stated, "I knew that when both MEDEVACs are needed there may be multiple patients. I also knew that 0437 local was an unlikely time to receive a routine MEDEVAC call."[124] Heavy firing still ringed COP Kahler as the MEDEVAC flights headed in. Madill remembered he "heard our pilots communicating with the Apache crews who were engaging a large enemy force on the east side of the valley."[125] This was the enemy force that was located to the east of the OP and still attacking

OP Topside. He also recalled, "En route to the COP Kahler OP I heard the ground element (Chosen 6 [Myer]) guiding our pilots to their location. I heard machine gun fire during the ground elements' radio transmissions and saw plumes of smoke on the ground in the area of COP Kahler from explosions."[126]

Both MEDEVAC helicopters reported observing AAF on the ground in close proximity to the LZs as they arrived over Wanat. The ground troops marked the LZs with violet smoke and VS-17 ground recognition panels. McDonald, in Dustoff 36, recalled the dramatic sights and smells he witnessed once he landed, stating, "The perimeter of the LZ was on fire to the north. There was yelling and screaming coming from the back of the aircraft. I could smell the gunpowder that was spent from rounds expended in the firefight."[127]

As Dustoff 35 came in to land at the LZ south of COP Kahler, its pilots had trouble identifying the landing site because heavy smoke from the nearby TOW fire obscured it. The smoke and dust was so thick that Dustoff 35 needed two passes before it could safely put down. The aircraft received ground fire on its approach and landing, to include one noticeable "boom" that rattled the helicopter frame. Staff Sergeant Atwon Thompkins, part of the aircraft crew, remembered that he had seen an insurgent within "three yards" of the southern concertina wire perimeter.[128]

After Dustoff 35 loaded five wounded men and departed, the second MEDEVAC helicopter, Dustoff 36, came forward. Because of airspace management issues, only one MEDEVAC aircraft at a time could operate at Wanat. Dustoff 36 approached the OP where it had been directed to perform a hoist evacuation. This entailed the use of a heavy anchor shaped piece of equipment that could be winched down from the helicopter. The hoist could only retrieve one man at a time and required the helicopter to hover over the scene while the equipment was operated. Although the paratroopers at the OP threw a smoke grenade, the pilots were unable to identify it, and the helicopter had to turn to the east and attempt another landing. On their second approach, the crewmembers were able to observe another smoke grenade and the pilots took the initiative to land instead on a single terrace to the south of the OP that was just large and flat enough. This eliminated the need for the hoist and the dangerous stationary hover.[129]

Dustoff 36 landed and the crew began the arduous task of loading the wounded while crossing uneven terrain. Staff Sergeant Matthew S. Kinney (the flight medic) and Staff Sergeant William R. Helfrich (the crew chief) were the first crewmembers off the helicopter and had to traverse a series of "four to six foot tall terraces" with the wounded to return to the helicopter. Kinney remembered simply stepping through the single strand of concertina wire around the OP. One man pushed and the other one pulled and it was exhausting work in body armor. The flight medic further recalled that by the end of the day, "I was smoked."[130]

Madill followed the two NCOs, taking in the scene of the battlefield near the OP. Stopping at a machine gun position he observed Garcia lying on the ground and realized that he could do nothing for him. On the terrace below lay three other dead men from the 2d Platoon. Madill recalled, "A US Soldier approached me and I asked him if there were any other patients. He responded, 'No.' I pointed to the KIA and asked 'are they dead?' He looked at me and stated, 'they're gone.'"[131] However, there were other wounded to be evacuated from the OP area. Dustoff 36 ultimately departed with four wounded men from the OP location, including Pitts, the only remaining member of the original garrison who was still at the OP.[132]

Of the dead who had fought at OP Topside, two Soldiers were found away from the OP. Specialist Gunnar Zwilling was found two terraces down about 15 yards from the center of the OP. Myer found Specialist Jason Bogar beyond the sleeping terrace to the northwest of the OP in the direction of the nearest buildings.[133]

Both MEDEVAC helicopters took their patients to the medical facility at Camp Wright in Asadabad, less than 15 miles away. Following these first flights, two additional MEDEVAC helicopters, Dustoff 34 and Profit 71, joined them for subsequent medical evacuations. All four helicopters repeatedly returned to Wanat. Chief Warrant Officer 4 Joseph Callaway was the pilot-in-charge of Dustoff 34 with Chief Warrant Officer 2 Nicholas Dance as co-pilot. When the Asadabad medical station reached capacity, these Blackhawks took casualties from Wanat to a larger facility at Jalalabad.[134]

After the first two MEDEVAC flights departed Wanat, Profit 71 arrived. Captain Kevin King, the physician's assistant onboard, recalled, "As we came in for a landing, I heard the pilot ask someone on the ground where we should land the helicopter, the shaky voice on the other end said, 'Don't care, just land.'"[135] The crew was able to take advantage of a momentary lapse in the fighting and landed at the LZ to the south of the main COP. They quickly loaded five wounded men including the badly burned ANA soldier. Initially intended for Asadabad, the flight was diverted to Jalalabad because King became seriously concerned with the condition of the Afghan. Chief Warrant Officer 2 Isaac Smith, one of the pilots, remembered:

That was when Captain King said, "How long is it going to take us to get back to Jalalabad Airfield?" I informed him of an approximate time, 20 minutes or so, and he said, "It needs to be as fast as possible because this guy in the back isn't looking very good at all." Our escorts were the close combat elements so they couldn't keep up with us at this point. I instructed Captain Minnie to go to 100 percent torque on both engines and fly as fast as possible. I then informed [the Apaches] that if we didn't get back now, there's a heavy possibility that one of the Soldiers would die. So, we flew back, single ship, through the Konar, back into JAF.[136]

King simply noted of his patient's deteriorating condition, "I needed to get him out of there, so I told the pilot to put his foot down and he did."[137]

Throughout the day, additional MEDEVAC helicopters rotated through Wanat, first evacuating the wounded, and then the bodies of those who had died on the battlefield. Prophet 71, Dustoff 35, and Dustoff 36 all returned at least twice to Wanat. Stockard remembered, "There was so many MEDEVAC birds that came in, I lost count how many birds actually came in that day."[138] Soldiers on the ground loading their wounded comrades, continuously changing priorities as more seriously wounded troopers were shifted to be placed sooner on the aircraft. Aboard the helicopters, the medics were far too absorbed in the effort to save the badly wounded men, who were covered in blood and dirt, to even learn their identities. Additional UH-60 utility helicopters were later pressed into service as impromptu MEDEVACs. All this resulted in a certain amount of administrative confusion concerning the order of evacuation but all the wounded were evacuated according to the severity of their condition. No more paratroopers died at Wanat after the arrival of the first MEDEVAC helicopter.[139]

In total, MEDEVAC crews evacuated 16 American and 4 ANA Soldiers from the battlefield. The professionalism of the MEDEVAC crews and their courage in flying into the smoke of burning vehicles and buildings and the heavy ground fire undoubtedly saved many lives.[140] That courage impressed the badly wounded Pitts:

I've seen a lot of MEDEVACs but I've never seen anything like what they did. It was one of the most amazing things I've ever seen. I actually wrote the crew chief of the bird I was on [Staff Sergeant Kinney]. I couldn't believe the pilots landed where they did, that exposed. I couldn't believe it. The Apaches were doing gun runs about 30 meters away.[141]

Hissong echoed Pitts' opinion:

> We were still taking fire when I saw the MEDEVAC birds come in. What they did next was the single greatest thing I have ever seen a pilot do. Instead of landing down at the COP, they landed on an extremely small flat spot next to OP Topside. They were taking heavy fire the whole time but managed to get our critical casualties evacuated. They landed in that same spot about 10 more times before the end of the day.[142]

The Consolidation at COP Kahler

TF *Rock* responded aggressively to the situation at Wanat by sending additional units as QRFs as transportation assets became available. The second QRF that TF *Rock* dispatched consisted of the 3d Platoon of A Company, that company's tactical command post (TAC), and a section from the battalion scout platoon. The commander of Able Company, Captain David Nelson, commanded the forces that arrived at Wanat in six HMMWVs at 0820 after a drive from an outpost on the Pech River beyond Camp Blessing. Nelson then assumed command of the defense of the COP. Elsewhere in the battalion, Battle Company Commander Captain Daniel Kearney, alerted his entire unit in the Korengal Valley for an impending move to Wanat. However, Kearney only had to dispatch his 3d Platoon, led by First Lieutenant Michael Moad, to COP Kahler. Moad's platoon moved via CH-47 Chinook helicopters, arriving at approximately 1330. Nelson gave Moad specific responsibility for the OP Topside area.[143]

Moad and his platoon sergeant, David Barbaret, were extremely displeased with the location of OP Topside. As Barbaret observed, "My initial perception on the battlefield was why are we in the low ground, where are the fortifications, and why don't we own any high ground?"[144] Moad and Barbaret felt that the dead ground to the north and east could not be adequately covered from the OP and they immediately scouted for a better location. Moad recalled:

> I took the remainder of my platoon to the large compound about 150 meters to the east of OP Topside in the high ground. The compound offered dominating observation above the village of Wanat and a good majority of avenues of approach into the proposed combat outpost. Moreover, this position was previously used as an attack position against Chosen Company evident by the large amount of expended AK-47 brass. Lastly, we were not actually first to this location; however, one squad from the Able Company QRF had occupied and maintained this position until we relieved them in the mid afternoon.[145]

The platoon then began to improve the position in the compound and gather information:

> Once in position, I had my platoon re-clear the compound and then selected positions for my Soldiers to man while offering them the best cover and concealment. We used the compound as our defensive position and then sent out reconnaissance and surveillance teams to search the nearby area [for any intelligence information]. We set out claymores in all likely avenues of approach and began to use surrounding rocks and sandbags we had carried into Wanat to build up defendable positions. Once in position, my platoon forward observer and I conducted terrain denial operations by using the 120-mm, which was still in operation around the Chosen command post.[146]

By the time the sun went down on 13 July, Moad and his platoon had completely evacuated OP Topside, established the new OP in the compound, and integrated the scout section into the position.[147]

Using a helicopter provided by Deputy CJTF-101 Commander Brigadier General Milley, Ostlund flew to Wanat from Camp Blessing on the afternoon of 13 July. Both Ostlund and Colonel Charles Preysler, the TF *Bayonet* commander, later visited Wanat several times but neither remained on site. However, as previously mentioned, Ostlund did dispatch his S3, Major Scott Himes, and the battalion TAC, to take overall command at Wanat. Milley had arrived at Blessing earlier in the day at the urging of his boss, Major General Schloesser, after a stop at the TF *Bayonet* headquarters at Jalalabad. Once there, he recalled that after lending his helicopter to Ostlund he "operated from the TF *Rock* [TOC] since it had sufficient radios so that I could exercise effective [command and control] back to the CJTF."[148]

Additional assets continued to flow into Wanat throughout the day. New arrivals included a large force of ANA commandos and a small US Special Forces element that advised the ANA unit. The Afghan commandos were highly experienced and extremely well trained special operations soldiers. Their arrival swelled the force at Wanat to over 200. On the next day, 14 July, a platoon of pathfinders from the 101st Airborne Division deployed to assist in the clearance of the high ground around the COP.[149]

At first light on 14 July, the ANA commandos conducted a meticulous house-to-house search of Wanat, gathering considerable intelligence information, and performing a careful analysis of battle damage. The

Wanat District Center, the hub of local government, provided the biggest surprise. The district center, which also served as the headquarters for a 20 man local police force, contained a large arsenal of weapons. The majority of these weapons had been recently fired. Also present were a large quantity of 7.62-mm ammunition and RPGs.[150]

Even though their police station was located nearby, the Wanat contingent of the Afghan National Police (ANP) played no significant role in the battle, and the ANP did not in any way support the defense of Wanat. One Chosen Company sergeant specifically recalled that during the later stages of the engagement on 13 July, "We pushed past COP Kahler down the road and received fire from alleyways and a house on the other side of the draw and we returned fire. The ANP compound was in the vicinity to my left about 200 meters. There was no fire coming from there. They were not engaging the enemy though they could have. After the fight, I saw ANP walking around like nothing had happened. Their uniforms were all clean."[151]

TOW squad leader Grimm had a chance to visit the district center after the battle. Grimm recalled:

In the Wanat ANP compound I saw it was *untouched* [his emphasis], though it was on the ingress/egress route of the AAF [anti-Afghan force] that attacked from the mosque and bazaar. I saw a lot of expended brass inside their perimeter, southwest side (facing us). ANA commandoes found a lot of bloody uniforms. All the ANP were in fresh brand new uniforms, which is unusual since they are only issued one uniform and usually they are dirty. They also appeared freshly shaven with razor nicks on their faces. There were also over 100 weapons, including AKs, PKMs, PRKs, RPGs, pistols, and shotguns. They were dirty and had recently been fired.[152]

The discovery of such an arsenal provided very strong evidence of ANP collusion with the insurgents. In short order the Afghan Government relieved the district police chief of his duties and arrested him, while disarming and dissolving the local police detachment. The Afghans also arrested the district governor after replacing him, although he was later released.[153]

The commandos searched over 100 structures in Wanat. All were vacant the day after the battle. Inside one house there was a large cache of medical supplies along with used BDUs. Another building yielded four AK-47 automatic rifles, two Realistic© model TRC-222 40-channel hand held radios, floodlights, blasting caps hidden inside a first aid kit, detonator cord, and a video camcorder with the tape still inside it. Grimm noted that in one house, "I saw about six ANP ID cards, a four inch stack of laminate, loose photos, everything to make ID cards. There was a camcorder and weapons."[154] The search of Wanat provided overwhelming evidence that the town had been completely infiltrated by the insurgents and used as a base from which to launch the attack.[155]

Skirmishes between the Coalition and insurgent forces in the Waygal region continued throughout the remainder of 13-14 July. Indeed, several times during that night, small enemy groups probed the American perimeter looking for gaps in the defenses. The vigorous application of overwhelming American firepower, including fire from an AC-130 gunship on station overhead quickly ended these probes. Other attacks involved small parties of insurgents who were in hiding or were attempting to exfiltrate the area. By the evening of 13 July, ISR (intelligence, surveillance, and reconnaissance) assets, including a Predator UAV, were scouring the countryside adjacent to COP Kahler, and rapidly identifying AAF forces that the Americans then engaged with mortars, field artillery, and CAS. The Coalition forces implemented careful fire support controls and made optimal use of field artillery, helicopter gunships, and CAS.[156]

By the afternoon of 15 July, the Americans had expended a large amount of munitions in and around Wanat, including almost 100 155-mm artillery rounds; numerous bombs from various types of airplanes including A-10 and F-15 attack jets and AC-130 gunships; hundreds of 30-mm cannon rounds; several score of 2.75-inch rockets; two Hellfire missiles delivered by the Apaches; and additional Hellfires delivered by other assets including UAVs. However, with the exception of a number of artillery projectiles and the majority of the Apache strikes, nearly all of this ordnance had been expended after 0630 on 13 July.[157]

By 15 July, there was also a considerable amount of combat power and command presence in the Wanat area. Himes, the TF *Rock* S3, commanded this force which included elements from three TF *Rock* companies plus additional Afghan and American special operations forces. Upon his arrival on the afternoon of 13 July, Himes stated that he "found the [US Special Forces] team leader and discussed the way ahead. The [Special Forces officer's] initial desire was to conduct an approach march to the northeast along the valley floor with a march objective of Qalay-e-gal [Kegal] [four miles] to the east."[158] The Special Forces (SF) commander wanted to aggressively maneuver to seal off the major route of enemy egress, an exit route that ran down the deep defile of the Wayskawdi Creek, by seizing the small village of Qualay-e-gal which entirely commanded every route through the creek valley. If adopted, this tactical approach was certainly risky, although the massive quantity of American firepower and ISR assets would have mitigated such risks. Still, there was the potential to inflict a significant, if not crushing defeat on the insurgents. Himes, however, worried that there were insufficient Coalition forces to secure their northern flank in the region and did not support the SF team leader's plan. Instead the American and Afghan Special Forces created a 40 man QRF within Wanat and pushed out other elements after dark in all directions to occupy high ground to the northwest, northeast, and southeast. With an AC-130 gunship now also on station at night, Wanat was relatively secure. Certainly, in the aftermath of the 13 July attack, this approach was the prudent course of action.[159]

The Withdrawal from the Waygal Valley

Ostlund gave Himes a pair of alternatives at 1700 on 14 July: either continue with the construction of a permanent COP in Wanat or withdraw from the town. The officers on the ground began to plan for both options. Several hours later, the senior American commanders made the decision to withdraw.

Just as a variety of factors had influenced the decision to establish COP Kahler at Wanat, a range of factors influenced the decision to evacuate. Myer made the original recommendation for withdrawal, stating that the following considerations led him to that judgment:

> After the fight on July 13th in Wanat, the situation for occupation was drastically changed. No matter how much Coalition forces conducted [information operations] to explain/battle the circumstances for occupation of Wanat, it would be viewed as hostile. The population in and around Wanat had clearly supported the enemy and did not maintain the conditions for Coalition force support and projects. Wanat is ideal because of the ground LOC [line of communication] open to the rest of the BN [battalion] but that would take significant manpower to keep open.[160]

Ostlund explained that after 13 July, the situation in Wanat was not favorable for success:

> Working [the lines of operation] was going to take an incredible influx of resources for security. The district governor was going to need to be replaced, the market was shot up [in fact one section of the bazaar was burned to the ground] and

we were not going to reward the area with $1.4 million in projects. The conditions radically changed on the morning of 13 July 2008 and the Wanat population priced themselves out of our desire to assist them at that time.[161]

Ostlund recommended that the Coalition pull out of the area, finish paving the road between Nangalam and Wanat, replace the local Afghan leadership, retrain the ANP, and then re-engage the population. The TF *Rock* commander noted that TF *Duke*, the unit deploying into northeast Afghanistan to replace TF *Bayonet*, had reservations about manning COP Kahler. Downplaying objections to a withdrawal based on casualty lists, Ostlund commented that, "I thought the argument, 'we paid too much to abandon this place' was a DUMB emotional versus logical, tactical, and supportable argument."[162]

On 14 July, Colonel Preysler and the CJTF-101 staff presented Major General Schloesser with four options: attack, withdraw, hold, or battle hand-off to TF *Duke*. Schloesser described the process he used to reach the final decision:

> The next day, the 14th, I had a staff recommendation from my staff at the CJTF level. When Preysler briefed me, he had Ostlund's as well as Captain Myer's recommendations, and they were all to evacuate. . . . This is Myer's recommendation to me; "After 13 July, the tactical problem set reference, geography and human terrain changed. The land is no longer technically tenable. We need more defensible land, which would displace the population and require a much larger force to hold and build. The population proved corrupted or intimidated. The land and human terrain are no longer tenable." He states it tactically but operationally, when I took that thought process – and again, Ostlund felt the same way, so did Preysler. They weighed it against what we were actually able to achieve with the people there in the Waygal Valley and it didn't make good tactical or operational sense to maintain that presence.[163]

Schloesser thought that his overall lack of resources severely constrained what his command could achieve in the Waygal Valley:

> The truth is I also did not have the resources to be able to go in and do what I knew was necessary which was to relocate to higher ground. In other words, we would be moving away from the people so we could have enough force there that we could

not only defend the base, which would be required, but also so we could be dismounted and be able to patrol and through those patrols actually influence the people. Frankly, my staff was divided. The ops, I believe, was basically of the same mind that we did not have the resources and it didn't make a cost-benefit ratio, didn't make sense for counterinsurgency. We were not going to achieve the effects we needed. We were obviously not separating the people from the enemy. We were not achieving any transformational types of things with the economy nor was there much promise. We could not link the people to a totally corrupt ANP, and the ANA were not wanted there. They were outsiders just like we were.[164]

Although the CJTF commander acknowledged that his intelligence section recommended a Coalition presence in the Waygal Valley to prevent insurgent movement into the Pech Valley, the CJTF-101 commander decided to withdraw all forces from Wanat and the valley.[165]

Early on the morning of 15 July, instructions came down from CJTF-101 through TF *Bayonet* to TF *Rock* to evacuate Wanat. The American force there immediately began the process of withdrawal. Helicopters began arriving and trucks began pouring in from Camp Blessing. The retrograde movement was executed as rapidly as transportation assets could be moved to Wanat and supplies could be loaded. Unlike the limitations during the establishment of COP Kahler, there were plentiful resources available for the withdrawal. The final helicopter flight, which departed in the early morning of 15 July, contained the seven remaining C Company mortarmen and their mortars. With all of the Americans having returned safely to their respective original bases, only a few partially destroyed fighting positions remained at the former site of COP Kahler.[166]

Aftermath

At dusk on 13 July, both sides at Wanat had sustained heavy losses. American casualties were nine killed and 27 wounded, with 16 of the latter requiring evacuation. Five ANA soldiers were wounded, with four evacuated. This total represents the highest casualty rate in any American battle in the Afghan War to date. All of the American deaths were sustained in the first two hours of combat (between 0420 and 0630). AAF casualties are, of course speculative but, based on the effects of American firepower, had to be significantly higher. The insurgents were highly skilled at evacuating their wounded and dead from the battlefield and recovering their casualties is an extremely high priority. It was rare that Coalition forces ever found more than a few scattered blood trails.[167]

Only a single enemy corpse was recovered from the battlefield. An American found the body of this insurgent in the concertina wire at the OP where he had become entangled. This is almost certainly the insurgent that McKaig killed with his claymore. The paratrooper who recovered this corpse later recalled, "I seen an enemy KIA in the wire . . . we pulled him out of the wire he was wearing a chest rig and off white clothing and a BDU coat under his top after getting him out of the wire. We pulled him down over near the OP and searched him. The enemy KIA had three AK-47 mag[azine]s on him, all were empty. No AK-47 was found. Nothing else was on the enemy KIA."[168] Later the Afghan commandos identified the dead insurgent as being Arab rather than Afghan, strongly intimating that he was a foreign fighter. Based on various intelligence sources, US estimates of enemy fatalities ranged from 21 to 52, with another 45 believed to have been wounded.[169]

Since 2006, the Coalition had attempted to gain control of the Waygal Valley by asserting military power and using reconstruction and other programs to win the support of the population. For many reasons, by mid 2008 those efforts had not borne fruit. Some would argue that the battle at Wanat on 13 July 2008 was the most direct evidence of that failure. Moreover, that action had convinced senior US military leaders that the price for success in the Waygal Valley was too dear and would hinder more successful efforts elsewhere. The choice to withdraw was difficult and serves as an excellent example of the tough decisions that US commanders had to make on a regular basis in Afghanistan in 2007-2008.

Notes

1. Sergeant John Hayes, interview by Douglas R. Cubbison, Combat Studies Institute, Fort Leavenworth, KS, 21 April 2009, 9; Corporal Tyler M. Stafford, interview by Douglas R. Cubbison, Combat Studies Institute, Fort Leavenworth, KS, 10 February 2009, 9–10; Sergeant Jason Oakes, interview by Douglas R. Cubbison, Combat Studies Institute, Fort Leavenworth, KS, 18 February 2009, 6.

2. Exhibit 38 (SPC, 2d Plt, C/2-503d IN, statement), CJTF-101, "Army Regulation 15-6 Investigation into Battle of Wanat (Redacted, Unclassified Version)" (Camp Blessing, Afghanistan, 16 October 2008), 2; Exhibit 34 (SSG, 1st Plt, D/2-503d IN, statement), CJTF-101, "Army Regulation 15-6 Investigation into the Battle of Wanat (Redacted, Unclassified Version) (Camp Blessing, Afghanistan, 16 October 2008), 1.

3. Exhibit 10 (SFC, 1st Plt, C/2-503d IN, statement), CJTF-101, "Army Regulation 15-6 Investigation into Battle of Wanat (Redacted, Unclassified Version)" (Korengal Outpost, Afghanistan, 16 October 2008), 1.

4. Exhibit 34, CJTF-101, "Army Regulation 15-6 Investigation into Battle of Wanat, 5-6.

5. Exhibit 10, CJTF-101, "Army Regulation 15-6 Investigation into Battle of Wanat, 1."

6. Exhibit 49 (SPC, 1st Plt, D/2-503d IN, statement), CJTF-101, "Army Regulation 15-6 Investigation into Battle of Wanat (Redacted, Unclassified Version)" (Camp Blessing, Afghanistan, 16 October 2008), 1-2; Exhibit 34, CJTF-101, "Army Regulation 15-6 Investigation into Battle of Wanat (Redacted, Unclassified Version), "2.

7. Phillips' section consisted of himself, Sergeant Hector Chavez, Sergeant Jared Gilmore, Staff Sergeant Jesse Queck, Specialist Sergio Abad, and Private First Class Scott Stenoski.

8. Exhibit 17 (SGT, Mortar Section, C/2-503d IN, statement), CJTF-101, "Army Regulation 15-6 Investigation into Battle of Wanat (Redacted, Unclassified Version)"(Landstuhl Regional Medical Center, Germany, 17 July 2008)," 2-3; Sergeant Hector Chavez, interview by Douglas R. Cubbison, Combat Studies Institute, Fort Leavenworth, KS, 19 March 2009, 6, 12; Kate Wiltrout, "Soldier from Eastern Shore Recounts Deadly Battle in Afghanistan, SSG Jesse L. Queck," *Hampton Roads Virginian–Pilot,* 19 July 2008, http://hamptonroads.com/2008/07/soldier-eastern-shore-recounts-deadly-battle-afghanistan (accessed 2 February 2009); Private First Class Scott Stenoski, interview by Matt Matthews, Combat Studies Institute, Fort Leavenworth, KS, 4 November 2008, 2.

9. Exhibit 17, CJTF-101, "Army Regulation 15-6 Investigation into Battle of Wanat (Redacted, Unclassified Version)," 3-4. Chavez, interview, 6–7, 12; Exhibit 64 (SSG, Mortar Section, C/2-503d IN, statement), CJTF-101, "Army Regulation 15-6 Investigation into Battle of Wanat (Redacted, Unclassified Version)" (Landstuhl Regional Medical Center, Germany, 16 July 2008), 4-5.

10. Sergeant First Class David Dzwik, interview by Matt Matthews, Combat Studies Institute, Fort Leavenworth, KS, 21 October 2008, 6.

11. Exhibit 17, CJTF-101, "Army Regulation 15-6 Investigation into Battle of Wanat (Redacted, Unclassified Version)," 3-4; ; Exhibit 62 (SSG, Mortar Section, C/2-503d IN, statement), CJTF-101, "Army Regulation 15-6 Investigation into Battle of Wanat (Redacted, Unclassified Version)" (Camp Blessing, Afghanistan, 16 July 2008), 1, 5; Sergeant First Class David Dzwik, interview by Douglas R. Cubbison, Combat Studies Institute, Fort Leavenworth, KS, 2 April 2009, 12; Chavez , interview, 19 March 2008, 6–7, 12; Exhibit 64 (SSG, Mortar Section, C/2-503d IN, statement), CJTF-101, "Army Regulation 15-6 Investigation into Battle of Wanat (Redacted, Unclassified Version)" (Landstuhl Regional Medical Center, Germany, 16 July 2008), 4-5.

12. Exhibit 64, CJTF-101, "Army Regulation 15-6 Investigation into Battle of Wanat (Redacted, Unclassified Version)," 6; Stenoski, interview, 4 November 2008, 1, 5; Exhibit 62, CJTF-101, "Army Regulation 15-6 Investigation into Battle of Wanat (Redacted, Unclassified Version)," 4.

13. Exhibit 18 (SPC, C/62d Eng Bn, statement), CJTF-101, "Army Regulation 15-6 Investigation into Battle of Wanat (Redacted, Unclassified Version)" (Camp Blessing, Afghanistan, 16 July 2008), 3.

14. Sergeant Erik Aass, interview by Matt Matthews, Combat Studies Institute, Fort Leavenworth, KS, 13 January 2009, 6.

15. Exhibit 70, (Specialist, 2d Squad, 2d Platoon, C/2-503d IN, statement), CJTF-101, "Army Regulation 15-6 Investigation into Battle of Wanat (Redacted, Unclassified Version)" (Camp Blessing, Afghanistan, 16 July 2008), 2-3; Sergeant Jeffrey Scantlin, interview by Douglas R. Cubbison, Combat Studies Institute, Fort Leavenworth, KS, 20 August 2009, 2–3.

16. Aass onterview, 13 January 2009, 7; Chief Warrant Officer 2 Isaac Smith, interview by Douglas R. Cubbison, Combat Studies Institute, Fort Leavenworth, KS, 19 May 2009, 4. The intensity of the fabric fire was confirmed by Sergeant Nicholas Ehler, UH-60 crew chief. Sergeant Nicholas Ehler, interview by Douglas R. Cubbison, Combat Studies Institute, Fort Leavenworth, KS, 18 July 2009, 5.

17. Captain Matthew Myer, interview by Matt Matthews, Combat Studies Institute, Fort Leavenworth, KS, 1 December 2008, 10.

18. Captain James Fisher and Captain (P) Ryan Berdiner, interview by Douglas R. Cubbison, Combat Studies Institute, Fort Leavenworth, KS, 16 July 2009, 1–2; Colonel William Ostlund, e-mails to Douglas R. Cubbison, Combat Studies Institute, Fort Leavenworth, KS, 24 February 2009 and 8 May 2009.

19. Lieutenant Colonel Stephen J. Maranian, "Field Artillery Fires in the Mountains of Afghanistan," Fires (July–September 2008): 36.

20. Fisher and Berdiner, interview, 16 July 2009, 1–2.

21. Exhibit 36, CENTCOM, "Re-investigation into the Combat Action at Wanat Village," 128. Qualified US Air Force forward air controllers (FACs) were not routinely assigned to infantry companies or platoons in Afghanistan.

22. Aass, interview, 13 January 2009, 6.

23. Exhibit 64, CJTF-101, "Army Regulation 15-6 Investigation into Battle of Wanat (Redacted, Unclassified Version)," 7.

24. Staff Sergeant Jonathan Benton, interview by Douglas R. Cubbison, Combat Studies Institute, Fort Leavenworth, KS, 4 August 2009, 8–9. The available sources dispute the presence of an ANA DShK heavy machine gun at Wanat. While one ETT member claims the gun was present, the more experienced and senior ETT NCOIC (noncommissioned officer in charge) states that the unit's DShK, which had been previously used at Bella, was down for maintenance at Camp Blessing during the Wanat fight. See Exhibit 38a (Sergeant, USMC, ETT 5-3, interview) to US Central Command (CENTCOM), "Re-investigation into the Combat Action at Wanat Village, Wygal District, Nuristan Province, Afghanistan, on 13 July 2008 (Redacted), 28; See Exhibit 42b (Staff Sergeant, USMC, ETT 5-3, interview) to US Central Command (CENTCOM), "Re-investigation into the Combat Action at Wanat Village, Wygal District, Nuristan Province, Afghanistan, on 13 July 2008 (Redacted), 27.

25. Exhibit 32 (SPC, C/2-503d IN, statement), CJTF-101, "Army Regulation 15-6 Investigation into Battle of Wanat (Redacted, Unclassified Version)" (Camp Blessing, Afghanistan, 16 July 2008), 2. CLP refers to Break-Free brand CLP— cleaner, lubricant, and preservative, the standard and tactical weapons cleaner and lubricant.

26. Exhibit 64, CJTF-101, "Army Regulation 15-6 Investigation into Battle of Wanat (Redacted, Unclassified Version)," 5.

27. Aass, interview, 13 January 2009, 11.

28. Exhibit 47 (PFC, C/2-503d IN, statement), CJTF-101, "Army Regulation 15-6 Investigation into Battle of Wanat (Redacted, Unclassified Version)" (Camp Blessing, Afghanistan, 16 July 2008), 4.

29. Sergeant Brian C. Hissong, personal statement, "Combat Outpost Kahler, July 8–15," (not dated).

30. Exhibit 36 (SPC, 2/C/2-503d IN, statement), CJTF-101, "Army Regulation 15-6 Investigation into Battle of Wanat (Redacted, Unclassified Version)" (Camp Blessing, Afghanistan, 16 July 2008), 2.

31. Exhibit 36 (SPC, 2/C/2-503d IN, statement), CJTF-101.

32. Hissong, personal statement.

33. Exhibit 36, CJTF-101, "Army Regulation 15-6 Investigation into Battle of Wanat," 2-3; Exhibit 67 (SSG, 2/C/2-503d IN, statement), CJTF-101, "Army Regulation 15-6 Investigation into Battle of Wanat (Redacted, Unclassified Version)" (Landstuhl Region Medical Center, Germany, 17 July 2008), 4; Exhibit 41 (SGT, 2/C/2-503d IN, statement), CJTF-101, "Army Regulation 15-6 Investigation into Battle of Wanat (Redacted, Unclassified Version)" (Camp Blessing, Afghanistan, 16 July 2008), 2.

34. Chavez, interview, 19 March 2008, 11.

35. Dzwik, interview, 21 October 2008, 7.

36. Hissong, personal statement.

37. Staff Sergeant Luis Repreza, interview by Douglas R. Cubbison, Combat Studies Institute, Fort Leavenworth, KS, 23 February 2009, 8. According to at least one of the Marine ETT members, the ANA did have certain limitations and problems, however. Their fire was inaccurate and erratic. The Afghan who was badly burned by the TOW explosion had left his fighting position. And it seemed to the Marine that the insurgents were not targeting the ANAs, shooting over them at Americans. See Exhibit 38a (Sergeant, USMC, ETT 5-3, interview) to US Central Command (CENTCOM), "Re-investigation into the Combat Action at Wanat Village, Wygal District, Nuristan Province, Afghanistan, on 13 July 2008 (Redacted), 11, 21.

38. Exhibit 42b (Staff Sergeant, USMC, ETT 5-3, interview) to US Central Command (CENTCOM), "Re-investigation into the Combat Action at Wanat Village, Wygal District, Nuristan Province, Afghanistan, on 13 July 2008 (Redacted), 38-42.

39. The defense of OP Topside is described in the following sources: Sergeant Ryan Pitts, interview by Matt Matthews, Combat Studies Institute, Fort Leavenworth, KS, 14 January 2009; Specialist Chris McKaig, interview by Matt Matthews, Combat Studies Institute, Fort Leavenworth, KS, 19 November 2008; Stafford, interview; and Exhibits 27, 50, 63, and 77(C/2-503d IN, statements), CJTF-101, "Army Regulation 15-6 Investigation into Battle of Wanat."

40. Captain Benjamin Pry, interview by Douglas R. Cubbison, Combat Studies Institute, Fort Leavenworth, KS, 6 May 2009, 10.

41. Exhibit 34, CJTF-101, "Army Regulation 15-6 Investigation into Battle of Wanat, 5-6.

42. Exhibit 34, CJTF-101, 6.

43. Stafford, interview, 10 February 2009, 10.

44. Stafford, interview, 10 February 2009, 10–11.

45. Stafford, interview, 10 February 2009, 11.

46. Stafford, interview, 10 February 2009, 11.

47. Pitts, interview, 14 January 2009, 9.

48. Stafford, interview, 10 February 2009, 13.

49. Stafford, interview, 10 February 2009, 13.

50. Stafford, interview, 10 February 2009, 13.

51. McKaig, interview, 19 November 2008, 3; Specialist Chris McKaig, "Stand to at Wanat," e-mail to Matt Matthews, Combat Studies Institute, Fort Leavenworth, KS, 22 January 2009. It should be remembered that all time estimates provided by the Soldiers involved in intense combat are relative and generally inaccurate.

52. McKaig, interview, 19 November 2008, 3.

53. McKaig, e-mail, 22 January 2009.

54. McKaig, interview, 19 November 2008, 4.

55. Stafford, interview, 10 February 2009, 10–12.

56. Stafford, interview, 10 February 2009, 10–12.

57. Pitts, interview, 14 January 2009, 13.

58. Stafford, interview, 10 February 2009, 12.

59. Exhibit 63 (SGT C/2-503d IN, statement), CJTF-101, "Army Regulation 15-6 Investigation into Battle of Wanat (Redacted, Unclassified Version)" (Landstuhl Regional Medical Center, Germany, 17 October 2008), 6.

60. Pitts, interview, 14 January 2009, 10.

61. Myer, interview, 1 December 2008, 11.

62. Benton, interview, 4 August 2009, 11.

63. Exhibit 39 (SPC HHC/2-503d IN, statement), CJTF-101, "Army Regulation 15-6 Investigation into Battle of Wanat (Redacted, Unclassified Version)" (Landstuhl Regional Medical Center, Germany, 18 October 2008), 2; Pitts interview, 14 January 2009, 10-11.

64. Stafford, interview, 10 February 2009, 14.

65. McKaig, e-mail, 22 January 2009; McKaig, interview, 19 November 2008, 5.

66. Exhibits 118, 119, 120, 121 (Autopsy Reports), CJTF-101, "Army Regulation 15-6 Investigation into Battle of Wanat (Redacted, Unclassified Version)" (22 July 2008).

67. Exhibit 27 (SGT C/2-503d IN, statement), CJTF-101, "Army Regulation 15-6 Investigation into Battle of Wanat (Redacted, Unclassified Version)" (Landstuhl Regional Medical Center, Germany, 18 October 2008), 3.

68. Stafford, interview, 10 February 2009, 13; Exhibit 77 (SPC C/2-503d IN, statement), CJTF-101, "Army Regulation 15-6 Investigation into Battle of Wanat (Redacted, Unclassified Version)" (Landstuhl Regional Medical Center, Germany, 17 October 2008), 2.

69. McKaig, interview, 19 November 2008, 4.

70. McKaig, e-mail, 22 January 2009; McKaig, interview, 19 November 2008, 4.

71. McKaig, interview, 19 November 2008, 5.

72. McKaig, interview.

73. McKaig, interview.

74. Stafford, interview, 10 February 2009, 14–15.

75. Stafford, interview, 10 February 2009, 13–15.

76. Stafford, interview, 10 February 2009, 14–15; Exhibit 27, CJTF-101, "Army Regulation 15-6 Investigation into Battle of Wanat", 4.

77. Pitts, interview, 14 January 2009, 11; Exhibit 63, CJTF-101, "Army Regulation 15-6 Investigation into Battle of Wanat", 6.

78. Pitts, interview, 14 January 2009, 11.

79. Pitts, interview, 14 January 2009, 11.

80. Exhibit 13 (SSG C/2-503d IN, statement), CJTF-101, "Army Regulation 15-6 Investigation into Battle of Wanat (Redacted, Unclassified Version)" (Camp Blessing, Afghanistan, 16 October 2008), 4.

81. Exhibit 67 (SSG C/2-503d IN, statement), CJTF-101, "Army Regulation 15-6 Investigation into Battle of Wanat (Redacted, Unclassified Version)" (Landstuhl Regional Medical Center, Germany, 17 October 2008), 4-5.

82. Exhibit 67 (SSG C/2-503d IN, statement), CJTF-101, Army Regulation 15-6 Investigation into Battle of Wanat, 4.

83. Exhibit 21, (SPC, C/2-503d IN, statement), CJTF-101, "Army Regulation 15-6 Investigation into Battle of Wanat (Redacted, Unclassified Version)" (Landstuhl Region Medical Center, Germany, 17 July 2008), 2. The reference to mortar fire is only mentioned in passing. If the AAF used mortars at Wanat, it was sparingly. Almost all AAF fires were via direct, line-of-sight weapons.

84. Exhibit 21, CJTF-101, "Army Regulation 15-6 Investigation into Battle of Wanat", 2.

85. Pitts, interview, 14 January 2009, 12.

86. Pitts, interview, 14 January 2009, 12.

87. Exhibit 21, CJTF-101, "Army Regulation 15-6 Investigation into Battle of Wanat", 3.

88. Pitts, interview, 14 January 2009, 12.

89. Dzwik, interview, 2 April 2009, 14; Exhibit 24 (SFC C/2-503d IN, statement), CJTF-101, "Army Regulation 15-6 Investigation into Battle of Wanat (Redacted, Unclassified Version)" (Bagram AB, Afghanistan, 25 July 2008), 1; Benton, interview, 4 August 2009, 10–12.

90. AH-64 Guntapes of Engagement at Wanat, 13 July 2008.

91. AH-64 Guntapes of Engagement at Wanat, 13 July 2008.

92. First Lieutenant Michael Moad, e-mail to Douglas R. Cubbison, Combat Studies Institute, Fort Leavenworth, KS, 17 March 2009.

93. AH-64 Guntapes of Engagement at Wanat, 13 July 2008.

94. Lieutenant Colonel John Lynch, interview by Douglas R. Cubbison, Combat Studies Institute, Fort Leavenworth, KS, 12 May 2009, 1; Exhibit 46a (WO1, Brigade Airspace Manager, HHC, 173d ABCT, interview) to US Central Command (CENTCOM), "Re-investigation into the Combat Action at Wanat Village, Wygal District, Nuristan Province, Afghanistan, on 13 July 2008 (Redacted), 4.

95. Lynch, interview, 12 May 2009, 12.

96. Chief Warrant Officer 3 Brian Townsend, interview by Douglas R. Cubbison, Combat Studies Institute, Fort Leavenworth, KS, 24 June 2009, 4–5.

97. Townsend, interview, 24 June 2009, 5; Chief Warrant Officer 3 John Gauvreau, interview by Douglas R. Cubbison, Combat Studies Institute, Fort Leavenworth, KS, 2 July 2009.

98. Aass, interview, 13 January 2009, 9.

99. First Lieutenant Matthew A. Colley, e-mail to Douglas R. Cubbison, Combat Studies Institute, Fort Leavenworth, KS, 25 March 2009; Exhibit 38a (WO1, Brigade Airspace Manager, HHC, 173d ABCT, interview) to US Central Command (CENTCOM), "Re-investigation into the Combat Action at Wanat Village, Wygal District, Nuristan Province, Afghanistan, on 13 July 2008 (Redacted), 17-18.

100. Exhibit 55 (CPT C/2-503d IN, statement), CJTF-101, "Army Regulation 15-6 Investigation into Battle of Wanat (Redacted, Unclassified Version)" (Camp Blessing, Afghanistan, 16 July 2008), 2; Myer, interview, 1 December 2008, 10, 13; Aass, interview, 13 January 2009, 9.

101. Exhibit 50 (SPC C/2-503d IN, statement), CJTF-101, "Army Regulation 15-6 Investigation into Battle of Wanat (Redacted, Unclassified Version)" (Wanat, Afghanistan, 13 July 2008), 1; Exhibit 70, CJTF-101, "Army Regulation 15-6 Investigation into Battle of Wanat (Redacted, Unclassified Version)," 2-3.

102. AH-64 Guntapes of Engagement at Wanat, 13 July 2008.

103. AH-64 Guntapes of Engagement at Wanat, 13 July 2008.

104. Sergeant First Class William Stockard interview by Matt Matthews, Combat Studies Institute, Fort Leavenworth, KS, 21 October 2008, 3.

105. Myer, interview, 1 December 2008, 10; AH-64 Guntapes of Engagement at Wanat, 13 July 2008.

106. AH-64 Guntapes of Engagement at Wanat, 13 July 2008.

107. Hissong, personal statement; Exhibit 16 (SPC, 1st Plt, C/2-503d IN, statement), CJTF-101, "Army Regulation 15-6 Investigation into Battle of Wanat (Redacted, Unclassified Version)" (Camp Blessing, Afghanistan, 16 July 2008), 1; Exhibit 30 (SGT, 1st Plt, C/2-503d IN, statement), CJTF-101, "Army Regulation 15-6 Investigation into Battle of Wanat (Redacted, Unclassified Version)" (Camp Blessing, Afghanistan, 18 July 2008), 1; Exhibit 33 (SPC, 1st Plt, C/2-503d IN, statement), CJTF-101, "Army Regulation 15-6 Investigation into Battle of Wanat (Redacted, Unclassified Version)" (Camp Blessing, Afghanistan, 16 July 2008), 1; Exhibit 35 (SPC, 1st Plt, C/2-503d IN, statement), CJTF-101, "Army Regulation 15-6 Investigation into Battle of Wanat (Redacted, Unclassified Version)" (Camp Blessing, Afghanistan, 16 July 2008), 1; Exhibit 48 (SPC, 1st Plt, C/2-503d IN, statement), CJTF-101, "Army Regulation 15-6 Investigation into Battle of Wanat (Redacted, Unclassified Version)" (Camp Blessing, Afghanistan, 16 July 2008), 1; Exhibit 53 (SPC, 1st Plt, C/2-503d IN, statement), CJTF-101, "Army Regulation 15-6 Investigation into Battle of Wanat (Redacted, Unclassified Version)" (Camp Blessing, Afghanistan, 16 July 2008), 1; Exhibit 59 (SPC, 1st Plt, C/2-503d IN, statement), CJTF-101, "Army Regulation 15-6 Investigation into Battle of Wanat (Redacted, Unclassified Version)" (Camp Blessing, Afghanistan, 16 July 2008), 1; Exhibit 79, CJTF-101, "Army Regulation 15-6 Investigation into Battle of Wanat (Redacted, Unclassified Version)," 1.

108. Hissong, personal statement.

109. Exhibit 11 (1SG C/2-503d IN, statement), CJTF-101, "Army Regulation 15-6 Investigation into Battle of Wanat (Redacted, Unclassified Version)" (Wanat, Afghanistan, 13 July 2008), 1.

110. Exhibit 35, CJTF-101, "Army Regulation 15-6 Investigation into Battle of Wanat", 1.

111. Exhibit 16 (SPC, 1st Plt, C/2-503d IN, statement), CJTF-101, "Army Regulation 15-6 Investigation into Battle of Wanat (Redacted, Unclassified Version)" (Camp Blessing, Afghanistan, 16 July 2008), 1.

112. Exhibit 83 (SPC, 1st Plt, C/2-503d IN, statement), CJTF-101, "Army Regulation 15-6 Investigation into Battle of Wanat (Redacted, Unclassified Version)" (Camp Blessing, Afghanistan, 16 July 2008), 1.

113. Exhibit 14, CJTF-101, "Army Regulation 15-6 Investigation into Battle of Wanat", 1.

114. Hissong, personal statement.

115. Aass, interview, 13 January 2009, 10.

116. Exhibit 73 (SSG, 1st Plt, C/2-503d IN, statement), CJTF-101, "Army Regulation 15-6 Investigation into Battle of Wanat (Redacted, Unclassified Version)" (Camp Blessing, Afghanistan, 16 July 2008), 1.

117. Exhibit 73 (SSG, 1st Plt, C/2-503d IN, statement), CJTF-101, 1-2.

118. Exhibit 11, CJTF-101, "Army Regulation 15-6 Investigation into Battle of Wanat", 1.

119. Exhibit 53, CJTF-101, "Army Regulation 15-6 Investigation into Battle of Wanat", 1.

120. Exhibit 53, CJTF-101, "Army Regulation 15-6 Investigation into Battle of Wanat", 1.

121. Exhibit 53, CJTF-101, "Army Regulation 15-6 Investigation into Battle of Wanat", 1.

122. AH-64 Guntapes of Engagement at Wanat, 13 July 2008.

123. Captain Justin J. Madill, Sworn Statement, FOB Fenty, Jalalabad Airfield, Afghanistan, 17 July 2008; Captain Justin J. Madill, "Battle of Wanat," e-mail to Douglas R. Cubbison, Combat Studies Institute, Fort Leavenworth, KS, 19 May 2009; Chief Warrant Officer 2 Wayne A. McDonald, Sworn Statement, FOB Fenty, Jalalabad Airfield, Afghanistan, 14 July 2008.

124. Madill, Sworn Statement, 17 July 2008.

125. Madill.

126. Madill.

127. McDonald, Sworn Statement, 14 July 2008.

128. Staff Sergeant Atwon Thompkins, Sworn Statement, FOB Fenty, Jalalabad Airfield, Afghanistan, 14 July 2008.

129. Staff Sergeant Matthew Kinney, interview by Douglas R. Cubbison, Combat Studies Institute, Fort Leavenworth, KS, 20 May 2009, 1; Chief Warrant

Officer 3 Christopher Hill, Sworn Statement on Wanat, FOB Fenty, Afghanistan, 13 July 2008.

130. Kinney, interview, 20 May 2009, 2.

131. Madill, Sworn Statement, 17 July 2008.

132. Kinney, interview, 20 May 2009, 2; Pitts, interview, 14 January 2009, 12–13.

133. Dzwik interview, 2 April 2009, 15; Myer interview, 1 December 2008, 14, 16.

134. Captain Ben Seipel, Sworn Statement on Wanat, FOB Fenty, Afghanistan, 14 July 2008. The rest of the crew of Dustoff 34 consisted of crew chief Sergeant Aaron Tuten, and flight medic Sergeant Adam Cannaughton.

135. Captain Kevin King, "Wanat" e-mail to Douglas R. Cubbison, Combat Studies Institute, Fort Leavenworth, KS, 14 May 2009.

136. Smith, interview, 19 May 2009, 5.

137. King, e-mail, 14 May 2009.

138. Exhibit 79, CJTF-101, "Army Regulation 15-6 Investigation into Battle of Wanat", 1.

139. Kinney, interview, 20 May 2009, 1–2.

140. Madill, Sworn Statement, 17 July 2008; Kinney, interview, 20 May 2009, 1–2.

141. Pitts, interview, 14 January 2009, 12–13.

142. Hissong, personal statement.

143. Captain Dan Kearny, interview by Douglas R. Cubbison, Combat Studies Institute, Fort Leavenworth, KS, 3–4 March 2009, 7–8; Moad, e-mail, 17 March 2009.

144. Exhibit 10, CJTF-101, "Army Regulation 15-6 Investigation into Battle of Wanat", 1.

145. Moad, e-mail, 17 March 2009.

146. Moad e-mail.

147. Moad e-mail.

148. Brigadier General Mark Milley, interview by Douglas R. Cubbison and Dr. William G. Robertson, Combat Studies Institute, Fort Leavenworth, KS, 18 and 20 August 2009, 45; Himes, interview, 25 April 2009, 10–11.

149. Major Scott Himes, interview by Douglas R. Cubbison, Combat Studies Institute, Fort Leavenworth, KS, 25 April 2009, 10.

150. The weapons found at the ANP post in Wanat included 76 AK-47 automatic rifles, 11 RPK 7.62-mm light machine guns, 3 PKM 7.62-mm general purpose machine guns, 6 RPG launchers, 3 12-gauge shotguns, 1 grenade

launcher, and 6 9-mm pistols. See Exhibit 4 (Search Summary), CJTF-101, "Army Regulation 15-6 Investigation into Battle of Wanat".

151. Exhibit 30, CJTF-101, "Army Regulation 15-6 Investigation into Battle of Wanat", 1-2.

152. Exhibit 34, CJTF-101, "Army Regulation 15-6 Investigation into Battle of Wanat", 6.

153. Colonel William Ostlund and Captain Matthew Myer, joint e-mail to Douglas R. Cubbison, Combat Studies Institute, Fort Leavenworth, KS, 23 March 2009.

154. Exhibit 34, CJTF-101, "Army Regulation 15-6 Investigation into Battle of Wanat", 6.

155. Exhibit 10, CJTF-101, "Army Regulation 15-6 Investigation into Battle of Wanat", 1.

156. Exhibit 52 (1LT, B/2-503d IN, statement), CJTF-101, "Army Regulation 15-6 Investigation into Battle of Wanat (Redacted, Unclassified Version)" (Korengal Outpost, Afghanistan, 16 July 2008), 1.

157. 173d Airborne Brigade Combat Team, "Presentation of Collateral Investigation Results to the Family of First Lieutenant Jonathan P. Brostrom" Briefing (not dated).

158. Exhibit 40 (MAJ 2-503d IN, statement), CJTF-101, "Army Regulation 15-6 Investigation into Battle of Wanat (Redacted, Unclassified Version)" (Camp Blessing, Afghanistan, 16 July 2008), 1.

159. Exhibit 40 (MAJ 2-503d IN, statement), CJTF-101.

160. Ostlund and Myer, joint e-mail, 23 March 2009.

161. Ostlund Ibid.; Major General Jeffrey Schloesser, interview by Douglas R. Cubbison and Robert Ramsey, Combat Studies Institute, Fort Leavenworth, KS, 5 August 2009, 4–5.

162. Milley, interview, 18 and 20 August 2009, 46; Ostlund and Myer, joint e-mail, 23 March 2009.

163. Schloesser, interview, 5 August 2009, 13.

164. Schloesser interview.

165. Schloesser interview.

166. Exhibit 40, CJTF-101, "Army Regulation 15-6 Investigation into Battle of Wanat", 1-2.

167. Matthew Cole, "Watching Afghanistan Fall," Salon Magazine, 27 February 2007, http://www.salon.com/ news/feature/2007/02/27/afghanistan/ (accessed 17 July 2008).

168. Exhibit 43(SGT, 1st Plt, C/2-503d IN, statement), CJTF-101, "Army Regulation 15-6 Investigation into Battle of Wanat (Redacted, Unclassified Version)" (Camp Blessing, Afghanistan, 18 July 2008), 1.

169. Exhibit 4 (Search Summary), CJTF-101, "Army Regulation 15-6 Investigation into Battle of Wanat (Redacted, Unclassified Version);" 173d ABCT,

"Presentation of Collateral Investigation Results" Briefing; Pry interview, 6 May 2009, 9-10.

Chapter 4

Conclusions

Overview

The engagement at Wanat on 13 July 2008 has generated a great deal of interest and scrutiny among military professionals and from outside observers. The primary force behind this interest was the significant number of Coalition casualties that resulted from the engagement. During the battle, insurgent action killed nine American Soldiers and wounded 27, with 16 of the wounded requiring immediate evacuation. Additionally, four of the 24 ANA (Afghan National Army) soldiers at the combat outpost (COP) were wounded. Discounting helicopter crashes, the nine US deaths at Wanat represented the highest American fatality total to date from any single engagement since US operations began in the country in 2001.

As illustrated throughout this work, the events and conditions that led to the engagement and the course of the battle itself are very complicated. At the strategic level, by 2008 Afghanistan had become an economy of force theater in the larger Global War on Terrorism. At the operational level, this meant that the Coalition forces and the security forces of the Afghan Government were dispersed widely across the country in an attempt to secure and win support from the population. As a result, small platoon sized contingents, normally numbering under 75 Soldiers, manned most Coalition bases. Under the right circumstances, the insurgents were able to mass numerically superior forces against the smaller bases and gain a temporary but significant advantage that could lead to casualties on the Coalition side. In some regions of Afghanistan where the population was also distributed across difficult terrain and enemy forces were equally dispersed, insurgent leaders required time to mass forces for strikes against the Coalition. In the case of the Waygal Valley in Nuristan province, US and Afghan forces in 2006 and 2007 were able to man and sustain small bases near the town of Aranas, a recognized center of insurgent activity in Nuristan, and in the hamlet of Bella. However, in 2008, when the Coalition headquarters consolidated its Waygal Valley presence onto one COP in the village of Wanat, the insurgents launched a large scale attack within days of its establishment. Arguably, the enemy had taken two years to mass sufficient forces to threaten the local civilians in the Waygal Valley enough to co-opt the civil authorities and exert control over activities in the town. This achievement made the attack on COP Kahler feasible.

What enemy success there was at Wanat was primarily predicated on one factor, tactical surprise. Press reports have referred to the action at Wanat as an "ambush" and declared that the Coalition force was "overrun" during the battle. Neither characterization is accurate. The Army defines an ambush as a "form of attack by fire or other destructive means from concealed positions on a moving or temporarily halted enemy."[1] While the insurgents did achieve tactical surprise, their attack was against a stationary US and ANA force, which was fighting from defensive positions. Clearly, the term ambush is inappropriate for this battle. Overrun is not an official Army term but in general military usage it means "to defeat decisively and occupy the positions of."[2] Applying the term in relation to the Battle of Wanat is, therefore, clearly inappropriate as the insurgents neither achieved a decisive victory nor occupied any of the American positions, even those at OP Topside.[3]

Still, the insurgents managed to gain an advantage over Coalition forces with the momentary and unexpected shock of their attack. While some members of the 2d Platoon, Chosen Company, seem to have had a certain late tour dread about the prospects of establishing a COP at Wanat, the chain of command did not expect the enemy to attack in the manner in which they ultimately did. Instead, as discussed in the first two chapters of this study, commanders from platoon level up through the senior Coalition command in Afghanistan expected the insurgents to increase their pressure on COP Kahler incrementally over time before committing to a large attack. This assumption was based on past actions of the insurgents in other places in the region, particularly at COP Ranch House near Aranas and at the COP in Bella. In previous instances, the insurgents had proven to be very deliberate in their operations. Coalition assumptions about enemy intent and capabilities played a critical role in the engagement at Wanat and will be assessed further in later sections of this chapter.[4]

Despite the tactical surprise, the US Soldiers reacted quickly and fought back valiantly. It was the courage and professionalism of the Americans and their two dozen Afghan allies that repelled a determined and coordinated assault by approximately 150 heavily armed insurgents who had stealthily managed to approach within yards of the Coalition positions before initiating their attack. For the most part, the battle took the form of a firefight at close range in which time was on the American side. When AH-64 Apache attack helicopters arrived followed closely by ground reinforcements, Coalition forces gained the upper hand. This paradigm, the placement of platoon sized positions supported extensively by fire support assets and a complex scheme of reinforcement, allowed the

US forces to maintain small outposts near local political and population centers per current US Army counterinsurgency (COIN) doctrine. This model worked well enough to allow the Coalition to retain control of the base at Wanat after the assault began on 13 July.

At OP (Observation Post) Topside, however, the terrain and positioning of forces created difficulties. While the large boulders eased the task of constructing the OP, they were not located on the military crest of the ridge. This unfortunate fact thus precluded observation of the ravine to the immediate north. Here, the ravine formed by Wayskawdi Creek approached very near to the American position, allowing the insurgents to get within hand grenade range of the position undetected. The insurgents' opening volley knocked out one machine gun and stunned the garrison, wounding almost all of them. In the ensuing firefight, the defenders did not regain the upper hand until two waves of ad hoc quick reaction forces (QRFs) arrived. Nevertheless, even at Topside, where the effects of tactical surprise were their greatest, the insurgents were unable to effectively overrun the position. Without a doubt, the enemy penetrated the OP. At one point, only a badly wounded Sergeant Ryan Pitts remained alive and fighting in the position. While the insurgents created a volume of fire that forced the evacuation of the OP by its walking wounded, the defense of the position was such that despite several perimeter penetrations, the insurgents were unable to follow up on their success. Although enemy fire was intense, it was mostly inaccurate, making the insurgents incapable of successfully isolating the OP from reinforcements. This failure blunted the AAF's efforts even as they inflicted a relatively high number of casualties on the US contingent fighting at the OP.

Despite initial disadvantages, the members of C Company and its supporting elements fought well at Wanat. The main COP position held its own against insurgent pressure from all sides. US and ANA firepower remained at levels that allowed the American leadership to dispatch several waves of reinforcements to the OP. This defensive stand bought enough time for the arrival of direct fire support assets such as the Apache helicopters. The Apaches were able to effectively engage insurgent fighters who had approached dangerously close to friendly positions. With the defense so enhanced, the arrival of the first ground reinforcements allowed the Americans to counterattack, clear enemy positions in the bazaar and hotel complexes close to the COP, and evacuate the wounded and dead.

While Coalition forces successfully repelled the insurgent attack at Wanat, Coalition military leaders had to reassess their plans in the Waygal Valley. Just days after the attack on COP Kahler, senior commanders decided to withdraw all their forces from the Waygal District. This decision was based on a number of factors, including the capacity of TF *Duke*, the unit moving into northeast Afghanistan to replace TF *Bayonet*, to man a base at Wanat. Still, the withdrawal had negative effects. The move effectively abandoned friends of the Afghan Central Government and the Coalition. Further it provided the insurgency with a sanctuary area relatively close to the population centers along the Pech, Konar, Alingar, and Kabul River valleys. However, insurgent success in this period may prove to be fleeting. Reports from the district in late 2009 indicate that the Waygal Valley's isolation from Coalition support has estranged the local populace from the insurgents.[5]

Several factors were instrumental in the successful defense of COP Kahler. The first was the effort made by the members of the 2d Platoon in the days before the attack. A combination of concertina obstacles, sandbags, and HESCO barriers buttressed the main COP to the extent that the insurgents were unable to penetrate the main perimeter despite being very close to it at the start of the action. Although several of the HESCOs were not completely filled with dirt, most were and all provided cover and concealment for key positions such as the mortar pit. The defenders used the available hand tools to the maximum extent possible, and the positions were excavated to the greatest depth feasible with these tools. The COP would not have survived the determined attack made on the morning of 13 July without basic fortifications which the 2d Platoon constructed, even under the severe constraints under which the paratroopers labored.

The enemy was able to destroy or suppress the mortars, the TOW (tube-launched, optically tracked, wire guided) missile launcher and one of the light machine guns at the OP at the start of the action. However, the Coalition forces freely employed the remaining crew-served weapons. The vehicle mounted systems; two M2 .50-caliber machine guns and two Mk-19 automatic grenade launchers, as well as the remaining ground mounted M240 machine gun at the OP, and the Marine ETT's (embedded training team) M240 offered enough firepower to keep the enemy at bay and allow the repositioning of forces to reinforce the threatened Topside position. These weapons systems, particularly the ones mounted on vehicles, played a key role in retaining freedom of action for the entire force at the COP. Despite being under intense enemy fire, most of the force remained in action long enough to keep the insurgents away from the main COP perimeter. Prior to the battle, Lieutenant Brostrom and Sergeant Dzwik, the platoon leader and platoon sergeant, had ensured that the maximum amount of ammunition was available for these weapons. In the initial movement to Wanat, each HMMWV (high-mobility multipurpose wheeled vehicle) carried extra ammunition and more arrived by helicopter the next day. During the engagement, the actions of the platoon were never constrained by lack of ammunition. Also, the 1st Platoon QRF brought additional ammunition, which allowed the defenders to continue the high rates of fire that were necessary to maintain the successful defense.[6]

Additionally, the importance of stand-to cannot be overemphasized. The force at COP Kahler was fully awake and alert at least 45 minutes before dawn, so, although tactically surprised, the Coalition force was manning all weapons and in position when the insurgents initiated the firefight. A traditional US Army defensive technique, stand-to was significant because of the insurgents' preference for night movements followed by dawn attacks. While the intensity and closeness of the insurgent fire surprised the US Soldiers, the predawn period was the expected time for such an attack. Despite losses in the first volley based on the enemy's ability to fire unimpeded by return fire, the defenders of the COP were able to regain their composure quickly and fight back effectively.

The defenders also displayed great flexibility in responding to the attack. As soon as it became obvious that OP Topside was the most vulnerable point in the American defense, tactical level leaders at the COP focused on organizing, dispatching, and leading ad hoc QRFs to the assistance of that position. Dzwik noted that even while he "was reduced to a rifleman for most of the fight . . . even when their current leadership was wounded or doing something else, each individual paratrooper acted as if he was an NCO."[7] Company RTO (radio-telephone operator) Aass agreed with this assessment, "Whenever one leader went down, there was always somebody to take over in his position. Then when somebody who was senior to that person showed up at whatever point, there was yet another seamless transition. There were never any arguments over who was in charge. Somebody was always in charge."[8] Wanat showed the flexibility of the US Army at the tactical level and exemplified the high standards of NCO (noncommissioned officer) initiative and leadership.

Finally, the last ingredient essential to the successful defense of COP Kahler was the bravery of the individual warriors, a quality displayed by every paratrooper, engineer, Marine, and Afghan soldier present. Individual exploits of bravery are too numerous to document comprehensively in this discussion. Still, a few examples are illustrative: Private First Class Sergio Abad, although severely wounded, continued to hand rifle ammunition to Sergeant Hector Chavez in the mortar pit at the start of the action. Chavez, in turn, on the evacuation of the mortar position, continued to drag Abad to safety at the COP command post area even after he himself was seriously wounded. Staff Sergeant Erich Phillips threw a smoldering TOW missile away from fellow Soldiers while under intense enemy fire. Brostrom and Specialist Jason Hovater sprinted past enemy machine gun fire and through an insurgent occupied bazaar complex to rush to the assistance of those at OP Topside. At the OP, Private First Class Jonathan Ayers and Specialist Christopher McKaig continued to expose themselves to return fire at the insurgents, even after Ayers was shot directly in his helmet. In the midst of heavy fire, Myer, the company commander, moved to the OP to assess the number and condition of his men who had been wounded in the fighting there. Additionally, the MEDEVAC (medical evacuation) crews landed their helicopters on a small terrace under accurate and intense enemy fire through heavy obscuring smoke to treat and evacuate wounded Soldiers. The Army recognized the valor of the defenders with 13 Silver Star medals, 23 Bronze Stars, and one pending recommendation for the Distinguished Service Cross.[9]

The sections that follow address in more detail the factors that contributed to the setting and outcome of the battle at Wanat on 13 July 2008. The previous chapters of this study have discussed these factors in the course of providing a historical narrative. This conclusion seeks to emphasize those points in the form of a discussion that begins with the broader context of the counterinsurgency (COIN) campaign in northeast Afghanistan and then addresses the contributing factors specific to the situation in Konar, the Waygal Valley, and finally the situation at COP Kahler on the morning of 13 July 2008. This discussion is designed to generate insights of utility to military professionals of today and tomorrow. The authors of this study further hope that the historical narrative and conclusions do justice to the professionalism and valor of the American and Afghan Soldiers who fought on that day.

Counterinsurgency in Northeast Afghanistan, 2007-2008

Combined Joint Task Force (CJTF)-101 had tasked TF *Bayonet* and by extension TF *Rock*, to conduct a COIN campaign in the northeast provinces of Afghanistan. Over the course of the 15 month deployment in 2007-2008, both Colonel Charles Preysler, the TF *Bayonet* commander, and Lieutenant Colonel William Ostlund, the TF *Rock* commander, designed campaigns intended to win over the population of these provinces by providing security from the insurgents and opportunities for economic and political progress. In this effort, provincial reconstruction teams (PRTs) became as important as infantry companies, as commanders struggled to achieve the right balance of lethal and nonlethal operations. Preysler, for example, focused on a comprehensive economic and political effort in Nangarhar Province. His "Nangarhar Inc." project attempted to improve infrastructure as well as agricultural conditions to transform the province into a model of economic development. The TF *Bayonet* commander hoped that the increasing economic opportunities would win support from the population for the cause of the Coalition and Afghan Government. At the same time, Preysler realized that for "Nangarhar Inc." to work, he had to have a stable security environment and that required aggressive operations against committed insurgent forces.[10]

The leaders of TF *Rock* also hoped to create the kind of stability that would lead to economic and political progress in their area of operation (AO). For Ostlund, the main site of progress was the Pech Valley which became the focus of a successful economic effort launched by TF *Rock* and the Konar PRT. Enemy attacks in the Pech Valley had decreased between 2006 and early 2008, an accomplishment attributed to road construction and the resulting increase in jobs. However, to secure the valley and protect its progress, Ostlund believed that TF *Rock* had to assert its presence in the main capillary valleys to the north and south of the Pech. For this reason, Ostlund's subordinate companies found themselves in the Korengal, Watapor, and Waygal Valleys where the paratroopers often engaged in combat with an implacable insurgent enemy.

Enemy activity in the Waygal Valley was less constant than in the Korengal or Pech valleys. While there were major combat actions in the Waygal Valley in 2007 and 2008, these were the exception and not the rule. Both US and insurgent forces in the valley were small in comparison to other areas and for the most part, the Waygal Valley was marked by extended periods of relative inactivity. When this calm was interrupted by violence, it was the insurgents and not the Coalition, who initiated the action. For example, after almost 90 days of relative inaction for the TF *Rock* paratroopers at Aranas in the summer of 2007, the enemy suddenly attacked COP Ranch House in August. After the battle, the valley was inactive again until the insurgents attacked a Chosen Company patrol near Bella in November 2007. This patrol was returning from a *shura* in Aranas at which the Americans were trying to assess the town's winter needs. After the ambush, there was very little activity until the following May 2008 when the AAF (anti-Afghanistan Forces) attacked Bella with increasing volleys of mortars and rockets in obvious preparation for a ground assault.

The mission of the patrol that was ambushed near Bella reflected the most common activity for TF *Rock* Soldiers; nonlethal missions such as attending shuras, opening schools, buying goods from the local populace, and supporting reconstruction projects. In fact, TF *Rock* conducted over 9,500 patrols during its 15 month tour, with only 1,100 enemy contacts on the patrols, a rate of slightly more than one contact per every 10 patrols. Ostlund emphasized the role of these nonlethal operations as part of his overall COIN campaign. Much of the success TF *Rock* achieved in the Pech Valley and elsewhere came through a partnership with the Konar PRT that brought invaluable resources and expertise to the reconstruction effort. However, TF *Rock* itself committed \$2.2 million in the battalion Commander's Emergency Response Program (CERP) funds for infrastructure and economic projects in its AO. Of this amount, \$110,000 went to support projects in the Waygal district, an expenditure that ranked fourth in the 11 districts for which TF *Rock* was responsible. This figure is significant because the Waygal district had the smallest population of all the districts in the TF *Rock* AO.[11]

Despite these efforts, the Chosen Company paratroopers operating at COPs in Bella and Aranas had relatively little success in winning support from the population of the Waygal Valley. As outlined in the first chapter, the people of the valley were generally suspicious of outsiders, whether Westerners or fellow Afghans. Moreover, within the valley communities, there had been hundreds of years of intertribal and intercommunity conflict, magnified by hundreds of years of geographic and cultural isolation. Understanding the cultural antagonisms and commonalities present in the Waygal Valley and Wanat between the Nuristanis and the Safi Pashtuns and among the Nuristanis themselves was difficult and complicated. On a more practical note, the Ranch House and Bella COPs were totally air-centric in terms of logistical support. When the risk involved in sustaining them proved greater than the benefits gained by their occupation, it was time to rethink their locations. Movement to the district center of Wanat was the result.

This natural antagonism meant that the general population met TF *Rock* initiatives with caution or sometimes overt hostility. The insurgent groups in the valley used violence to oppose Coalition efforts, lashing out at the paratroopers and their Afghan allies in aggressive attacks. Ostlund recognized that even after months of effort, TF *Rock* had not made progress in the Waygal Valley, asserting, "no matter what we did [in the Waygal Valley] we were just not effective."[12] At least part of that ineffectiveness could be attributed to the overall lack of Coalition forces in the Waygal Valley. TF *Rock* could only commit one American platoon, roughly 40 Soldiers, to the valley at any one time. This small contingent could operate in only one or two communities within the valley, leaving the remainder exposed to insurgent influence and control. Even if the population had been more open to Coalition projects and plans, the simple fact that the local insurgent groups outnumbered US forces made any collaboration with TF *Rock* potentially dangerous to the residents of the valley. Thus, intimidation by the enemy was a major obstacle for the members of TF *Rock* to overcome. Certainly, the local leaders of Wanat had either sided with insurgent forces before the battle or felt they had no choice but to allow the enemy to infiltrate their town. The discovery of bloody uniforms, recently fired weapons and other equipment in the police station, as noted in chapter 3, was clear evidence that even the local agencies of the Afghan central government had been co-opted and had not favorably responded to coalition efforts to establish security and governmental legitimacy.

Despite previous problems with the valley population, TF *Rock* and Chosen Company did not abandon their COIN approach. Between the Ranch House attack in late 2007 and the engagement at Wanat, Ostlund and Chosen Company continued to meet with local leaders in the valley and attempted to use reconstruction projects as an inducement for their participation in creating security. When this initiative met with little success, the TF *Rock* leadership decided to move forward with the transfer of the COP from Bella to Wanat. The new COP would be located near the district center where the main north-south river road met an important east-west trail and where a major market was located. For this reason, it would serve as the base from which the Coalition could renew efforts to bring reconstruction projects to the valley and further the legitimacy and reach of the Afghan central government. Thus, the new COP at Wanat served as a symbol in the belief that the Coalition forces and their Afghan allies would still win over the population in the valley.

Enemy Disposition and Intent: Situational Awareness in the Waygal Valley

On the morning of 13 July 2008, the insurgent enemy in the Waygal Valley launched a violent assault on TF *Rock*'s new base in Wanat. The proximate cause of the casualties was the insurgents' ability to arrive at Wanat essentially undetected and infiltrate into positions literally yards from the main COP and the OP. How was the enemy able to obtain this degree of tactical surprise? The general response to this question must invoke the role of uncertainty, a factor that is inseparable from any military operation. Even in the twenty first century, Army staff officers and commanders continue to work in a world where the term "fog of war" applies. The "fog" persists even in an age in which a military force fields a large number of electronic devices to provide an ever increasing amount of situational awareness to commanders.

In the planning for Operation ROCK MOVE and in the first days after the establishment of COP Kahler, US military leaders made decisions in the absence of highly precise information about enemy dispositions and enemy intent. First, the insurgent situation had changed in the Waygal Valley. Whereas in 2006 and 2007 the Americans were able to place two half-platoon positions at Aranas and at Bella, the enemy in 2008 was far better mobilized to resist Coalition efforts in the area. The much more defensible and far less remote Wanat position actually had become less defensible than the smaller, more eccentrically designed Ranch House position had been in 2006. The Coalition presence in their midst no longer surprised the insurgent leaders. Apparently they had resolved to do whatever was necessary to remove that presence which had disrupted their operations and recruitment. For this purpose, by June 2008, Mullah Osman and other insurgent leaders had massed forces to attack Bella. The infrastructure was now in place to conduct a systematic and extended campaign to intimidate and exert control over the local civilian population. The number of Coalition forces on the ground facilitated these enemy actions. The American presence was thin. In fact, US forces had withdrawn from Aranas in late 2007 and by early July 2008 were preparing to evacuate COP Bella. Thus, it was evident to the valley population that the Coalition security commitment to specific communities was less than constant.

Coalition leaders also had difficulty understanding the political situation in Wanat. Certainly, tactical level commanders in TF *Rock* acknowledged that many within the Wanat population harbored anti Coalition sentiments. Several shuras between the Americans and Wanat leaders in the spring and summer of 2008 had gone poorly and one was followed by an insurgent ambush on Coalition vehicles returning to Camp Blessing. However, no one in the US leadership appears to have understood the willingness of village leaders to cooperate, willingly or unwillingly, with the AAF in a large attack against Coalition forces.

In place of precise information about the enemy, the Coalition chain of command from the platoon level to senior officers in the CJTF, made assumptions about insurgent dispositions and intent. At the tactical level, 15 months of experience in the region had led to an expectation that any enemy attack on a new base would develop gradually with harassing fires preceding any deliberate attack. Myer used the August 2007 Ranch House attack as an example of how the "typical" attack evolved:

> There are things that customarily happen and then it kind of builds up to a large event. What we eventually saw was

a pattern of about 90 to 120 days of build up until a large scale event happened. . . . What we anticipated was that they were going to first attack us with rockets because that was something they could do that didn't take a lot of personnel to do it. If we had a new area occupied, they could try to affect us and try to dial in those rockets like they had done at Bella. They had shot rockets at Bella over time and then eventually they could get them inside the wire pretty consistently.[13]

Myer then stated succinctly, "So, we thought if they were going to do a large scale attack [at Wanat], they're going to first refine all the assets they wanted to utilize to do that and then after something like 90 days, then they're going to try to do a large scale attack like they did at the Ranch House."[14]

In his expectation that the enemy would respond in a systematic gradual manner to the American presence at Wanat, Myer was not alone. Reflecting the views of the TF *Rock* S2, the ROCK MOVE operations order briefing indicated that the enemy would try to "disrupt the construction of [a Coalition Forces] base in the village of Wanat."[15] Before any general attack, the insurgents were expected to gradually establish a series of positions and weapons caches near Wanat. ROCK MOVE considered that the most dangerous enemy action would be an ambush of US forces as they moved into Wanat. However, this was not the insurgents' most probable action. Before the attack, Lieutenant Colley, the TF *Rock* Assistant S2, felt that "the most likely enemy course of action would be to conduct probing attacks of the new US position in order to discover any weaknesses."[16] Reflecting on the enemy reaction after the battle, Lieutenant Colonel Ostlund, echoed the beliefs of his staff and subordinates, "I think that the perception across the task force is that probes would come long before a deliberate effort [by the enemy]."[17] He then stated that in his opinion "there was enough force protection and combat power [at COP Kahler] to dissuade any anticipated attack."[18] In terms of expectations of enemy actions, Ostlund and Myer were supported by Colonel Preysler, their brigade commander, and Generals Milley and Schloesser at CJTF-101. These officers all felt that a large attack at Wanat was unlikely, at least in the near future.[19]

The enemy response to Operation ROCK MOVE reinforced US assumptions. To the TF *Rock* planners, the most dangerous part of the operation was the withdrawal from Bella and the initial occupation of Wanat. An insurgent attack at Bella while helicopters were evacuating the position could have proven devastating. A complex ambush against the newly arriving troops at Wanat could have been equally disastrous. However, neither event occurred. The timing of the evacuation of Bella with the occupation of Wanat seemingly confused the enemy. The Americans had achieved tactical surprise against the insurgents in both phases of the operation. No helicopters were shot down at Bella and the Coalition force arrived in Wanat without any opposition.[20]

Given the history of operations in the Waygal Valley during the TF *Rock* deployment, there was good reason to expect no large enemy operations after the successful execution of ROCK MOVE. Chosen Company had seen only two major attacks during its operations in the Waygal Valley, the assault on Ranch House in August 2007 and the ambush near Bella in November of that year. The overall level of enemy activity in the valley was much less than in other parts of the battalion sector. As measured by troops in contact (TICs) incidents, the Korengal Valley, B Company's sector, was three times as active as the Waygal Valley. In that valley, B Company had three bases including the Korengal Outpost and COP Restrepo. Able Company's sector along the Pech River and in the Watapor and Shigal Valleys was more than twice as active. A large enemy attack shortly after the unopposed occupation of the Wanat position would have been an unprecedented action on the part of the insurgents. This belief was reinforced when, after the successful movement to Wanat and closure of Bella, Wanat was quiet in the four days leading up to the attack. In that same four day period, the battalion's 12 additional bases registered daily enemy contacts and attacks.[21]

The insurgents in the Waygal Valley, of course, did not act according to precedent. Two factors played key roles in the enemy's almost immediate strike on COP Kahler. The first was the availability of a massed force of insurgents near Bella. The second was the Coalition's lack of operational security and operational surprise in the move to Wanat. In addition, the massing of insurgent forces was a combination of two additional factors. July was the middle of the insurgent campaigning season and each year the insurgents focused their efforts on one Coalition site. In the later days of the previous season, the insurgents had directed their efforts at Ranch House. In 2008 the enemy planned to strike at Bella. Intelligence indicators for several months before ROCK MOVE had indicated this enemy intention. The objective was either to disrupt a Coalition withdrawal or to take credit for the Coalition withdrawal after it occurred. The insurgent leaders did not want to let a campaigning season go by without at least one major attack against a fixed American location. When this did not happen at Bella and Coalition forces began arriving at Wanat, it appears the new outpost became the fresh target.[22]

Before this shift, the enemy concentration against Bella did not go unobserved. The TF *Rock* S2 section noticed the increased enemy activities around the isolated post. Specifically during the period 1-4 July, there were indicators that the insurgent leadership intended to attack Bella at the first opportunity with at least 300 fighters. The Apache strike on the insurgent mortar teams on 4 July possibly disrupted the attack against Bella and probably wounded Osman, the insurgent leader. In addition, Captain Pry, the TF *Rock* S2 officer, felt that the land use discussions in Wanat had forced Osman, or his successor, to divide his forces between Bella and Wanat. The resulting pressure on the civilian population at Wanat was evident at the shuras held there on 26 May and 8 June. However, the need to target two places meant that the enemy was unable to assemble sufficient forces to attack either.[23]

Although Pry thought that the force massed to attack Bella could be used to attack Wanat instead, he was uncertain that this would be the immediate insurgent response. Pry was certain that the enemy had to react to the Coalition move into Wanat because such a development would threaten the insurgents' freedom of action. If the AAF knew in advance when an occupation would take place, they would try to disrupt it or prevent it. Moreover, a position at Wanat would be most vulnerable during its initial occupation. Pry had some indications that Osman had already begun to take measures to prepare for operations at Wanat, such as the caching of supplies and weapons.[24]

Once ROCK MOVE had succeeded, the enemy reaction was less certain. Before Chosen's 2d Platoon went to Wanat, Myer and Pry discussed the situation. The result of these discussions was inconclusive. While Pry felt the enemy had the capability to conduct a large attack, there was no direct evidence that they would do so. Myer agreed that a large scale assault was unlikely, although he felt the Coalition force at Wanat was adequate to repulse any attack if one did take place. After Bella was closed on 9 July, the enemy had a significant amount of fighters and resources in the Bella/Wanat area and only one Coalition post left to target; the newly established position at Wanat.[25]

Because of the nature of COIN operations in Afghanistan, with their inherent interaction with local populations of mixed loyalties, operational security and operational surprise were difficult if not impossible to attain. This was the case at Wanat where the Coalition forces desired to accommodate local sensibilities before placing a new camp near the village. As early as their 2007 predeployment site visit, TF *Rock* leaders had looked at the Wanat area as the site of a potential COP. Since existing

US Army procedures required the negotiation of land use with local ownership, the US forces could not simply occupy the site. Seizure of land for military purposes in wartime has been a longstanding military tradition. Nevertheless, in Afghanistan in 2008, despite the presence of a determined enemy in the countryside, there was an established set of procedures for taking local land for military use. While generally designed to accommodate local sensitivities, the Wanat negotiations had the opposite effect of antagonizing community leaders who were under pressure from the insurgents to avoid overt cooperation with the Coalition. Ironically, in this instance, the Wanat elders would have preferred that the US forces simply seize the land and reimburse them later.[26]

The land negotiations telegraphed the Coalition intention to move into the Wanat area. However, after the enemy began to intimidate the local citizenry, the negotiations became extended. On both sides, the Coalition occupation of Wanat became more of an event on the horizon rather than a reality. While the Wanat elders and the insurgent leaders knew that the Coalition intended to establish itself in the town, TF *Rock* leaders did not explain when or how this move would be made. Even so, the land negotiations did include the discussion of the location of the new base with the local civilian leadership. The geography of the village and valley restricted the options available to TF *Rock* and in a land ownership document negotiated between Ostlund and the district governor on 20 April 2008, the TF *Rock* commander provided the governor with the intended site for the proposed COP. In retrospect, the TF *Rock* commander considered the district governor to be "an informant for the AAF."[27] Still, given the situation where Coalition officials negotiated for the use of specific plots of land, it was unavoidable that local nationals with unknown loyalty would become aware of which plots were to be used. This was a risk inherent to COIN operations in which the counterinsurgent forces strive to avoid unnecessarily alienating local populations.[28]

By withholding the specific timing of ROCK MOVE, TF *Rock* surprised the insurgents. This coup prevented the enemy from disrupting the initial establishment of COP Kahler when Coalition forces were most vulnerable. However, the combination of an available force in the region and some foreknowledge of the Coalition intent in Wanat greatly facilitated the insurgents' capacity to transform a planned attack on Bella into an attack on Wanat without the usual and methodical escalation of contact. Although tactically surprised by the American occupation of Wanat on 8 July, the enemy was able in turn to tactically surprise Coalition forces at COP Kahler on 13 July.

Although the Americans did not expect any attack larger than a limited probe or harassing indirect fire, the Coalition chain of command believed that the force placed at Wanat and the fire support it had arranged could repel any unexpected assault. The force at COP Kahler, equivalent to two platoons of infantry with on site indirect fire and engineer support, was twice the size of the element that had successfully defended the Ranch House position 10 months earlier. Additionally, TF *Rock* had given to the Wanat garrison the priority of field artillery fires from the two 155-mm artillery pieces stationed at Camp Blessing and an additional two howitzers at Asadabad. The battalion QRF, Chosen Company's 1st Platoon, was available for immediate reinforcement of Wanat. How the Coalition chain of command, from platoon to CJTF levels, understood the enemy situation in the Wanat area is salient to this discussion. That state of affairs evolved quickly between the arrival of US forces on the evening of 8 July through the morning of 13 July when the insurgents launched their attack. How did the Coalition forces gather information about their surroundings in the days between their arrival and the attack?

The ISR (intelligence, surveillance, and reconnaissance) assets assigned by CJTF-101 to support Operation ROCK MOVE were important to the understanding of the situation in and around Wanat. Systems such as the Predator UAV that provided full motion video (FMV) and the Red Ridge aircraft that offered signals intelligence (SIGINT) were few in number and in high demand across Afghanistan in 2008. These assets were controlled by CJTF-101 which carefully managed their apportionment. For Coalition forces in Regional Command–East (RC-East), an area amounting to close to 50,000 square miles, only a single Predator UAV and a single Warrior-Alpha UAV were available. In the Waygal Valley, the Predator UAV and other ISR assets controlled by the CJTF were critical because the UAVs belonging to the brigade and battalion could not operate there. TF *Rock*'s assigned Raven UAVs, for example, were small and fragile systems that were highly susceptible to the wind conditions in the valleys of Nuristan. TF *Rock* S2 Pry described the Raven as a "liability" in the Waygal Valley. Similarly, the high elevation and steep slopes of the Waygal Valley also prevented the employment of the brigade level Hunter UAV system over Wanat.[29]

Operation ROCK MOVE had a high priority at the CJTF-level. That status led the CJTF ISR managers to apportion a great deal of FMV and SIGINT coverage to Wanat in the first 72 hours of the operation. In the period from 9 July through the morning of 11 July, the Predator and Red Ridge systems collected information on the Waygal Valley. On each of these days, the FMV support amounted to 15 hours of coverage and the SIGINT to eight hours. These amounts are impressive but it is important to note that on each day, at least some of the FMV coverage of Wanat was reduced because the UAV system had to be shifted to combat operations in which Coalition forces were in contact with insurgents. During the three day period beginning on the morning of 9 July, neither the FMV nor the SIGINT systems detected any indicators of an enemy force that was massing around Wanat with intent to attack COP Kahler.

CJTF-101 ISR managers made apportionment schedules 72 hours in advance. Before ROCK MOVE had begun, they had ensured that ISR coverage over Wanat would be substantial in the first three days of COP Kahler's operations. Once the disestablishment of COP Bella, considered the most risky part of ROCK MOVE, was complete and the situation around Wanat appeared stable, the priorities at CJTF-101 changed. In the second week of July, CJTF Commander Schloesser and his staff were managing a number of large scale operations and crises including a major offensive operation in the Tangi Valley of Wardak Province where Coalition forces were actively seeking insurgent groups that had tortured, killed, and mutilated three American Army National Guardsmen. In the two weeks before the Wanat attack and the two weeks following that assault, there were over 60 insurgent attacks in southern Paktika and Khowst provinces and an additional 20 attacks along the Konar and Nangarhar provincial border areas. Compounding the challenges posed by the constant demands of these combat actions were poor weather conditions which after 11 July significantly reduced the amount of ISR available across Afghanistan. On 11 July, the force at Wanat was supposed to have received some FMV coverage but incidents near the city of Khowst and in the Tangi Valley in which Coalition forces were in contact with the enemy took precedence and no UAV missions were flown over Wanat. Poor weather on 12 July grounded most of the FMV systems but four hours of SIGINT coverage was given to COP Kahler. This support ended at 1630 on 12 July.[30]

On 10 July, Pry had learned that the ISR coverage over COP Kahler was no longer guaranteed after 11 July and would likely diminish as other priorities became more important. While Pry and key staff in TF *Rock* and TF *Bayonet* vociferously protested the change in ISR apportionment and demanded that the CJTF continue to give significant FMV and SIGINT support to COP Kahler, the very real priorities noted above trumped their concerns. Without these external ISR resources, Chosen Company had to depend on its own sensors. The ITAS (Improved Target Acquisition System) component of the TOW missile system and the LRAS3 (Long

Range Advanced Scout Surveillance System) Ostlund had given to the unit were available for detection of visual threats. The Low Level Voice Intercept (LLVI) team and the ICOM scanners at battalion level continued to search for enemy communications that might indicate impending action against the new combat outpost.

Whether or not the Predator would have detected the movement of the insurgent force into Wanat after dark on 12/13 July is questionable. Using their LRAS3 and ITAS, the 2d Platoon identified a potential threat on that night just before the enemy attack began. This lack of detection suggests that the insurgents had moved onto the high ground surrounding Wanat as well as into the town itself in small groups that were not easily detected by the CJTF-level ISR assets. Having the UAV and other ISR assets overhead on the morning of 13 July may have enhanced the situational awareness of the force at COP Kahler but it is far from clear that those assets would have played a decisive role in disrupting the insurgent attack.

The members of the 2d Platoon also used simple observation to collect information of the developing situation. The most important observation they made during this period was that the number of military aged Afghan men was growing in Wanat while the women and children seemed to disappear. Moreover, a number of the paratroopers at COP Kahler asserted that many of these men appeared to be closely watching the activities at the COP. However, based on prior experience, Myer had expected such scrutiny. Perhaps more alarming was the lack of support from the governmental and local leaders at Wanat during the first few days of the operation. The Afghans had rebuffed all attempts by Brostrom to arrange a meeting with them. On 12 July, Brostrom discovered that the local Afghan leaders were holding a *shura* at the district center without an American presence. His concern then increased after he interrupted the meeting and was met with hostility. Finally, on the evening of 12 July, Myer received what could be interpreted as a veiled, if not relatively typical, warning of an imminent attack from a Wanat family that was supportive of the Coalition.

The TF *Rock* staff acknowledged receiving a report about the suspicious *shura* on 12 July but Myer did not report the Wanat elder's warning he received on the eve of the insurgent attack. Myer discounted its significance. The local elder who gave it "was a guy that always said that in general terms we were going to get attacked. So I didn't report anything because that is not what I thought."[31] Accordingly, the collected data did not decisively indicate to either Myer or his superiors that enemy forces were massing in and around Wanat for an attack. More precisely, it is probable that the observations made by the force at COP Kahler did not override the lack of indications from the CJTF-level ISR assets or the widely held assumptions about how the enemy would begin any attack on Wanat.

The expectation of limited enemy action at Wanat shaped all Coalition actions in the days before the attack. When examining the thoughts and actions of key leaders and staff at the platoon, company, and battalion levels, it would be useful to assess further why assumptions about enemy intent were not reevaluated, given developing intelligence on the ground. There was no single certain indicator that the enemy had massed for an imminent attack. Certainly, neither the SIGINT nor IMINT detected such activity.There were signs, however, of growing insurgent activity in Wanat and its environs that might have generated new assessments in the days before the attack.

The Delays in Construction of COP Kahler

Once the Coalition force arrived on 8 and 9 July, the defenses of the base grew steadily but slowly. The most glaring problem was the delay in the arrival of the Afghan companies contracted to deliver the majority of the manpower, supplies, and equipment with which the COP would be constructed. There was nothing out of the ordinary in the use of Afghan contractors in this situation. Military engineer assets were in high demand across Afghanistan and Coalition units sought to hire contractors from the general area to offer employment that might help garner support from the population. However, no Afghan contractors in the Waygal Valley could provide the required construction services. Thus, TF *Rock* chose a contractor that had done similar work for the Army elsewhere in Konar province and, within the norms of the Afghan work environment, could be expected to perform to standard.

While security concerns and communications problems delayed the arrival of the construction companies, Ostlund and Myer knew this before the commencement of ROCK MOVE and chose to risk going forward with the operation anyway. This was a calculated decision based on the lunar illumination cycle which would provide safer flying conditions for the aerial extraction of the Bella garrison and an attempt to have the new position established with the maximum number of days before the follow on unit took over AO Rock. Given the enemy's prior deliberate actions, this seemed to be a reasonable chance to take at the time.[32]

Lacking the heavy equipment and construction materials that would have been provided by the Afghan companies, the 2d Platoon and the squad from the 62d Engineer Battalion labored in the first four days to construct an initial defensive perimeter that was smaller in scale and protective capacity than was originally planned. To construct their positions, the paratroopers of the 2d Platoon relied on hand excavating tools (which they had to share), sandbags, concertina wire, and the HESCOs. Of course, the engineer squad did much of the heavier work, even while the Bobcat was inoperable. The Bobcat, even if it had remained operational throughout the whole preparatory period, could not have ascended the terraces that led to the OP to improve the position there.

In this labor, the hot weather and the developing shortage of bottled water slowed the ability of the men at COP Kahler to complete the work. They had brought as much bottled water as they could load in their vehicles along with all their other supplies. While Dzwik, the 2d Platoon sergeant, admitted he had miscalculated the amount of water required for the weather conditions, the five days of supply dictated in the operations order required aerial or ground resupply to accumulate from stockpiles at Camp Blessing. In the first days of COP Kahler, however, expected resupply was limited by a shortage of available aircraft and security on the ground route between Blessing and Wanat. The heat and water status was never so dire that the paratroopers completely ceased working. In fact, they had filters and iodine tablets that would have enabled them to draw water from a nearby well or the Waygal River if the water situation had become an emergency. However, with the resupply situation being unclear and more limited than expected, the platoon leadership reprioritized and asked for a resupply of bottled water from TF *Rock* while limiting labor to the cooler parts of the day rather than collect water from local sources. The requested bottled water soon arrived when several civilian trucks arrived from Camp Blessing with the cargo. This resupply was followed by an additional water shipment which came by Chinook helicopter with Myer on the day before the battle.[33]

Certainly, an earlier arrival of the Afghan construction companies with additional barrier material (sandbags, concertina wire, etc.) and more excavation tools would have enabled the US and Afghan troops to build more complete positions and allowed for the construction of overhead cover for the fighting positions. This supplementary protection may have afforded greater cover from the small arms fire and rocket-propelled grenade (RPG) fragments that rained down on the Americans from insurgent positions on the roofs of buildings or on ridgelines. Nevertheless, the 2d Platoon and the ANA, while not able to build an impregnable defense in the days before the attack, surely did construct adequate defenses which managed to repulse the ensuing enemy assault.

The most important effect of the platoon's focus on constructing the COP, and the self imposed restrictions on labor in the hot weather, is that the platoon leader did not believe he could spare any element to mount regular patrols in the town and its immediate vicinity. Brostrom did lead a patrol to the Wanat district headquarters on 12 July where he found the local Afghan leaders holding a meeting. Other than this instance, the platoon leader apparently felt that he could not spare any of his men to conduct security patrols. Benton, the 2d Squad leader, stated, "We just did not have the assets to support ourselves moving much farther away [from the town center]. Moving a kilometer away from what we had, you were just signing your own death warrant at that point."[34]

These concerns were real. The lack of regular patrols, however, meant Coalition forces at Wanat were not interacting with the population of the town to foster relationships and collect intelligence, both of which are critical to successful counterinsurgency operations. Moreover, the lack of patrols meant that for much of the four days they were in Wanat, the Coalition forces had little understanding of what was occurring in much of the town and on key terrain such as the deep ravine to the north of OP Topside.

Only on the morning of 13 July did Brostrom, at Myer's urging, prepare to lead a second patrol. The purpose of this patrol, which included both US and Afghan troops, was to locate a potential site for a new OP. As the patrol prepared to leave the COP before dawn on 13 July, the insurgent attack began. The opportunity to detect the insurgents maneuvering on the high ground around Wanat or their infiltration into the town in the days before the assault had thus been lost.

The Timing of Operation ROCK MOVE: The Relief by TF *Duke*

Some of the paratroopers in TF *Rock*, including members of the 2d Platoon, Chosen Company, contended that the relief in place (RIP) operation in early July 2008 ultimately affected the planning and execution of ROCK MOVE. The relief of TF *Bayonet* and TF *Rock* by TF *Duke* (3d Brigade Combat Team, 1st Infantry Division) and TF *Blue Spaders* (1st Battalion, 26th Infantry) was a complex operation that was to take place over a number of weeks between 7 July and early August. The execution of the RIP complicated operations at the battalion level during the period immediately prior to the Wanat attack. The staff had to plan for both current tactical operations and the imminent redeployment. Moreover, some key personnel such as the brigade engineer, had redeployed early to facilitate the return to home station.[35]

Certainly, some leaders in the 2d Platoon believed the RIP distracted TF *Rock*. Dzwik described the timing of ROCK MOVE as problematic, if only because the RIP involved moving thousands of unit members around Afghanistan with helicopters, assets that were in short supply even without an ongoing relief. Other observers have noted that the traditional winter lull in combat operations presented a better time to establish a new COP in the Waygal Valley. TF *Rock* might have considered doing exactly this during the winter months of late 2007 and early 2008. However, at that time the unit was still committed to operating at COP Bella and Chosen Company had only one platoon available for manning outposts in the Waygal Valley. Thus, that winter would have been a difficult time to establish a second COP in the valley.[36]

The Coalition command could have tasked the incoming unit, TF *Duke*, with the mission of establishing the COP at Wanat, either immediately after the RIP or in the latter months of 2008 when the fighting season waned. The higher echelons of command at division, brigade, and battalion levels however, believed that TF *Rock* was a better choice for the job and that the end of that unit's deployment was a better time. They did not want to pass this mission to a new unit which lacked the experience of TF *Rock* and organizationally had fewer troops and other resources than Ostlund's command. Brigadier General Milley recalled that both the brigade commander and battalion commander believed that their units were the right force to establish the COP at Wanat. Milley remembered that Preysler "absolutely did not want, and strongly recommended against, handing that task off to the incoming brigade."[37] Milley considered the potential problems presented by executing ROCK MOVE while the RIP was ongoing. Ultimately, Schloesser and Milley decided that because Preysler and Ostlund had over 15 months of experience in the region and had been developing the operation for months, TF *Rock* was the right team to establish the COP at Wanat.[38]

Defensive Positioning

While contextual factors like the RIP contributed to the conditions extant prior to the attack at Wanat, far more important to the course of the engagement was the tactical situation at COP Kahler itself. Specifically, the positioning of the defenders and the placement of weapons had a direct effect on the unfolding of events. The size of the Wanat garrison is the best starting point for this discussion. C Company had placed two platoons, one US and one ANA (with three US Marine advisors), amounting to 56 infantrymen plus a medic and a forward observer, at Wanat. This force was supported by a small composite mortar section consisting of a single

120-mm mortar, one 60-mm mortar, and six men. The battalion also augmented the garrison with a three man TOW missile squad attached from D Company to provide highly accurate direct fire support. TF *Rock* also attached an engineer squad (six men) from the supporting 62d Engineer Battalion to Chosen Company in order to build fighting positions at COP Kahler. Counting Meyer and Aass, this total force of 73 Soldiers was significantly stronger and more capable than the half-platoons from Chosen Company that had earlier garrisoned the more isolated Ranch House and Bella outposts. Further, the contingent at COP Kahler was larger than all those that manned TF *Rock*'s other separate bases, with the exception of Camp Blessing, in July 2008.[39]

The leaders of the Wanat garrison found a position with great potential and significant vulnerabilities. Most of the populated areas in Nuristan were in valleys surrounded by steep sided mountains. Thus, any position in or near these communities was by definition dominated by high ground. Wanat was no exception. However, the village, located as it was only five miles north of Camp Blessing near Nangalam, was far less remote than the previous outposts at Bella and Aranas. Further, a reasonably good road that reinforcements used on the day of the battle connected Wanat to Nangalam. When helicopter support was necessary, the aircraft found fewer terrain hazards around Wanat than at Bella and Ranch House. The position of COP Kahler itself, on the edge of the town, offered good fields of fire in several directions and was compact enough that units could easily be shifted around it.

The positioning of squad and weapon positions within the larger COP is yet another issue. The establishment of fighting positions is part of the art of infantry leadership. Because of the myriad of factors involved, there is no single correct manner of establishing a COP. At Wanat the ultimate repulse of the enemy attack vindicates the defensive arrangements to a degree. Still, salient facts about the tactical placement of squads and weapon positions contributed to the way in which the battle unfolded. The merits of the precise position of the COP as well as the location of vehicles and crew-served weapons, for example, require further discussion. The comments of the platoon sergeant of the reinforcing platoon from B Company, fresh from the Korengal Valley, focused on the weaknesses of the positions at COP Kahler, including the vulnerabilities of the OP. He noted:

> My initial perception of the battlefield was why are we in the low ground, where are the fortifications, and why don't we own any high ground? All of the gun trucks appeared

to be set within a distance of 50-75 meters of one another. . . The [enemy] had made use of all available dead space and buildings surrounding the area where COP Kahler was established and the high grounds on all sides. The OP was open to fires from the high ground on its north and west sides. . . The bazaar separated the OP from the main element where additional [enemy] personnel were located, further separating the US forces.[40]

The general location of the COP, the dead space surrounding it, the positioning of the vehicles and the OP, and the insurgent use of nearby buildings, form the core of the discussion that follows.

COIN principles and Coalition land use policies created several paradoxes for the Soldiers at COP Kahler. While the best terrain for defense was on the high ground surrounding the town, any outpost placed on the ridges would be separated in time and distance from that community. This separation would have violated COIN imperatives that directed counterinsurgent forces to live with and be near the local people. That proximity would allow the Coalition to have a greater understanding of the situation in the settlement and would foster positive relationships between the Coalition and town residents. Therefore, COP Kahler needed to be as close to Wanat as possible. Contributing to this decision about location of the COP was an assumption that the proximity of a large number of civilians to some extent would deter the insurgents from launching major assaults on the outpost. This belief, while perhaps true in the abstract, was negated in practice by the insurgents' success in intimidating the Wanat residents and infiltrating into the town immediately prior to the attack.

The restricted space on the main COP made the positioning of the 120-mm and 60-mm mortars problematic, particularly once the insurgents occupied positions in the nearby buildings. Given the surrounding high ground, the nearby buildings, and the size of the COP, there were no real sites for the mortars that would not be subjected to direct small arms and RPG fire. However, in the cases of both systems, there were better alternatives. While the mortar section placed its 120-mm mortar in a large protected firing position, which also served as the platoon ammunition point, the site was located on the perimeter of the COP protected from enemy fire and ground assault solely by the concertina wire and the incompletely filled HESCO barrier encircling the position.

While US Army mortar crews are expected to be able to defend themselves, their primary mission is to fire the mortars. Accordingly, placing the tubes behind the protection of infantry squad fighting positions would have facilitated the execution of this primary mission. Once the battle started, the mortar section found itself consumed with self defense. The proximity of the ammunition point and firing pit to the COP perimeter meant that the Soldiers designated to man the mortar were too close to the enemy to employ their main weapon system without risking their survival.

The 60-mm mortar was also poorly emplaced and employed. Left in an unmanned position in the center of the COP, the location provided no cover or concealment. Effective enemy small arms fire isolated the tube's position. The 60-mm was designed for quick emplacement and portability but it remained on a site exposed to concentrated enemy fire. Accordingly, this small, portable, and very valuable weapon system remained unused throughout the battle.

The positioning and use of the ANA platoon also merits discussion. Typically, the ANA played a key role in Coalition operations through its ability to communicate with the local population and provide security while US forces accomplish other tasks. During the Coalition's operations in 2006 in Wanat, the ANA played an important role in the defense, occupying key OP positions on high ground around the main position and conducting security patrols and interaction with the local civilians. In July 2008, the activities of the ANA platoon were restricted to constructing and manning three fighting positions on the north side of the COP and a traffic control point (TCP) on the main road just south of the COP. This TCP was redundant as it was backed up by an American TCP a short distance down the same road. On his arrival at Wanat, Myer noted that his interaction with the ANA was restricted to looking at "the ANA sector of fire to ensure that they would have good fire control measures to keep them from firing at US forces."[41] However, as noted above, Myer and Brostrom eventually planned to use the ANA for the patrol tasked with reconnoitering sites for a new OP on high ground overlooking the COP. The insurgents attacked before this patrol began.

After their arrival on 9 July, the 24 Afghan soldiers and their three USMC advisors were certainly available to perform a variety of patrols as well as man OPs. The Marines believed that the Afghan soldiers possessed adequate training and skills to perform effective dismounted patrolling. With the structures so close to the COP perimeter, an ANA presence in the town could possibly have prevented the enemy occupation of the bazaar and other nearby structures. The ANA might have detected many of the signs of enemy infiltration in the town or picked up other indications of the impending attack. Unfortunately, the C Company paratroopers generally distrusted the ANA, holding them in the same low regard as the Afghan Security Guards (ASG) who had failed the company at Ranch House and had killed 2d Platoon's Sergeant First Class Kahler at Bella.[42]

The disposition and use of weapons systems at the COP also shaped the course of the battle. The 2d Platoon had a relatively large number of crew-served direct fire weapons as well as smaller squad automatic weapons (SAWs) at the outpost. The vehicle mounted weapons and the machine guns were key to the defense of any outpost such as COP Kahler. In the case of the 13 July battle at Wanat, these weapons and their crews unleashed a great amount of suppressive fire throughout the engagement. It is important to note that none of the vehicle mounted weapons could directly support the men at OP Topside. This is probably why the platoon leadership chose to place both of the unit's M240 machine guns at the OP.

During the engagement, some of the platoon's weapons failed. A superficial examination of these failures may lead to the conclusion that the root causes were either inherent to the weapons' design or lay in poor maintenance by the operators. However, a more systematic analysis of weapons usage shows that almost all of the weapons that failed did so after firing a high volume of rounds in a short period. While about a fifth of the weapons failed sometime during the action, all but one of these cases occurred after the weapons were fired at a high rate for a number of minutes. The one exception was a SAW from the engineer squad that initially failed to fire but after a routine barrel change was back in action. Several other SAWs also jammed but their operators were able to put them back into working order. There is no conclusive evidence that the weapons' failures led to any of the casualties at COP Kahler.

The concept of employment of weapons in an infantry platoon directed crew-served weapons to provide high rates of fire capable of suppressing enemy positions. These weapons, M240 machine guns and SAWs especially, were designed for such use and were equipped with belt-fed ammunition and extra barrels. No M240s failed in the action and the SAWs that jammed, did so after firing a great number of rounds. As noted above, these jams were fixed when the operators changed barrels. In fact, most of the weapons that jammed at Wanat were M4 carbines. The M4 was the basic individual weapon carried by US Soldiers in Afghanistan and was not designed to fire at the maximum or cyclic rate for extended periods. Enemy action and weapons dispositions forced the defenders of COP Kahler and OP Topside to use their M4s in uncharacteristic roles. This, not weapons maintenance deficiencies or inherent weaknesses in weapons design, was the reason a number of weapons jammed during the battle. The maintenance of a high rate of fire was critical to retaining fire superiority and to prevent positions (particularly OP Topside) from being overrun by determined and continuous insurgent assaults.

During the insurgent attack, the amount of suppressive fire from the crew-served weapons might have been greater but enemy fire, not mechanical failures, hindered their effectiveness. The two mortars were positioned in such a manner that the enemy was able to place direct small arms fire onto their locations. RPG fire at the beginning of the action destroyed the vehicle mounted TOW. The crew of one of the M240 machine guns at the OP was severely wounded by RPG fire at the first enemy volley and the operator of the sniper rifle was killed early. The two M240s at the OP were left unmanned for long periods because one crew was out of action and the other had run out of ammunition, not realizing there was additional ammunition available in the OP from the unmanned weapon. When reinforcements arrived and attempted to use the M240 manned by the wounded or killed Soldiers, they were killed before they could fire the weapon. The other M240 remained unmanned until the second QRF arrived. The Marine advisors also had an M240, which was used throughout the action and was later moved to the OP position.

The main position had two Mk-19 grenade launchers mounted on HMMWVs and a .50-caliber machine gun mounted on the platoon leader's HMMWV. Of these, one Mk-19 jammed but was repaired and fired for the remainder of the action. The other was fired until enemy fire destroyed it. The platoon leader's .50-caliber machine gun fired continuously throughout the action. An additional M2 machine gun mounted on a HMMWV was stationed at the traffic control point and fired until knocked out by enemy fire.

Fire support external to C Company, along with the ability of the Americans to freely shift forces around and between defensive positions, proved to be decisive at Wanat. The arrival of the AH-64 Apache attack helicopters specifically, appears to have been a key moment in the engagement. The fire directed by the Apaches at the insurgent locations near the OP gave enough of a breathing space for the force at COP Kahler to consolidate and redistribute its strength. From that moment forward, the insurgents were essentially on the defensive.

This success is not to argue that the fire support plan was executed smoothly. The enemy's ability to move very close to the Coalition positions prior to the start of the fight negated most of the preplanned fires making fire support an improvised process. Moreover, the absence of the company fire support officer (FSO) and the isolation of the platoon forward observer at the OP hindered the coordination of support, especially the AH-64 Apaches, forcing Myer to devote most of his attention to such issues. On 12 July, Myer had left the FSO at Camp Blessing because he believed Pitts, the platoon forward observer, was extremely competent. He had no idea that Pitts would be fighting for his life at Topside during most of the engagement. Accordingly, Myer was forced to focus on managing air support (CAS), indirect fire assets, and MEDEVAC assets during the major part of the action. This limited his direct influence on tactical decisions. However, what impact the absence of the company FSO had on fire support is speculative, at best. Myer managed to obtain both fire and MEDEVAC assets for Wanat as soon as possible and, with only a single platoon from his company on the ground, this was undoubtedly his most important role in the battle.

The first Apaches arrived about an hour after the start of the action. Since the critical part of ROCK MOVE had already passed, the limited number of Apaches was providing a general support role for all of TF *Bayonet* based out of the centrally located airbase at Jalalabad. The direct flight time to Wanat was about 30 minutes. However, the Apaches were delayed by the requirement to escort the MEDEVAC Blackhawk helicopters, also located at Jalalabad, which were alerted after the Apaches were. The AH-64s then had to loiter around Camp Blessing until the field artillery barrage was halted so they could safely approach Wanat. Attack aviation arrived at Wanat as quickly as it could.

The placement of the OP is perhaps the most important factor contributing to the course of the engagement at Wanat. As documented in the second chapter, the leadership of the 2d Platoon was concerned that troops at the main COP had only limited fields of vision to the east because the bazaar blocked that view. Also of concern was the inability to see to the north, especially toward the bridges over the river from the COP. The view in this direction was blocked by the town's buildings. Any OP location had to offer relatively clear views in both these directions. Accordingly, beginning in April, C Company commander Myer, 2d Platoon leader Brostrom and platoon sergeant Dzwik began looking at the ridgeline that OP Topside ultimately was placed on as the general location for an OP position.[43]

Some consideration was given to establishing an OP on top of or inside the hotel. However, that decision would have entailed moving the residents out of the building and thus risked alienating the population. Finally, while Brostrom and Dzwik believed the OP needed to be on higher ground, Brostrom also thought it could not be so far up the rise of the slope that travel between the location and the main COP would become too dangerous or time consuming. Put simply, Brostrom and Dzwik believed that if attacked, the OP had to be close enough for quick and easy reinforcement. An additional factor was a rocky outcropping partway up the ridge to the east of the bazaar. This outcropping consisted of three large rocks arranged in a roughly triangular configuration and a large shady tree. The paratroopers felt that the rocks would enhance the OP position by providing a certain amount of natural protection. The position of the rocks, however, was not on the military crest of the ridge, a fact that ultimately affected fields of observation. Brostrom eventually went along with this point, even defending the decision later with Myer, his company commander.[44]

All these factors led Brostrom to choose a spot on the side of the ridgeline approximately 60 yards east-northeast of the main COP. While that location offered good fields of vision eastward and distantly to the north, it was separated from the COP by the bazaar. This not only made OP Topside difficult to see from the main COP but also forced any travel between the OP and the main COP to go around the bazaar buildings which might complicate the movement of any reinforcing unit. More importantly, OP Topside was potentially fatally vulnerable because of the proximity of the deep ravine directly to its north and the dead space that this terrain feature created to within ten yards of the northern position of the OP. Enemy elements approaching westward down the Wayskawdi Creek toward Wanat could use the concealment offered by the dead space to get within grenade range of the OP when they initiated their attack.

The 2d Platoon did not adequately cover this dead space either through the use of mines, early warning devices, or by patrolling. The platoon leader's decision against mounting patrols has been discussed earlier in this chapter. The mine available to cover dead space was the Claymore antipersonnel mine. The Claymores used at OP Topside were not employed in this capacity but rather emplaced closer to the OP to repulse ground assaults during periods of limited visibility. In this role, the Claymores had a mixed record. More passive measures, such as tripwire flares or other movement detection devices do not seem to have been available to the platoon. Nor did the unit place expedient early warning devices in the dead space. However, the platoon leadership was quite aware of the problem and planned to use indirect fire to engage any enemy element detected in that low ground. The mortars were the most responsive indirect fire weapons for this mission but enemy action precluded the early use of the best indirect fire systems available to cover the space. The 155-mm howitzers at Camp Blessing were also available but during the battle the proximity of the enemy to the OP made their use dangerous.

After the battle, both Myer and Dzwik expressed reservations about the location of the OP primarily because of the dead space but also because higher ground overlooked it. On his arrival at COP Kahler on 12 July, Captain Myer determined that the site of the OP was not optimal and planned to shift it to a better location at the earliest opportunity. Because Myer did not believe an attack was imminent, this shift was to take place the morning of the attack. Such a site would have likely been farther to the east along the same ridge in a position better able to observe the ravine of the Wayskawdi Creek. That position would have been harder to reinforce than OP Topside proved to be. However, if Brostrom and Dzwik had redefined the mission of the OP to be a small post that would provide early warning of enemy movements rather than a relatively larger post that had a robust ability (two M240 machine guns) to not just detect but fight the enemy, the need for reinforcement may have been precluded. The reinforcing platoon from B Company did, in fact, move the OP to this position on higher ground at its first opportunity.[45]

Summary

All operations in war require a certain amount of risk because there are variables in play that could impact operations. These variables include the weather, the effects of terrain and, most importantly, the actions of the enemy. In COIN, the actions of the civilian population must be added to this list. At Wanat, a very experienced American infantry unit executed a complicated operation to establish a new post several days before the end of their deployment. The insurgent enemy, already prepared to attack the now abandoned Bella outpost, shifted gears against almost all American expectations, and attacked the new Wanat position within days of its establishment. The American and ANA forces defeated this attack but suffered nine combat deaths and over two dozen wounded in that defense. The Coalition then withdrew from the area. This final section summarizes the reasons for and the results of the actions on 13 July 2008 in Wanat, Afghanistan.

Counterinsurgency Operations

Across its large AO, TF *Rock* clearly pursued a COIN campaign. The unit's operations were a combination of lethal and nonlethal missions, all focused on winning support from the local population. The TF had great success in the Pech Valley by using road construction and other building projects. In the Korengal and Waygal Valleys, there was less success in winning support. The xenophobia of the Waygal population was one reason for this lack of success. Nuristanis have historically shown suspicion of and sometimes hostility toward outsiders. This hostility could be defined as tightly as distrust of a neighboring village and as loosely as hatred of any foreigners.

Compounding this cultural factor was the relatively minimal force projected by the Coalition into the valley. Because TF *Rock*'s units were stretched across a huge and mountainous region, Chosen Company, the element responsible for the Waygal Valley, could only afford to commit one US platoon to the valley at any given time. In a COIN campaign, such decentralization automatically incurred risk. In order to minimize the inherent risk, TF *Rock*'s leadership attempted to reallocate forces and other assets to meet changing demands and enemy actions. In fact, one can argue that leaders in CJTF-101, TF *Bayonet*, and TF *Rock* decided to conduct ROCK MOVE because they were felt strongly that COP Bella was too risky too maintain. Lieutenant Colonel Ostlund and his staff further attempted to mitigate risk generally by establishing quick reaction forces as well as positioning supporting units such as field artillery and combat aviation in places where they could best assist the small outposts. This was a difficult balancing act and one that had to be done on almost a daily basis.

Decentralized operations also meant that the Coalition could offer only promises of comprehensive security to the population in many communities. The reality was that local insurgents in the Korengal, Waygal, and other valleys often held a great amount of influence over loyalties and actions of local populations. The enemy presence in Wanat was so great that it turned the town's leaders against the government that had appointed them and into accomplices in the attack on COP Kahler. TF *Rock* never fully gained a strong foothold in the Waygal Valley. The small elements that manned the COPs at Bella and Aranas were never large enough to provide security and win the support of the populations of those small settlements. The establishment of COP Kahler was TF *Rock*'s attempt to remedy the situation by building a new outpost in the district center. The leadership in TF *Rock* recognized that the insurgents held power in Wanat but believed that Operation ROCK MOVE was a way to mitigate this influence in Wanat and, over time, reverse this condition. Further, the base at Wanat would not only be more secure because of its proximity to Camp Blessing but it would serve as the platform from which TF *Rock* and TF *Duke*, the incoming US brigade in the region, could begin efforts to win support from the population of the Waygal Valley.

Combat Outpost Stationing in TF Rock

This work has attempted to place the battle at Wanat into the historical context of operations in the Waygal Valley. Over the course of 2007 and early 2008, the Coalition outposts were gradually moved nearer the main regional base at Camp Blessing. Wanat was the least remote post in the Waygal Valley. It was located less than five miles from Camp Blessing, far closer to the battalion headquarters than many other platoon sized positions in the TF *Rock* AO. Platoon COPs were the most common type of position in the TF *Rock* AO. Several such positions, including COP Kahler, also contained a company headquarters element as well as a combat platoon. With 74 Soldiers including the Afghan unit and other US attachments, the force at COP Kahler on 13 July was actually larger than that which manned typical outposts in the eastern part of Afghanistan.

Operations in AO Rock were decentralized to the company and platoon levels. The position at Wanat was a US and ANA platoon position. The platoon leader, assisted by his platoon sergeant, was the appropriate level of command. However, both the ANA and 2-503d Infantry deployed company headquarters to the position after a couple of days. This was appropriate considering that the platoons had been augmented with company and battalion level assets (mortars, TOW, and engineers). Command and control was simplified by collocating company commanders to the location. Whether higher level commanders (battalion, brigade, division) should have come to Wanat in the short period before the battle is problematic. To the chain of command, the most dangerous part of ROCK MOVE was the initial occupation of the position. Once this happened successfully, Wanat became a lesser priority than places under continual enemy contact such as the Korengal and Pech Valley regions.

While TF *Rock* had intelligence indicators of massed insurgents, these were thought to have been brought together to attack the long established COP Bella. After air attacks blunted such an attack on 4 July and the move to Wanat was successfully executed several days later, most US observers felt that the enemy would have to have a preparatory period before attacking Wanat by ground assault. This was the enemy pattern in the past.

The decision to conduct ROCK MOVE during the beginning of the relief in place, transfer of authority (RIPTOA) process was clearly a calculated risk. However, the American chain of command strongly believed that such a maneuver was less risky if conducted by the departing experienced unit, rather than the new inexperienced unit, TF *Blue Spaders*. Therefore, having Chosen Company conduct ROCK MOVE was actually considered the less risky action.

Although the battalion and brigade commanders did not visit Wanat before the battle and Myer only arrived the day before, this was hardly an example of command neglect. These commanders had busy schedules and multiple operations going on during the period 8-12 July. On 11 July, Ostlund escorted Admiral Michael Mullen, the senior American military officer, in a tour of the Korengal Valley and otherwise had a full slate of meetings with local officials and leaders throughout the AO Rock region. Myer personally directed the evacuation of Bella on 8 and 9 July and was diverted to Camp Blessing for the investigation of the 4 July Apache incident in which he played a major role. 12 July was the earliest he could get to Wanat given the investigation and the availability of transportation. Given that the Waygal Valley was quiet during the Bella evacuation and the first days of the Wanat occupation, it seems reasonable that these officers' attentions were devoted to more pressing matters.

Insurgent Performance

The preparations made by the insurgents at Wanat appear to have been thorough. Troops apparently assembled, received arms and ammunition, and marched to preparatory positions without any problems. In this, they were aided both by the illumination cycle and, critically, the American expectation that any overt action by the enemy would begin with probing attacks. However, once the battle started, usual insurgent deficiencies became apparent. Enemy fire control was almost nonexistent with volume substituting for accuracy and although the AAF massed forces at Wanat, they were not all committed initially to provide the maximum effect. Nevertheless, initial enemy fire was accurate enough to target effectively COP Kahler's most powerful weapon systems. The TOW vehicle was destroyed by several RPG hits fired at short range. None actually hit the TOW system itself, which theoretically could have been removed from the vehicle and mounted on the ground until the ammunition caught fire. While insurgent fire neutralized the mortars, it also damaged the enemy position in the bazaar. Although the enemy fire's intensity was high, its relative inaccuracy allowed the Americans to shift troops around the position and reinforce the OP several times. If the insurgents had not been firing from positions so close to the Americans, this advantage in volume would likely have been lost as well.

While the insurgents massed a relatively large force to attack Wanat, not all their forces appear to have been committed at the same time. Had they done so, the effect may have been decisive. Instead, the enemy was able to stay in the firefight for an extended period of time despite the likelihood of incurring significant casualties. This left some of their fresh troops exposed to American firepower when air support and reinforcements arrived. The insurgents would have been better served to have used their entire force in one massive strike at the beginning of the action. As it was, the survivors were exposed to concentrated fires from Coalition CAS as they withdrew from the battle area.

The Outcome at Wanat

At the tactical level, American and ANA troops successfully defended COP Kahler. The key factor in the defense was that the forces employed, particularly when supported with additional firepower assets and a stream of reinforcements, were adequate to defend the positions. The defenders were able to maintain sufficient fires throughout the action, allowing leaders at the base to shift forces to protect the most threatened areas, particularly the OP. This achievement came in spite of the neutralization of the unit's mortars and TOW, the limited value of field artillery in the region, and the hour required by the AH-64 Apaches to travel to Wanat. The Coalition's defense of Wanat vindicated an approach that featured reserves of air power and ground troops made readily available to areas under attack.

Following the battle at Wanat, Major General Schloesser, the CJTF-101 commander, decided to remove Coalition forces from the Waygal valley. His reasoning behind this decision rested on his understanding that the population in Wanat did not support the Coalition generally and would not support a COP within the limits of the town. Further, he believed that CJTF-101 did not have the troops and other resources necessary to place a new COP on the high ground above Wanat, from which a successful campaign to win over the town population might be possible. This evacuation was more of a relocation of the available forces than a retreat. Both TF *Rock* and its successor unit TF *Blue Spaders*, had responsibility for a large AO that included the most densely population areas of the Konar and Pech River valleys as well as the dangerous Korengal Valley. The RIP between TF *Rock* and TF *Blue Spaders* was not a one for one relief. The new unit was a modular combined arms battalion reconfigured to light infantry status for duty in Afghanistan. As such, it was slightly smaller than the airborne infantry battalion it was replacing. Without an influx of additional troops into the region, the US presence in this AO, already limited, would necessarily become smaller.

Events subsequent to the battle make the decision to evacuate the Waygal valley more difficult to assess. After the attack on COP Kahler, the US command adopted an indirect approach to deal with the Waygal

Valley. Rather than creating small outposts with the limited number of troops available in the valley, the command decided to isolate the area and use the troops in more populated areas. On assuming his duties in June 2009, General Stanley McChrystal, the American theater commander in Afghanistan, adopted a similar policy on a broader basis which resulted in the withdrawal of US forces from many capillary valleys in Northeast Afghanistan.

At the strategic level, Wanat will only prove to have negative effects if ultimately the United States departs Afghanistan because the nation becomes convinced that the overall effort is not worth the cost, with Wanat being used as one piece of evidence in such an argument. As such, the battle's importance could rise to a level far greater than its actual military significance.

Casualties at Wanat

The relatively high American casualty rate on 13 July 2008 has been attributed to a number of causes. These include weapons failures, command neglect, intelligence failures, logistics deficiencies, slow air support, and a failure to conduct COIN operations. A detailed analysis of these assertions shows that weapons did not fail and that problems with logistical support, while possibly hindering the creation of an impregnable defense, did not hinder the creation of an adequate defense. Air support was dispatched as quickly as possible with any delays based on a combination of limited air assets and the geography of northeastern Afghanistan.

The major cause of American casualties sits squarely in the realm of situational awareness, more specifically the Coalition leadership's understanding of the insurgent enemy capability and intent. This situational awareness is better described not as a failure but as one of the persistent risks in warfare that so far has not been eliminated by advanced military technology. The enemy reacted in a way the Americans did not expect. While an adequate force and quick reaction system was in place to prevent a more complete disaster, this miscalculation did contribute to the high number of casualties.

Intelligence is not simply a matter of information collection. It is also a matter of information interpretation. By July 2008, all the officers in the TF *Rock* and TF *Bayonet* chain of command were experienced veterans of the war with these insurgents. They expected the enemy forces to react in the same way they had in the past. The insurgents had never attacked a position so soon after its establishment. They had never induced the population of a town to depart and allow that community to be turned into a base for immediate operations. While Coalition intelligence indicated that the enemy intended to attack in the Waygal Valley, the insurgents showed an uncharacteristic flexibility in shifting their focus immediately from Bella to Wanat and then in executing the attack.

The hot and cold nature of operations in the Waygal Valley played into the insurgents' hands and was a major reason for the American interpretation. While the district saw three of the biggest battles in TF *Rock*'s tour in northeast Afghanistan, the area was virtually inactive between these events, particularly when compared to other valleys. When the dangerous portion of ROCK MOVE, the withdrawal from COP Bella, was successfully completed, the Waygal Valley seemed to have reverted to a cold status. Limited intelligence assets were moved elsewhere and signs that the enemy had assembled large forces were interpreted to mean an eventual attack, not an immediate one.

A secondary cause for the large number of casualties was the positioning of OP Topside, the site where eight of the nine deaths occurred. Observers will understandably argue about whether or not the platoon leadership made an accurate risk assessment which included key factors such as terrain, weapons emplacement and employment, dead space, and fields of fire. However, the overriding consideration is whether the benefits that the location of the OP gave to the force at COP Kahler outweighed its weaknesses. To be sure, the OP allowed for observation of the bridges to the north and up the slopes to the east and northeast. The platoon leader had magnified the capabilities of the OP by placing the platoon forward observer (FO) and LRAS3 there. Additionally, for an OP, Topside was manned by a sizable force that had two M240 machine guns along with other small arms. Finally, the OP was positioned near enough to the main COP to allow reinforcements to reach it relatively quickly. On the other hand, the force at the OP was too small and too isolated to maintain the firepower necessary to repulse, without casualties, any sizable enemy contingent that attacked from close proximity. This type of attack was possible because of the ravine directly to the north of the OP which the Soldiers could not observe. This inability to see into the ravine was a critical weakness and ultimately, that terrain served as a covered and concealed route for the insurgents during the battle. The initial insurgent volley of fire from small arms and RPGs, while effective elsewhere, was particularly devastating to the nine man position on the side of the ridge. After the opening fusillade and the insurgents' successful approach to the very edge of the OP, the initial fight at Topside became one of attrition in which the larger enemy force would probably win. This outcome became all the more likely when a large reinforcing element did not move immediately to the isolated OP once the fight began. All of the Soldiers at the main COP were busy reacting to enemy fire at that time. Instead, over the course of the first hour of the engagement, two smaller ad hoc QRFs arrived at the OP separately. Each of these forces took casualties, some incurred even before they arrived at Topside but these valorous actions and the arrival of the AH-64 Apache attack helicopters prevented the OP from being overrun by the enemy.

Closing Thoughts

Any military engagement if examined closely enough, will yield insights of potentially great value to serving Soldiers as they go forward to meet the challenges of their era. The engagement at Wanat, Afghanistan on 13 July 2008 is no exception. Different reviewers may use the same facts to reach different lists of insights or "lessons learned." Thus, such a list compiled by one individual is by its very nature incomplete when seen by a wider community. This truism notwithstanding, the creation of such a list may be a useful exercise at this stage of our understanding of the Wanat fight. What follows is an admittedly partial list of observations and potential insights from CSI's investigation of the engagement on 13 July 2008:[46]

1. In a country like Afghanistan, with its extremes of terrain, altitude, and weather, the positive effect of a relatively small infantry force can be multiplied several fold by committing what would normally be considered an excessive number of enablers such as aviation and engineer assets. In a war of small heavily fortified posts nestled amongst the population in nearly vertical terrain, aviation and engineer units can extend the reach, sustainability, and survivability of the maneuver formations committed to the fight.

2. In a COIN environment, where the emphasis is on interaction with the populace, units may find themselves distributed throughout a large area in small platoon or squad-sized outposts. When these smaller units are operating in a decentralized manner across a distributed battlefield, commanders at all levels must provide necessary capabilities or further assess risk when required capabilities are not available. Within risk assessments, it is critical to determine where risk is mitigated and where it is not, therefore identifying acceptable and unacceptable risk.

3. Soldiers at any level can be lulled into an unwarranted sense of security in regard to what they believe the enemy will do and give short shrift to what the enemy can do based upon previous experience. Virtually

everyone involved with Operation ROCK MOVE, from squad to CJTF, expected the enemy to respond in a particular way and that way was quite different from what actually happened. Military history is replete with examples of Soldiers turning threat analysis based on templates into ironclad paradigms, to their ultimate detriment. While the outcome at Wanat was not quite so catastrophic as some earlier examples of this phenomenon from American military history, the cost to 2d Platoon, Chosen Company was high in July 2008.

4. The normal progression of observations by low level units up the intelligence chain can lead to the loss of nuance and significance in the successive INTSUMs (intelligence summaries) ultimately reaching decision-makers. What the TF *Bayonet* G2 called "atmospherics" tended to drop out of the reporting of events as the multiple echelons recast and broadened their submissions. At least one general officer in the Wanat story has considered this phenomenon important enough to warrant possible structural changes in the reporting methodology.

5. When units rotate in and out of theater on a more or less fixed but staggered schedule, strong consideration should be given to the human effects such policies engender. Tasks given to both incoming and outgoing units should be balanced against both their capabilities and their expectations. At the higher echelons, these considerations seem to have been well balanced in regard to executing Operation ROCK MOVE during a complex RIP-TOA. Some of that understanding and balance, however, may not have penetrated to the company and platoon level where the policy had to be implemented at the end of a long, tiring, and dangerous tour in Afghanistan.

6. In a complex COIN environment, host nation forces will most likely be present and will also most likely not initially reach the level of professionalism thought to be necessary by their American counterparts. This disparity in capabilities can easily lead American personnel to underutilize the host nation units when attached to an American led operation, resulting in a potential loss of fighting power. The ANA platoon at Wanat, was still judged to be relatively immature as a unit, and thus was assigned solely to the construction of its own defensive positions.

7. Given the perceived need to co-locate with the population in a COIN-centric operation, Coalition forces must retain situational awareness beyond their perimeter. If true standoff distance cannot be obtained or is deemed counterproductive, some means to see beyond the next building periodically must be gained. At Wanat, regular patrolling was foregone in

the interest of advancing the state of the defensive fortifications, a difficult but understandable choice. Given the particular physical layout of the Wanat position, however, more aggressive patrolling may have been the only means to gain the necessary situational awareness to deny the enemy an unimpeded and concealed approach to the COP.

8. In small unit actions involving defensive positions, choices made early in micro-environments may have large consequences. Observation Post Topside, while sited to see the distant bridges, the higher mountains, and the southeast ridge upon whose lower slopes it sat, had absolutely no capability to see into the ravine of the Wayskawdi Creek or indeed into the dead ground little more than 10 yards in front of it. Thus the LRAS3 emplaced at Topside could see far but not near thereby permitting a concealed approach to both Topside and the village buildings between Topside and the main COP. While there seldom are perfect choices in defensive placement and the reasons for placing Topside where it was are understandable, the fact remains that an unobserved approach to within grenade range of the Coalition positions was left uncovered. Seen in that light, the formidable earth moving done by SGT Pitts's Topside garrison may have inadvertently provided a false sense of security for all, however well it sheltered the occupants of the OP. Throughout the history of infantry fighting, placement decisions of only a few yards difference occasionally make a vast difference in the outcome of the fight and Wanat was no exception.

9. Finally, in a point that hardly bears repeating, technological superiority does not always guarantee battlefield success at minimal cost. Full motion video and robust SIGINT are helpful but are not infallible panaceas even if available 24/7. Technological marvels like ITAS and LRAS3 marvelously extend our range of vision but cannot yet extend into dead ground 10 yards in our front. Eventually, technology often gives way to human factors: courage, fear, and fatigue to name but a few and we must rely upon what some have called "aggressive self rescue" by individual Soldiers to prevail. The engagement at Wanat is yet another example of that phenomenon.

War can be studied. Tremendous tools of technology can be applied to complex analyses. What is unpredictable and cannot be completely measured is the human factor. The opposing sides are composed of human beings whose actions and reactions can be projected but not completely predicted. At Wanat, the enemy did not act as expected. Nevertheless, the defenders, although relatively small in number and dispersed over two separate positions and without their most important crew-served weapons, fought harder than the enemy expected and defeated them.

American casualties in the Battle of Wanat, although still relatively small in comparison to similar actions in American military history, were higher than public expectations in the modern age. Accordingly, the media and the public have sought an explanation for the losses. However, such explanations are not necessarily clear cut. War is not a science but an art. It is a series of actions and reactions by opposing sides both of which are operating in an environment of uncertainty. Historically, a professional military force has served the United States well and the US Soldiers and Marines who fought at Wanat on 13 July 2008 maintained, and indeed, strengthened this tradition.

Notes

1. Department of the Army, Field Manual 1-02, *Operational Terms and Graphics* (Washington, DC: Government Printing Office, 2004), 1-10.

2. *Merriam Webster's Collegiate Dictionary*, 11th ed., s.v."1Overrun."

3. An example of even a semi-official government media outlet referring to an overrun at Wanat is "US, Afghan Troops Abandon Base Overrun by Militants," *Voice of America News*, 16 July 2008, http://www.globalsecurity.org/military/library/news/2008/07/mil-080716-voa01.htm (accessed on 31 August 2010). As late as June 2010, media outlets were still referring to Wanat incorrectly as an ambush. See Greg Jaffe, "Army Overrules Inquiry Faulting Officers in Wanat Ambush," *Washington Post,* 24 June 2010, http://www.washingtonpost.com/wp-dyn/content/article/2010/06/23/AR2010062305289.html (accessed on 31 August 2010).

4. Exhibit 16a (CPT, Company Commander, C/2-503d IN, interview) to US Central Command (CENTCOM), "Re-Investigation into the Combat Action at Wanat Village, Wygal District, Nuristan Province, Afghanistan, on 13 July 2008 (Redacted), 60-3, 68-9; Exhibit 11a (COL, Brigade Commander, 173d ABCT, interview) to US Central Command (CENTCOM), "Re-Investigation into the Combat Action at Wanat Village, Wygal District, Nuristan Province, Afghanistan, on 13 July 2008 (Redacted), 17-19; Exhibit 7a (LTC, Battalion Commander, 2-503d IN, interview) to US Central Command (CENTCOM), "Re-Investigation into the Combat Action at Wanat Village, Wygal District, Nuristan Province, Afghanistan, on 13 July 2008 (Redacted), 23, 50-1, 54-5; Exhibit 9a (MG, CJTF-101 Commander, 101st Airborne Division, interview) to US Central Command (CENTCOM), "Re-Investigation into the Combat Action at Wanat Village, Wygal District, Nuristan Province, Afghanistan, on 13 July 2008 (Redacted), 26, 29-30; Milley interview, 18 and 20 August 2009, 22-3.

5. Greg Jaffe, "'They Feel Like Outsiders and They Don't Want to Be:' The U.S. Hopes that Afghans in Areas Along the Pech River Will Embrace Progress, But Much Unrest Remains," *Washington Post*, 6 October 2009, http://www.washingtonpost.com/wp-dyn/content/article/2009/10/05/AR2009100503799_pf.html (accessed 14 December 2009).

6. The crew of one of the M240 machine guns at the OP perceived they had run out of ammunition, although the basic load of the other M240 positioned at the OP was available nearby for their use.

7. Sergeant First Class David Dzwik, interview by Matt Matthews, Combat Studies Institute, Fort Leavenworth, KS, 21 October 2008, 7.

8. Sergeant Erik Aass, interview by Matt Matthews, Combat Studies Institute, Fort Leavenworth, KS, 13 January 2009, 11.

9. The DSC recommendation was for SGT Ryan Pitts. The Silver Star awardees included, in alphabetical order: SPC Ayers (posthumous), 1LT Brostrom (posthumous), SPC Davis, SPC Denton, SGT Garcia (posthumous), SGT Gilmore,

SSG Grimm, SPC Hayes, CPL (USMC) Jones, CPT Myer, SSG E. Phillips, SGT Pitts (interim award), SSG Samaroo, and SPC Scantlin.

10. Carter Malkasian and Gerald Meyerle, *Provincial Reconstruction Teams: How Do We Know They Work?* (Carlisle Barracks, PA: Strategic Studies Institute, 2009), 19; TF *Rock, "*AO Rock Overview, 26 July 2008" Briefing, slide 92.

11. Colonel William Ostlund, e-mail to Donald P. Wright, Combat Studies Institute, Fort Leavenworth, KS, 15 September 2009; TF *Rock*, "AO ROCK Overview, 26 July 2008" Briefing, slide 31. Population figures are from 2000 and were found at http://geobase.org.af/maps/national/population/afgPopulationEstimates.xls (accessed 18 December 2009).

12. Colonel William Ostlund, interview by Contemporary Operations Study Team, Combat Studies Institute, Fort Leavenworth, KS, 19–20 March 2009, 10.

13. Captain Matthew Myer, interview by Matt Matthews, Combat Studies Institute, Fort Leavenworth, KS, 1 December 2008, 3, 8.

14. Myer, interview.

15. TF *Rock*, "CONOP ROCK MOVE, 2/3 ANA, C/2-503 IN (ABN) and 2-17 CAV, Level 1 CONOP, 8–9 July 08*"* Briefing, slide 6.

16. First Lieutenant Matthew Colley, statement to Douglas R. Cubbison, Combat Studies Institute, Fort Leavenworth, KS, undated 2009, 6; TF *Rock*, "CONOP ROCK MOVE" Briefing, slide 7.

17. Lieutenant Colonel William Ostlund, e-mail to Donald P. Wright, Combat Studies Institute, Fort Leavenworth, KS, 19 November 2009.

18. Ostlund e-mail.

19. Exhibit 9a (MG, CJTF-101 Commander, 101st Airborne Division, interview) to US Central Command (CENTCOM), "Re-Investigation into the Combat Action at Wanat Village, Wygal District, Nuristan Province, Afghanistan, on 13 July 2008 (Redacted), 26, 29-30; Milley interview, 18 and 20 August 2009, 22-3; Exhibit 11a (COL, Brigade Commander, 173d ABCT, interview) to US Central Command (CENTCOM), "Re-Investigation into the Combat Action at Wanat Village, Wygal District, Nuristan Province, Afghanistan, on 13 July 2008 (Redacted), 17-19

20. TF *Rock*, "CONOP ROCK MOVE" Briefing, slides 5 and 7. Lieutenant Colonel William Ostlund, e-mail to Douglas R. Cubbison, Combat Studies Institute, Fort Leavenworth, KS, 8 May 2009. After the 4 July incident, while no aircraft were fired upon at Bella, the AAF did periodically shoot RPGs at the outpost. Despite the lack of antiaircraft fire, TF *Rock* personnel were very anxious about this threat as intercepted enemy ICOM radio traffic indicated that the AAF was preparing to engage helicopters in the area. See TF *Bayonet*, "07 July 2008 Bayonet CUB Brief to CJTF-101," 7 July 2008.

21. TF *Rock*, "TIC Asset Tracker" Spreadsheet, 22 July 2008; General Charles Campbell, "Memorandum, Subject: Army Action on the Re-Investigation into the Combat Action at Wanat Village, Wygal District, Nuristan Province, Afghanistan, on 13 July 2008, 13 May 2010, 8-9, 11; TF *Rock*, "Rock Daily Snapshot-Thursday, July 10, 2008."

22. TF *Rock*, "CONOP ROCK MOVE" Briefing, slide 6; Lieutenant Colonel William Ostlund, "Battle of Wanat Storyboard and Brief" Briefing, 16 July 2008, slide 4; Myer, interview, 1 December 2008, 4.

23. Captain Benjamin Pry, interview by Douglas R. Cubbison, Combat Studies Institute, Fort Leavenworth, KS, 6 May 2009, 6; TF *Rock*, "CONOP ROCK MOVE" Briefing, slides 6 and 7.

24. Pry, interview, 6 May 2009, 8;

25. Pry; Myer, interview, 1 December 2008, 3.

26. Pry, interview, 6 May 2009, 7; Ostlund, "Battle of Wanat Storyboard and Brief" Briefing, slide 3.

27. Lieutenant Colonel William Ostlund Statement, CJTF-101, "Army Regulation 15-6 Investigation into Battle of Wanat (Redacted, Unclassified Version)" (Bagram Air Base, Afghanistan, 21 October 2008).

28. Pry, interview, 6 May 2009, 7.

29. Pry, interview, 6 May 2009, 12–13.

30. Brigadier General Mark Milley, interview by Douglas R. Cubbison and Dr. William G. Robertson, Combat Studies Institute, Fort Leavenworth, KS, 18 and 20 August 2009, 23; Seth G. Jones, *In the Graveyard of Empires, America's War in Afghanistan* (New York, NY: W.W. Norton and Company, 2009), 311–312; US Central Command (CENTCOM), "Re-investigation into the Combat Action at Wanat Village, Wygal District, Nuristan Province, Afghanistan, on 13 July 2008 (Redacted), 44-45.

31. Exhibit 16a (CPT, Company Commander, C/2-503d IN, interview) to US Central Command (CENTCOM), "Re-investigation into the Combat Action at Wanat Village, Wygal District, Nuristan Province, Afghanistan, on 13 July 2008 (Redacted), 64.

32. For a detailed discussion of these issues, see Major Brian T. Beckno, interview by Douglas R. Cubbison, Combat Studies Institute, Fort Leavenworth, KS, 2 July 2009, 3–7 and Exhibit 12a (COL, Commander, 101st Aviation Brigade, interview) to US Central Command (CENTCOM), "Re-Investigation into the Combat Action at Wanat Village, Wygal District, Nuristan Province, Afghanistan, on 13 July 2008 (Redacted), 8-9.

33. Captain Devin George, "Logistics at Wanat," e-mail to Douglas R. Cubbison, Combat Studies Institute, Fort Leavenworth, KS, 22 April 2009.

34. Staff Sergeant Jonathan G. Benton, interview by Douglas R. Cubbison, Combat Studies Institute, Fort Leavenworth, KS, 4 August 2009, 8.

35. Captain William Cromie, interview by Douglas R. Cubbison, Combat Studies Institute, Fort Leavenworth, KS, 13 August 2009. The transfer of authority between TF *Rock* and TF *Blue Spaders* ultimately took place on 24 July 2008.

36. Sergeant First Class David Dzwik, interview by Douglas R. Cubbison, Combat Studies Institute, Fort Leavenworth, KS, 2 April 2009, 4.

37. Milley, interview, 18 and 20 August 2009, 18.

38. Mille interview, 23.

39. Even in the volatile Korengal Valley, the reinforced B Company occupied three platoon-size outposts rather than one large company position.

40. Exhibit 10 (SFC, B/2-503d IN, statement)CJTF-101, "Army Regulation 15-6 Investigation into Battle of Wanat (Redacted, Unclassified Version)" (Korengal Outpost, Afghanistan, 16 July 2008), 1.

41. Captain Matthew Myer, Sworn Statement (Co C, 2d Battalion, 503d Infantry), CJTF-101, "AR 15-6 Investigation into Battle of Wanat, 21 July 2008."

42. Exhibit 42b (Staff Sergeant, USMC ETT 5-3, statement) to US Central Command (CENTCOM), "Re-Investigation into the Combat Action at Wanat Village, Wygal District, Nuristan Province, Afghanistan, on 13 July 2008 (Redacted), 39, 42.

43. Sergeant First Class David Dzwik, interview by Douglas R. Cubbison, Combat Studies Institute, Fort Leavenworth, KS, 9 July 2009, 2.

44. Exhibit 25 (SFC C/2-503d IN, statement), CJTF-101, "Army Regulation 15-6 Investigation into Battle of Wanat (Redacted, Unclassified Version)" (Camp Blessing, Afghanistan, 16 July 2008), 1; Exhibit 55 (CPT C/2-503d IN, statement), CJTF-101, "Army Regulation 15-6 Investigation into Battle of Wanat (Redacted, Unclassified Version)" (Camp Blessing, Afghanistan, 16 July 2008), 1; Dzwik, interview, 9 July 2009, 4–5; Lieutenant Colonel Kevin Anderson, interview by Douglas Cubbison, Combat Studies Institute, Fort Leavenworth, KS, 3 April 2009, 4.

45. Dzwik, interview, 9 July 2009, 4–5; Exhibit 55, CJTF-101, "Army Regulation 15-6 Investigation into Battle of Wanat", 1; Exhibit 52 (1LT B/2-503d IN, statement), CJTF-101, "Army Regulation 15-6 Investigation into Battle of Wanat (Redacted, Unclassified Version)" (Camp Blessing, Afghanistan, 16 July 2008), 1-2.

46. Exhibit 10a (BG, CJTF-101 Deputy Commander, 101st Airborne Division, interview) to US Central Command (CENTCOM), "Re-Investigation into the Combat Action at Wanat Village, Wygal District, Nuristan Province, Afghanistan, on 13 July 2008 (Redacted), 43; Exhibit 10c (BG, CJTF-101 Deputy Commander, 101st Airborne Division, interview) to US Central Command (CENTCOM), "Re-

Investigation into the Combat Action at Wanat Village, Wygal District, Nuristan Province, Afghanistan, on 13 July 2008 (Redacted), 31-34; Exhibit 19a (LTC, Brigade S2, 173d ABCT, interview) to US Central Command (CENTCOM), "Re-Investigation into the Combat Action at Wanat Village, Wygal District, Nuristan Province, Afghanistan, on 13 July 2008 (Redacted), 43

26, 29-30; Milley interview, 18 and 20 August 2009, 19-21; Exhibit 19c (LTC, Brigade S2, 173d ABCT, statement) to US Central Command (CENTCOM), "Re-Investigation into the Combat Action at Wanat Village, Wygal District, Nuristan Province, Afghanistan, on 13 July 2008 (Redacted), 4-5. The problem of templates unthinkingly becoming paradigms is well explored in Timothy Karcher, *Understanding the "Victory Disease," from the Little Bighorn to Mogadishu and Beyond*, Global War on Terrorism Occasional Paper No. 3, Fort Leavenworth: Combat Studies Institute Press, 2004.

Glossary

1LT	first lieutenant
AAF	Anti-Afghan Force (Afghanistan Insurgents)
AAR	after action review
ABCT	Airborne Brigade Combat Team
ACM	anti-Coalition militia (Afghanistan Insurgents)
ANA	Afghan National Army
ANP	Afghan National Police
AO	area of operation
AR	Army Regulation
ASF	Afghan Security Forces
ASG	Afghan Security Guard
ASP	ammunition supply point
BCT	brigade combat team
BDU	battle dress uniform
BMNT	begin morning nautical twilight
BN	battalion
CALL	Center for Army Lessons Learned
CAS	close air support
CCP	casualty collection point
CERP	Commander's Emergency Response Program
CG	commanding general
CJTF	combined joint task force
CLP	clcancr, lubricant, and preservative
CO	commanding officer
COIN	counterinsurgency
COL	colonel
COP	combat outpost
CP	command post
Cpl	corporal (USMC)
CPR	cardiopulmonary resuscitation
CPT	captain
CREST	Contingency Real Estate Support Team
DOD	Department of Defense
DSC	Distinguished Service Cross
EENT	end evening nautical twilight
ETT	embedded training team
FA	Field Artillery

FMV	full motion video
FO	forward observer
FOB	forward operating base
FRAGO	fragmentary order
FSO	fire support officer
GIROA	Government of the Islamic Republic of Afghanistan
GWOT	Global War on Terrorism
HE	high explosive
HHC	Headquarters and Headquarters Company
HiG	Hizb-i-Islami Gulbuddin
HMMWV	high-mobility multipurpose wheeled vehicle
HTT	human terrain team
HUMINT	human intelligence
HVT	high value target
IBA	individual body armor
ICOM	integrated communications
ID	Infantry Division; identification
IED	improvised explosive device
IN	Infantry
IO	information operations
IR	infrared
ISAF	International Security Assistance Force
ISI	Inter Services Intelligence
ISR	intelligence, surveillance, and reconnaissance
ITAS	Improved Target Acquisition System
J2	Intelligence Section at Joint Staff
J3	Operations Section at Joint Staff
JAF	Jalalabad Airfield
JMRC	Joint Multi-National Readiness Center (Hohenfels, Germany)
Kandak	ANA Battalion (Afghanistan name)
KIA	killed in action
LAW	light antitank weapon
LLVI	low level voice intercept
LN	local national
LOC	line of communication
LOO	line of operation
LRAS3	Long Range Advanced Scout Surveillance System

LTC	lieutenant colonel
LZ	landing zone
MBITR	multiband inter/intra team-radio
MEDEVAC	medical evacuation
MEU	Marine Expeditionary Unit
MILDEC	military deception
MRE	meal, ready to eat; mission-rehearsal exercise
MWR	morale, welfare, and recreation
NATO	North Atlantic Treaty Organization
NCO	noncommissioned officer
NCOIC	noncommissioned officer in charge
NGO	nongovernment organization
NOD	night observation device
NVA	North Vietnamese Army
OEF	Operation ENDURING FREEDOM
OIC	officer in charge
OIF	Operation IRAQI FREEDOM
OP	observation post
OPD	officer professional development
PDSS	predeployment site survey
PER	probable error of range
PFC	private first class
PID	positive identification
PRT	Provisional Reconstruction Team
PV2	private (Pay Grade 2)
QRF	quick reaction force
RC-East	Regional Command–East
RC-South	Regional Command–South
RIP	relief in place
RIPTOA	relief in place, transfer of authority
ROC	rehearsal of concept drill
ROTC	Reserve Officers' Training Corps
RPG	rocket propelled grenade
RSTA	reconnaissance surveillance and target acquisition
RTO	radio-telephone operator
S2	Intelligence Section at Brigade and Battalion Staff
S3	Operations Section at Brigade and Battalion Staff

SAF	small arms fire
SAW	squad automatic weapon
SEAL	Sea, Air, Land
SF	Special Forces
SFC	sergeant first class
SGT	sergeant
SIGINT	signal intelligence
SOF	Special Operations Forces
SPC	specialist
SSG	staff sergeant
SSgt	Staff Sergeant (USMC)
TAC	tactical command post
TACSAT	tactical satellite
TCP	traffic control point
"Terp"	Afghan Interpreter (nickname)
TF	task force
TIC	troops in contact
TOC	tactical operations center
TOW	tube launched, optically tracked, wire guided
TTP	tactics, techniques, and procedures
UAV	unmanned aerial vehicle
UEX	unit of execution
US	United States
USAID	US Agency for International Development
USMC	United States Marine Corps
WIA	wounded in action
XO	executive officer

Bibliography

Interviews, Discussions, Notes, and e-mail Correspondence

"Ahmad," Afghan Resident of Wanat, Waygal District, Nuristan, Afghanistan (real name withheld)

Drew Bowman, Team Leader, Human Terrain Team

Sami Nuristani, Afghan former resident of Nishai, Waygal District, Nuristan, Afghanistan (real name withheld)

Major General Jeffrey Schloesser

Brigadier General Mark Milley

Colonel Christopher Cavoli

Colonel William Ostlund

Colonel Christopher W. Pease

Colonel Charles Preysler

Colonel John Sutton

Lieutenant Colonel Kevin J. Anderson

Lieutenant Colonel William Butler

Lieutenant Colonel Pierre Gervais

Lieutenant Colonel David Hanselman

Lieutenant Colonel Rumi Nielson Green

Lieutenant Colonel Jimmy S. Hinton

Lieutenant Colonel John Lynch

Lieutenant Colonel Julian Smith

Major Shane Barna

Major Brian T. Beckno

Major Scott Himes

Major Ryker Horn

Major Brent Walter

Captain Ryan Berdiner

Captain Will Cromie

Captain James Fisher

Captain Jennifer Fortenberry

Captain Devin George

Captain Andrew Glenn

Captain Daniel Kearney

Captain Kevin King

Captain Justin J. Madill

Captain Duane A. Mantle

Captain Matthew Myer

Captain Benjamin Pry

Captain Walter Tompkins

Captain Amanda Wilson

First Lieutenant Matthew A. Colley

First Lieutenant Matthew C. Ferrara

First Lieutenant Erik Jorgensen

First Lieutenant Michael Moad

Chief Warrant Officer 3 John Gauvreau

Chief Warrant Officer 3 Brian Townsend

Chief Warrant Officer 3 Chuck Whitbeck

Chief Warrant Officer 2 Juan L. Guzman

Chief Warrant Officer 2 Isaac Smith

First Sergeant Scott Beeson

Sergeant First Class David Dzwik

Sergeant First Class Scott A. Grenier

Sergeant First Class Andrew Guerrero

Sergeant First Class William Stockard

Staff Sergeant Jonathan Benton

Staff Sergeant Matthew Kinney

Staff Sergeant Erich Phillips

Staff Sergeant Luis Repreza

Sergeant Erik Aass

Sergeant Hector Chavez

Sergeant Nicholas Ehler

Sergeant John Hayes

Sergeant Brian C. Hissong

Sergeant Michael Johnson

Sergeant Jason T. Oakes

Sergeant Ryan Pitts

Sergeant Jesse L. Queck

Sergeant Erick J. Rodas

Sergeant Jeffrey Scantlin

Corporal Tyler M. Stafford

Specialist Jason Baldwin

Specialist Charles Bell

Specialist Tyler Hanson

Specialist Sean Langevin

Specialist Chris McKaig

Specialist Jeffrey Shaw

Private First Class Scott Stenoski

United States Military

Briefings

2d Battalion (Airborne), 503d Infantry. "Thoughts on COIN OEF VIII" Briefing (not dated).
———. "2d Battalion (ABN), 503d IN, 173d ABCT, AO Rock Overview, 26 July 2008" Briefing.
173d Airborne Brigade. "Presentation of Collateral Investigation Results to the Family of First Lieutenant Jonathan P. Brostrom" Briefing (not dated).
CJTF-82. "CJTF-82 Command Brief," 14 February 2008.
———. "Tier I OPD AAR" Briefing, undated, "RC East Geometry" slide.
"TF Bayonet CDRs ROE Refresher" Briefing, 15 May 2007.
TF *Bayonet*, "Bayonet CUB [Combat Update Brief] to CJTF-101," 5-12 July 2008.
TF *Rock*. "CONOP ROCK MOVE, 2/3 ANA, C/2-503 IN (ABN) and 2-17 CAV, Level 1 CONOP, 8–9 July 2008" Briefing, 7 July 2008.

TF *Rock.* "AO Rock Overview, 26 July 2008" Briefing.

TF *Rock.* "AO Rock" PowerPoint slide, c. March 2008.

TF *Rock.* "NTC Observer Controller Briefing," 12 December 2007.

TF *Rock*, "TF Rock/ PRT Nuristan," PowerPoint briefing, June 2008.

TF *Rock*, "Rock Daily Snapshot-Thursday, July 10, 2008."

Ostlund, Lieutenant Colonel William. "Battle of Wanat Storyboard and Brief" Briefing, 16 July 2008.

Documents and Manuals

"1st Battalion, 32d Infantry Regiment" Web site. http://www.drum.army. mil/sites/tenants/division/3BCT/1-32INF/afghan.asp (accessed 22 September 2009).

173d ABCT. "Fallen Heroes." http://www.173abnbde.setaf.army.mil/ Fallen%20Heroes/PFC%20Timothy% 20Vimoto.htm (accessed 1 June 2009).

2d Battalion (Airborne), 503d Infantry, 173d Airborne Brigade Combat Team. "Bronze Star for Valor Citation, SFC David Dzwik."

———. "Silver Star Citation, Captain Matthew Myer."

———. "Silver Star Citation, Corporal Jonathan Ayers."

———. "Silver Star Citation, 1st Lieutenant Jonathan Brostrom."

———. "Silver Star Citation, Specialist Aaron Davis."

———. "Silver Star Citation, Specialist Michael Denton."

———. "Silver Star Citation, Sergeant Israel Garcia."

———. "Silver Star Citation, Sergeant Jared Gilmore."

———. "Silver Star Citation, Staff Sergeant Sean Samaroo."

3d Brigade Combat Team, 10th Mountain Division. *Spartan Review, After Action Report, Afghanistan 06–07.* Fort Drum, NY, May 2007.

AH-64 Guntapes of Engagement at Wanat, 13 July 2008.

Combined Joint Task Force-101. "US Army Response to US Congressman Neal Abercrombie, January 26, 2009." Washington, DC: Office of the Chief of Legislative Liaison.

———. "Statement on Waygal District/Nuristan" (e-mails to Mr. Matt Matthews, CSI, 3–4 April 2009).

Combined Joint Task Force-101 and 173d Airborne Brigade Combat Team. "Combined Responses, Prepared in Support of Briefing Provided by Colonel Charles Preysler to the Brostrom Family on 23–24 October 2008."

Crawley, Specialist Neil A., MEDEVAC. Personal Statement, FOB Fenty, Jalalabad Airfield, Afghanistan, 15 July 2008.

Department of the Army G3. *US Army Troop Levels in OEF Spreadsheet*, 2008.

Department of the Army. Field Manual (FM) 1-02, *Operational Terms and Graphics*. Washington, DC: Department of the Army, 2004.

_____. Field Manual (FM) 3-21.8 (FM 7-8), *The Infantry Rifle Platoon and Squad*. Washington, DC: Department of the Army, 2007.

_____. Field Manual (FM) 10-52, *Water Supply in Theaters of Operation*, Washington, DC: Department of the Army, 1990.

Hanselman, Lieutenant Colonel David. "April/May [2008] Trip Report to AO-Bayonet" (n.p., n.d.).

———. "Bella Ambush, 9–10 November 2007" (n.p., n.d.).

———. "History Collection Mission of the 173d ABCT, 17–30 October 2008" (e-mail to Dr. William G. Robertson, 12 November 2008).

———. "Operation Rock Avalanche, 25 October Deliberate Ambush of 1st Platoon, Battle Co, 2-503 PIR" (n.p., n.d.).

Helfrich, Sergeant William, MEDEVAC. Personal Statement on Wanat, FOB Fenty, Afghanistan, 14 July 2008.

Hill, Chief Warrant Officer 3 Christopher, MEDEVAC. Personal Statement on Wanat, FOB Fenty, Afghanistan, 13 July 2008.

Hissong, Sergeant Brian C. Personal Statement, "Combat Outpost Kahler, July 8–15, 2008" (n.d.).

Human Terrain Team—TF Warrior/1st MEB. "Notes from Meeting with Pashai *Shura* Representatives, 29 January 2009," 30 January 2009.

Madill, Captain Justin J., Flight Surgeon, MEDEVAC. Personal Statement, FOB Fenty, Jalalabad Airfield, Afghanistan, 17 July 2008.

McDonald, Chief Warrant Officer 2 Wayne A., MEDEVAC. Personal Statement, FOB Fenty, Jalalabad Airfield, Afghanistan, 14 July 2008.

Minnie, Captain Paul, MEDEVAC. Personal Statement on Wanat, FOB Fenty, Afghanistan, 15 July 2008.

Seipel, Captain Ben, MEDEVAC. Personal Statement on Wanat, FOB Fenty, Afghanistan, July 14, 2008.

Swanson, Sergeant Chad, MEDEVAC. Personal Statement on Wanat, FOB Fenty, Afghanistan, 22 July 2008.

TF *Pacemaker*, "Recon Results Brief, Proposed Wanat COP," 10 April 2008.

TF *Rock*, "TIC Asset Tracker" Spreadsheet, 22 July 2008.

TF *Rock*, *07 11 24 Aranus Shura (2) Posted*, 2 December 2007.

TF *Rock*, *07 12 15 Aranus SHURA_ 15DEC07*, 16 December 2007.

Thompkins, Staff Sergeant Atwon, MEDEVAC. Personal Statement, FOB Fenty, Jalalabad Airfield, Afghanistan, 14 July 2008.

US Army. "2007 Army Posture Statement, Addendum H, Army Force Generation." http://www.army.mil/aps/07/addendum/h.html (accessed 11 August 2009).

US Army Center for Health Promotion and Preventive Medicine. "Heat Injury Prevention." http://chppm-www.apgea.army.mil/heat/ (accessed 1 June 2009).

Official Investigations

Task Force Bayonet "AR 15-6 Investigation (Findings and Recommendations) –COP Bella Allegation of Non-Combatant Casualties, 4 July 2008," 26 July 2008.

US Central Command (CENTCOM), "Re-investigation into the Combat Action at Wanat Village, Wygal District, Nuristan Province, Afghanistan, on 13 July 2008 (Redacted), with 77 Exhibits and additional enclosures, 12 January 2010.

US Combined Joint Task Force-101."Army Regulation 15-6 Investigation into Battle of Wanat (Redacted, Unclassified Version)." Bagram Air Base, Afghanistan, 21 October 2008.

Books, Articles, and Reports

"The 173d Returns from Afghanistan." *Stars and Stripes*, September 2008.

ABC Nightline. "The Other War," 12 November 2007.

Afghanistan Research and Evaluation Unit. "Updated Population Estimates for Afghanistan." *Afghanistan Research Newsletter.* http://www.areu.org.af/index.php?option=com_frontpage&Itemid=25 (accessed 13 August 2009).

"Afghanistan Says U.S. Airstrike Hit Wedding Party." *New York Times,* 6 July 2008. http://www.nytimes. com/2008/07/06/world/asia/06iht-afghan.4.14278415.html (accessed 8 September 2009).

Aird, Sergeant Brandon. "Daily Maintenance Keeps UAV Eyes in the Sky." SpaceWar.com. http://www.spacewar.com/reports/Daily_Maintenance_Keeps_UAV_Eyes_In_The_Sky_999.html (accessed 19 February 2009).

———. "Medic Recognized for Actions During Insurgent Assault." *Outlook* 41, Issue 15 (15 April 2008).

———. "Sky Soldier Awarded Distinguished Service Cross." *Army.mil/news*. http://www.army.mil/-news/2008/09/17/12493-sky-soldier-awarded-distinguished-service-cross/ (accessed 19 February 2009).

Associated Press, July 2008, "N.C. Soldier among 9 Killed in Attack."
    http://militarytimes.com/valor/army-cpl-pruitt-a-rainey/3630793/
    (accessed 7 April 2010).

Breen, Bob. *First To Fight, Australian Diggers, New Zealand Kiwis and
    US Paratroopers in Vietnam, 1965–1966.* Nashville, TN: The
    Battery Press, 1988.

Burgess, Lieutenant Colonel Tony, ed. *Afghan Company Commander
    After Action Review Book, Operation Enduring Freedom VII.*
    West Point, NY: US Army Center for Company Level Leaders,
    US Military Academy, 2007.

Burns, Robert. "Mullen: Afghanistan Isn't Top Priority." *USA
    Today,* 11 December 2007. http://www.usatoday.com/news/
    washington/2007-12-11-3963072919_x.htm. (accessed 6
    November 2009).

Cadieu, Major Trevor. "Canadian Armour in Afghanistan." *Canadian
    Army Journal* 10, no. 4 (Winter 2008): 5–25.

Chivers, C.J. "In Afghanistan, Soldiers Bridge 2 Stages of War."
    New York Times, 13 April 2009. http://ebird.osd.mil/ebfiles/
    e20090413670023.html (accessed 13 April 2009).

Chultheis, Rob. *Night Letters, Inside Wartime Afghanistan.* New York
    Orion Books, 1992.

Clausewitz, General Carl von. *On War.* Michael Howard and Peter Paret,
    editors and translators. New York, NY: Alfred P. Knopf, 1973
    (Everyman's Library Edition).

Cole, Matthew. "Watching Afghanistan Fall." *Salon Magazine,* 27
    February 2007. http://www.salon.com/news/feature/2007/02/27/
    afghanistan/ (accessed 16 July 2008).

Coss, Colonel Michael A. "Operation Mountain Lion: CJTF-76 in
    Afghanistan, Spring 2006." *Military Review* (January–February
    2008): 22–29.

Cubbison, Douglas R. "'Look Out For Hell Some Place Soon,' The 2d
    Colorado Cavalry in Missouri, February–September, 1864."
    Military History of the West 32, no. 1 (Spring 2002): 1–24.

———. "The Crossed Swords Tribe of Afghanistan: The 10th Mountain
    Division and Counterinsurgency Excellence in Afghanistan,
    2006" (unpublished manuscript).

Darack, Edward. *Victory Point: Operations Red Wings and Whalers—
    The Marine Corps Battle for Freedom in Afghanistan.* New York:
    Berkley Caliber, 2009.

Demarest, Geoffrey. "19th Century Strategy and Its Applicability to
    Insurgent Warfare." *Small Wars Journal* (2009).
    www.smallwarsjournal.com (accessed 5 February 2010).

Dougherty, Kevin "10th Mountain Division Improves Base for Incoming Unit," Stars and Stripes, May 15, 2007, http://www.stripes.com/news/10th-mountain-division-improves-base-for-incoming-unit-1.64019 (accessed 17 August 2010).

Dornfield, Ann. "A Soldier Who Documented Lives in Conflict." *National Public Radio.* http://www.npr.org/templates/story/story.php?storyId=92757330 (accessed 10 April 2009).

Edelberg, Lennart. "The Nuristani House." In *Cultures of the Hindu-Kush, Selected Papers from the Hindu-Kush Cultural Conference Held at Moesgard 1970,* edited by Karl Jettmar. Wiesbaden, Germany: Franz Steiner Verlag, 1974.

Edwards, David B. *Before Taliban: Geneologies of the Afghan Jihad.* Berkeley: University of California Press, 2002.

Emanuel, Jeff. "An Alamo with a Different Ending." http://www.americanintelligence.us/News/ article/sid=5307.html (accessed 9 April 2009).

Farmer, Ben. "US Repels Taliban from Gates of Kabul." *Telegraph* (26 March 2009). http://www.telegraph.co.uk/news/worldnews/asia/afghanistan/5054906/US-repels-Taliban-from-the-gates-of-Kabul.html (accessed 20 August 2009).

Foust, Joshua. "Dispatches from FOBistan: Fixing Afghanistan Starts With Fixing Ourselves." *Registan.Net.* http://www.registan.net/index.php/2009/02/12/dispatches-from-fobistan-fixing-afghanistan-starts-with-fixing-ourselves/ (accessed 30 March 2009).

———. "Garrisons and Force Protection Crowd Out Other Objectives in Afghanistan." *Reuters News Service.* http://blogs.reuters.com/great-debate/author/joshuafoust/ (accessed 30 March 2009).

Fury, Dalton. *Kill Bin Laden, A Delta Force Commander's Account of the Hunt for the Worlds' Most Wanted Man.* New York, NY: St. Martin's Press, 2008.

Gall, Carlotta, and Abdul Waheed Wafa. "9 From One Family Die in U.S. Strike Near Kabul." *New York Times*, 6 March 2007. http://www.nytimes.com/2007/03/06/world/asia/06afghan.html?_r=1&scp=2&sq=march% 206%202007%20gall&st=cse (accessed 20 November 2009).

Garcia, Sergeant Israel. Memorial Web page. http://www.sgtisraelgarcia.com/ (accessed 13 July 2009).

Garamone, Jim. "Report Alleges Police Aided Taliban in Attack that Killed Nine." *Armed Forces Press Service,* 4 November 2008. http://www.defenselink.mil/news/newsarticle.aspx?id=51790 (accessed 4 February 2009).

Giustozzi, Antonio. *Koran, Kalashnikov and Laptop, The Neo-Taliban Insurgency in Afghanistan*. New York: Columbia University Press, 2008.

Grau, Colonel Lester W., ed. *The Bear Went Over the Mountain: Soviet Combat Tactics in Afghanistan*. Washington, DC: National Defense University Press, 1996.

"Guest Book for CPL Gunnar Zwilling." http://www.legacy.com/gb2/default.aspx?bookID=113839824&page=3 (accessed 1 May 2009).

"Guide to Water Purification." http://www.princeton.edu/~oa/manual/water.shtml (accessed 9 September 2009).

"Gunnar W. Zwilling." *Saint Louis Post-Dispatch,* 17 July 2008. http://afghanistan.pigstye.net/ article.php?story=GunnarWZwilling (accessed 1 May 2009).

Harris, Kent. "Most Patrols in Kunar Province Wind Up Being Routine." *Stars and Stripes,* 27 June 2008.

———. "Six Vicenza Soldiers Honored for Acts of Valor in Afghan Battle." *Stars and Stripes,* 21 March 2009. http://www.stripes.com/article.asp?section=104&article=61477 (accessed 31 March 2009).

Hemming, Jon. "Afghan President Orders Probe into Civilian Deaths." *Reuters India News,* 7 July 2008. http://in.reuters.com/article/southAsiaNews/idINIndia-34395620080706?sp=true (accessed 16 March 2009).

Hesco Bastion Ltd. Web site. http://www.hesco.com/enter.html (accessed 1 June 2009).

Holt, Frank L. *Into the Land of Bones, Alexander the Great in Afghanistan*. Los Angeles: University of California Press, 2005.

Human Rights Watch. *"Troops In Contact": Airstrikes and Civilian Deaths in Afghanistan*. New York: Human Rights Watch, 2008.

International Medical Corps Press Release. "International Medical Corps Mourns the Loss of Three Humanitarian Workers in Afghanistan; Another Injured." http://www.imcworldwide.org.uk/news.asp?pageid=5&nid=2 (accessed 14 August 2009).

Jaffe, Greg. "'They Feel Like Outsiders and They Don't Want to Be:' The U.S. Hopes that Afghans in Areas Along the Pech River Will Embrace Progress, But Much Unrest Remains." *Washington Post,* 6 October 2009. http://www.washingtonpost.com/wp-dyn/content/article/2009/10/05/AR2009100503799_pf.html (accessed 14 December 2009).

Jalali, Colonel Ali Ahmad, and Lester W. Grau, *The Other Side of the Mountain: Mujahidden Tactics in the Soviet-Afghan War.* Quantico, VA: US Marine Corps, 1995.

Jettmar, Karl, ed. *Cultures of the Hindu-Kush, Selected Papers from the Hindu-Kush Cultural Conference Held at Moesgard 1970.* Wiesbaden, Germany: Franz Steiner Verlag, 1974.

Johnson, Thomas H. "The Taliban Insurgency and an Analysis of *Shabnamah* (Night Letters)." *Small Wars and Insurgencies* 18, no. 3 (September 2007): 317–344.

Johnson, Thomas H., and M. Chris Mason. "No Sign until the Burst of Fire: Understanding the Pakistan-Afghanistan Frontier." *International Security* 32, no. 4 (Spring 2008): 41–77.

Jones, Schuyler. *Men of Influence in Nuristan: A Study of Social Control and Dispute Settlement in Waigal Valley, Afghanistan.* New York: Seminar Press, 1974.

Jones, Seth G. *In the Graveyard of Empires, America's War in Afghanistan.* New York: W.W. Norton & Company, 2009.

Junger, Sebastian. "Into the Valley of Death." *Vanity Fair,* January 2008. http://www.vanityfair.com/politics/features/2008/01/afghanistan200801 (accessed 2 February 2009).

———. "Return to the Valley of Death." *Vanity Fair,* October 2008. http://www.vanityfair.com/politics/features/2008/10/afghanistan200810 (accessed 2 February 2009).

———. *War.* New York: Hachette Book Group, 2010.

"Karzai 'Axes Leader for US Rebuke.'" *Al Jazeera.Net.* http://english.aljazeera.net/news/asia/2008/07/ 2008710134241675953.html (accessed 19 February 2009).

Katz, David J. "Kafir to Afghan: Religious Conversion, Political Incorporation and Ethnicity in the Vaygal Valley, Nuristan. "Ph.D. Thesis, University of California, Los Angeles, 1982.

Kilcullen, David. *The Accidental Guerrilla; Fighting Small Wars in the Midst of a Big One.* New York: Oxford University Press, 2009.

Klimburg, Max. "The Enclaved Culture of Parun in Former Kafiristan." *Asien* 104 (July 2007): 65–70.

———. "The Situation in Nuristan." *Central Asian Survey* 20, no. 3 (2001): 383–390.

Kozaryn, Linda D. "New Weapons Cache Found: Oruzgan Deaths Investigated." *Defend America*, 8 July 2002. http://www.defendamerica.mil/archive/2002-07/20020708.html (accessed 19 November 2009).

Levy, Sergeant First Class Jason. "Battalion Mortar Platoon Operations in Afghanistan." Infantry (July 2009): 23-32.

Luttrell, Marcus. *Lone Survivor:* The Eyewitness Account of Operation Redwing and the Lost Heroes of SEAL Team 10. New York: Little, Brown and Company, 2007.

Luzader, John F. *Saratoga, A Military History of the Decisive Campaign of the American Revolution.* New York, NY: Savas and Beatie, 2009.

Malkasian, Carter, and Gerald Meyerle. *Provincial Reconstruction Teams: How Do We Know They Work?* Carlisle Barracks, PA: Strategic Studies Institute, 2009.

Malmstrom, First Lieutenant Erik, 1-32 Infantry, 3d BCT, 10th Mountain Division. "Losing the Waigul Valley." *The Pennsylvania Gazette,* November/December 2008, 42–47.

Maranian, Lieutenant Colonel Stephen J. "Field Artillery Fires in the Mountains of Afghanistan." *Fires* (July–September 2008): 34–36.

Marine Corps Times. "Marine Receives Silver Star in Okinawa," 4 April 2009. http://www.marinecorpstimes.com/news/2009/04/marine_silverstar_040309w/ (accessed 6 April 2009).

"The Massacre at Aranas on the Waygal River, Nuristan Province." *RAWA News,* 16 July 2008. http://www.rawa.org/temp/runews/2008/07/16/the-massacre-at-aranas-on-the-waygal-river-nuristan-province.html?e=http:/amyru.h18.ru/images/cs.txt? (accessed 19 February 2009).

Masters, John. *Bugles and a Tiger, A Volume of Autobiography.* New York: The Viking Press, 1956.

Matthews, Matt M. *Operation AL FAJR: A Study in Army and Marine Corps Joint Operations.* Fort Leavenworth, KS: Combat Studies Institute Press, 2006.

McAfee, John P. *Slow Walk in a Sad Rain.* Alexander, NC: Alexander Books, 2002.

McGrath, John J. *Boots on the Ground: Troop Density in Contingency Operations.* Fort Leavenworth: Combat Studies Institute Press, 2006.

Miles, Donna. "Wounded Soldier Anxious to Return to Operation Enduring Freedom." *DefenseLink News,* 4 October 2005. http://www.defenselink.mil/news/newsarticle.aspx?id=18164 (accessed 4 February 2009).

Moore, Michael, and James Fussell *Afghanistan Report I: Kunar and Nuristan, Rethinking U.S. Counterinsurgency Operations.* Washington, DC: Institute for the Study of War, July 2009.

Morris, David J. "The Big Suck: Notes from the Jarhead Underground." *Virginia Quarterly Review* 83, no. 1 (Winter 2007): 144–169.

Mraz, Steve. "Soldiers Recount Deadly Account on Afghanistan Outpost." *Stars and Stripes,* 19 July 2008. http://www.stripes. com/article.asp?section=104&article=56237 (accessed 2 February 2009).

Mujahideen of Islamic Emirate of Afghanistan. "Attack American Invaders Base in Nooristan Province." http://theunjustmedia. com/clips/afgha/July08/noor/noor.htm (accessed 29 March 2009).

Murphy, Edward F. *Dak To, The 173d Airborne Brigade in South Vietnam's Central Highlands, June–November 1967.* Novata, CA: Presidio Press, 1993.

Narrative from Shok Valley Battle in Afghanistan," *Army Times,* 15 December 2008, http://www.armytimes.com/news/2008/12/ army_battlenarrative_121508w/ (accessed on 19 July 2010);

Nelson, Soraya Sarhaddi. "Westerners Play Pivotal Role in Afghan Rebuilding." *National Public Radio Morning Edition* transcript, 20 May 2008. http://www.npr.org/templates/transcript/transcript. php?storyId=90599416 (accessed 20 November 2009).

Noelle, Christine. *State and Tribe in Nineteenth-Century Afghanistan: The Reign of Amir Dost Muhammad Khan (1826-1863).* London: RoutledgeCurzon, 2004.

Ostlund, Colonel William B. "Tactical Leader Lessons Learned in Afghanistan: Operation Enduring Freedom VIII." *Military Review* (July–August 2009): 2–9.

"Pashai." *World Culture Encyclopedia.* http://www.everyculture.com/ Africa-Middle-East/Pashai.html (accessed 12 February 2009).

Prevas, John. *Envy of the Gods, Alexander the Great's Ill-Fated Journey Across Asia.* Cambridge, MA: Da Capo Press, 2004.

Preysler, Colonel Charles. "DOD News Briefing, October 17, 2007." http://www.defenselink.mil/transcripts/transcript. aspx?transcriptid=4062 (accessed 3 March 2009).

Rautenstrauch, Bill. "Battle at Wanat, Specialist Christopher McKaig." *LaGrand (Oregon) Observer,* 30 August 2008. http://www. lagrandeobserver.com/Features/Portraits/Battle-at-Wanat (accessed 2 February 2009).

Ricks, Thomas. "Inside An Afghan Battle Gone Wrong: What Happened at Wanat." http://ricks.foreignpolicy.com/posts/2009/01/28/ inside_an_afghan_battle_what_happened_at_wanat_last_july_i (accessed 2 February 2009).

Robertson, Dr. William Glenn. *Counterattack on the Naktong, 1950.* Leavenworth Paper No. 13 Fort Leavenworth: Combat Studies

Institute, US Army Command and General Staff College,
December 1985.

Rogers, Robert. *Journals of Major Robert Rogers.* 1765. Reprint, Ann
Arbor, MI: University Microfilms, 1966.

Roggio, Bill. "Al Qaeda's Paramilitary 'Shadow Army'" (9 February
2009). http://www.longwarjournal.org/archives/2009/02/al_
qaedas_paramilita.php (accessed 9 March 2009).

Roul, Animesh. "Gems, Timber and Jiziya: Pakistan's Taliban Harness
Resources to Fund Jihad." Terrorism Monitor 7, no. 11 (30 April
2009). http://www.jamestown.org/programs/gta/single/ ?tx_
ttnews[tt_news]=34928&tx_ttnews[backPid]=26&cHash=4d18a
44d9a (accessed 13 October 2009).

Rubin, Elizabeth. "Battle Company is Out There." *New York Times,*
24 February 2008. http://www.nytimes.com/2008/02/24/
magazine/24afghanistan-t.html?_r=2 (accessed 2 February
2009).

Sami, Omer, Moeed Hashimi, and Wali Salarzai. "NATO Airstrike Kills
22 Civilians in Nuristan.*" Pajhwok Afghan News*, 5 July 2008.
http://www.pajhwok.com/viewstory.asp?lng=eng&id=57969
(accessed 16 November 2009).

Sciutto, Jim. "'Relax, Brother': Exclusive Video Shows Taliban Attack
That Killed 9 U.S. Soldiers at Afghan Post July 2008 Incident
Shown From Taliban Viewpoint: 'We Attacked From 4 Sides,'"
12 November 2009. http://abcnews.go.com/WN/Afghanistan/
exclusive-video-shows-taliban-attack-killed-us-soldiers/
story?id=9068156 (accessed 7 December 2009).

Smith, General Rupert. *The Utility of Force, The Art of War in the
Modern World.* New York: Alfred A. Knopf, 2007.

Smith, Herschel. "Analysis of the Battle of Wanat." *The CPT's Journal*
(11 November 2008). http://www.CPTsjournal.com/2008/11/11/
analysis-of-the-battle-of-wanat/ (accessed 4 February 2009).

———. "Backwards Counterinsurgency in Afghanistan." *The CPT's
Journal.* http://www.CPTsjournal.com/2009/04/21/backwards-
counterinsurgency-in-afghanistan/ (accessed 21 April 2009).

———. "Opening a Combat Outpost for Business." *The CPT's Journal*
(2 February 2009). http://www.CPTsjournal.com/2009/02/02/
opening-a-combat-outpost-for-business/ (accessed 4 February
2009).

Smucker, Philip. "Asphalt Dreams." *The Atlantic Monthly* 301, no. 5
(June 2008): 24–25.

St. Clair, Mark. "Commander: Media Reports on Afghanistan Outpost Battle Were Exaggerated, COL Charles "Chip" Preysler, Commander of the 173d Airborne Brigade Combat Team." *Stars and Stripes,* 20 July 2008. http://www.stripes.com/article. asp?section=104&article=56252 (accessed 2 February 2009).

Strand, Richard F. "Notes on the Nuristani and Dardic Languages." *Journal of the American Oriental Society* 93, no. 3 (July–September 1973): 297–305.

———. "Richard Strand's Nuristan Site." http://users.sedona. net/~strand/Current.html (accessed 3 March 2009).

———. "The Changing Herding Economy of the Kom Nuristani." *Afghanistan Journal* 2, no. 4: 123–134.

———. "The Current Political Situation in Nuristan." http://users. sedona.net/~strand/Current.html (accessed 12 February 2009).

Tan, Michelle. "Dire Sunrise at Wanat." *Army Times,* 16 December 2008. http://www.armytimes.com/news/2008/12/army_ WanatMain_121408/ (accessed 2 February 2009).

Tanner, Stephen. *Afghanistan: A Military History from Alexander the Great to the Fall of the Taliban.* Cambridge, MA: Da Capo Press, 2002.

Tate, David. "US Had Warning of Attack in Nuristan." *A Battlefield Tourist,* 28 July 2008. http://www.battlefieldtourist.com/ content/2008/07/ (accessed 2 April 2009).

"Three Soldiers Killed in Enemy Attack," *DiversityinBusiness.com,* http://www.diversityinbusiness.com/Military/Casualties/2006/ Mil_Cas_20608.htm (accessed on 16 August 2010).

"Uphill Pursuit for Afghan Warlord," Christian Science Monitor, 22 December 2003, http://www.csmonitor.com/2003/1222/p06s01-wosc.html/(page)/CSM-Photo-Galleries/In-Pictures/Space-Photos-of-the-Day/Space-photos-of-the-day-06-22 (accessed 17 July 2010).

US Congress, Senate. *Statement of Secretary of Defense Robert M. Gates, Senate Armed Services Committee, Tuesday, September 23, 2008.*

US Department of Defense. *Unmanned Systems Roadmap, 2007–2032.* Washington, DC, 10 December 2007.

US Department of Defense Joint Chiefs of Staff. *Joint Planning Document 3-13.4, Military Deception.* Washington, DC, 13 July 2006.

"US Planes Hit Afghan Wedding Party, Killing 27." *The Sydney Morning Herald,* 7 July 2008. http://www.smh.com.au/news/world/us-planes-hit-afghan-wedding-party-killi ng-27/2008/07/07/1215282687896.html (accessed 8 September 2009).

Utley, Sergeant Major D. "Konar Valley." *Long Hard Road, NCO Experiences in Afghanistan and Iraq.* Fort Bliss, TX: US Army Sergeants Major Academy, October 2007.

Veterans of Foreign Wars. "Ambushed Soldiers Heroes VFW Chief Says; National Commander Visits Wounded at Landstuhl." http://www. vfw.org/index.cfm?fa=news.newsDtl&did=4631 (accessed 19 February 2009).

Wahab, Shaista, and Barry Youngerman. *A Brief History of Afghanistan.* New York: Facts on File, 2007.

Weekes, Richard V., ed. "Nuristani." In *Muslim Peoples, A World Ethnographic Survey.* Westport, CT: Greenwood Press, 1978.

Welcome, Specialist George. "The Art of Saving Lives, MEDEVAC View of the Battle of Wanat, Afghanistan." http://www.blackfive. net/MAIN/2008/07/MEDEVAC-VIEW-OF.HTML (accessed 2 February 2009).

Wiltrout, Kate. "Soldier from Eastern Shore Recounts Deadly Battle in Afghanistan, SSG Jesse L. Queck." *Hampton Roads Virginian-Pilot,* 19 July 2008. http://hamptonroads.com/2008/07/soldier-eastern-shore-recounts-deadly-battle-afghanistan (accessed 2 February 2009).

Wittman, George H. "Afghan Proving Ground." *The American Spectator,* 6 March 2009. http://spectator.org/archives/2009/03/06/afghan-proving-ground/print (accessed 6 March 2009).

Yousaf, Mohammad. *Afghanistan, The Bear Trap.* Havertown, PA: Casemate, 2001.